Parents
and the
Achieving
Child

Parents and the Achieving Child

Owen W. Cahoon
Alvin H. Price
A. Lynn Scoresby

Brigham Young University Press

Library of Congress Cataloging in Publication Data

Cahoon, Owen W   1937–
   Parents and the achieving child.
   Includes index.
   1. Parent and child.   2. Child development.
3. Home and school.   I. Price, Alvin H., 1935–
II. Scoresby, A. Lynn, joint author.   III. Title.
HQ772.C32   649'.1   78-32168
ISBN 0-8425-0856-2

International Standard Book Number: 0-8425-0856-2 (paper)
Library of Congress Catalog Number: 78-32168
Brigham Young University Press, Provo, Utah 84602
© 1979 by Brigham Young University Press. All rights reserved
Printed in the United States of America
79 5Mp 28016

CONTENTS

Editor's Note: To avoid the awkward repetition of constructions such as "he or she" throughout this book, we have chosen to use the masculine pronouns as neuter pronouns referring to both sexes.

CHAPTER 1
WHY PARENTS SHOULD TEACH:
AN INTRODUCTION

For many years people involved in the education of young children have known that teaching a child effectively requires establishing a close relationship with the child. In order to learn effectively, the child must be able to trust the teacher, must be able to know that the adult will be caring and warm; the teacher must provide a constant and consistent relationship. In addition, quality learning demands closeness. Teacher and child must experience mutual feelings: if both feel sad or happy, excited or loving, they will feel close, and learning can occur. The learning relationship is also characterized by openness. This means that both teacher and child feel free to talk about anything they wish to—especially about each other. When such a relationship exists, the child more readily learns to read and to write and to do arithmetic.

Because there are great numbers of children but limited educational resources, public schools have been forced to organize so that one teacher associates with as many as twenty to thirty-five children; occasionally a teacher will have even more than thirty-five pupils. As a result a child cannot speak as soon as an idea occurs to him, cannot write when he wishes, and very likely cannot draw as soon as he has the desire. Because of crowded conditions, the child is unable to learn at his own speed and instead must learn at a pace determined by the ability of average students in his class. Furthermore, he must compete with twenty or more other children to establish a trusting, close, and open relationship with the teacher. And the teacher, believing—and rightly so—that each child is as important as another, tries to give equal amounts of attention to each child. The usual result is that the teacher is able to build a close, trusting relationship with only some of the children. Considerable evidence suggests that children who succeed in school are those who are able to establish a close relationship with their teachers, so it seems likely that if all children were taught by a person they felt close to and trusted, all would learn more effectively.

What can be done to provide a better teacher-student relationship for more children? A number of school systems have tried various new approaches. Some have, for example, created *individualized learning situations* in which a teacher and an individual student relate with each other. Others have initiated flexible scheduling, which permits small groups of students to associate with a single teacher. All sorts of individualized books, tools, and learning materials have been made available. But in spite of these efforts, each teacher must still associate with, and be responsible for, at least twenty students.

Jean Mizer dramatizes in a true story how difficult it is for a teacher in a large school classroom to build a close relationship with each student:

It started with tragedy on a biting cold February morning. I was driving behind the Milford Corners bus as I did most snowy mornings on my way to school. It veered and stopped short at the hotel, which it had no business doing, and I was annoyed as I had to come to an unexpected stop. A boy lurched out of the bus, reeled, stumbled, and collapsed on the snowbank at the curb. The bus driver and I reached him at the same moment. His thin, hollow face was white even against the snow.

"He's dead," the driver whispered.

It didn't register for a minute. I glanced quickly at the scared young faces staring down at us from the school bus. "A doctor! Quick! I'll phone from the hotel!"

"No use. I tell you he's dead." The driver looked down at the boy's still form. "He never even said he felt bad," he muttered. "He

2

just tapped me on the shoulder and said, real quiet, 'I'm sorry, I have to get off at the hotel.' That's all, polite and apologizing like."

At school the giggling, shuffling morning noise quieted as the news went down the halls. I passed a huddle of girls. "Who was it? Who dropped dead on the way to school?" I heard one of them whisper.

"Don't know his name; some kid from Milford Corners," was the reply.

It was like that in the faculty room and the principal's office. "I'd appreciate your going out to tell the parents," the principal told me. "They haven't a phone and, anyway, somebody from school should go there in person. I'll cover your classes."

"Why me?" I asked. "Wouldn't it be better if you did it?"

"I didn't know the boy," the principal admitted levelly, "and in last year's sophomore personalities column I note that you were listed as his favorite teacher."

I drove through the snow and cold down the bad canyon road to the Evans' place and thought about Cliff Evans. "His favorite teacher!" He hadn't spoken two words to me in two years! I could see him in my mind's eye, all right, sitting back there in the last seat in my afternoon literature class. He came into the room by himself and left by himself. "Cliff Evans," I muttered to myself, "a boy who never talked." I thought a minute. "A boy who never smiled; I never saw him smile once."

The big ranch kitchen was clean and warm. I blurted out my news somehow. Mrs. Evans reached blindly toward a chair. "He never said anything about being ailing."

His stepfather snorted, "He ain't said nothin' about anything since I moved in here."

Mrs. Evans pushed a pan to the back of the stove and began to untie her apron. "Now hold on," her husband snapped. "I got to have breakfast before I go to town. Nothin' we can do now anyway. If Cliff hadn't been so dumb, he'd a' told us he didn't feel good."

After school I sat in the office and stared bleakly at the records spread out before me. I was to close the file and write the obituary for the school paper. The almost bare sheets mocked my effort. Cliff Evans, white, never legally adopted by stepfather, five young half brothers and sisters. These meager strands of information, and the list of D grades, were all the records had to offer.

Cliff Evans had silently come in the school door in the mornings and gone out the school door in the evenings, and that was all. He had never belonged to a club. He had never played on a team. He

3

had never held an office. As far as I could tell, he had never done one happy, noisy kid thing. He had never been anybody at all.

How do you go about making a boy into a zero? The grade school records showed me. The first and second grade teachers' annotations read, "Sweet, shy child"; "timid but eager." Then the third grade note opened the attack. Some teacher had written in a good, firm hand, "Cliff won't talk. Uncooperative. Slow learner." The other academic sheep had followed with "dull"; "slow-witted"; "low IQ." They became correct. The boy's IQ in the ninth grade was listed at 83. But his IQ in the third grade had been 106. The score didn't go under 100 until the seventh grade. Even shy, timid, sweet children have resilience. It takes time to break them.

I stomped to the typewriter and wrote a savage report pointing out what education had done to Cliff Evans. I slapped a copy on the principal's desk and another in the sad, dog-eared file. I banged the typewriter and slammed the file and crashed the door shut, but I didn't feel much better. A little boy kept walking after me, a little boy with a peaked, pale face; a skinny body in faded jeans; a little boy with big eyes that had looked and searched for a long time and then had become veiled.

I could guess how many times he'd been chosen last to play sides in a game, how many whispered child conversations had excluded him, how many times he hadn't been asked. I could see and hear the faces and voices that said over and over, "You're dumb, you're dumb. You're a nothing, Cliff Evans."

A child is a believing creature. Cliff undoubtedly believed them. Suddenly it seemed clear to me: When finally there was nothing left at all for Cliff Evans, he collapsed on a snowbank and went away. The doctor might list "heart failure" as the cause of death, but that wouldn't change my mind.

We couldn't find ten students in the school who had known Cliff well enough to attend the funeral as his friends. So the student body officers and a committee from the junior class went as a group to the church, being politely sad. I attended the services with them and sat through it with a lump of cold lead in my chest and a big resolve growing inside me.

I've never forgotten Cliff Evans nor that resolve. He has been my challenge year after year. I look up and down the rows carefully each September at the unfamiliar faces. I look for veiled eyes or bodies scrounged into a seat in an alien world. "Look, kids," I say silently, "I may not do anything else for you this year, but not one of you is going to come out of here a nobody. I'll work or fight to

4

the bitter end doing battle with society and the school board, but I won't have one of you coming out of here thinking himself a zero."

Most of the time—not always, but most of the time—I've succeeded. (Jean E. Mizer, "Cipher in the Snow," NEA Journal 52 [November 1964]:8–10).

The search for a program that provides a close learning relationship leads us to one of the most important and profound of schools: the home. In the home a child has the potential of an involved day-to-day association with adults and with other children. At home a child can learn at least one major principle: how to associate with his fellowman. And if parents can teach such a complex principle, it is also possible for parents to teach things that will improve a child's mental or intellectual development, increase his emotional maturity, and stimulate his creativity. Many parents believe they can't teach because they don't have enough knowledge of subject matter or they don't know *how* to teach or they don't have enough time. You may be surprised to learn that you know enough and that you have all the necessary resources right in your home and that, with a little training, you can be a very successful teacher. Parents cannot avoid teaching: children will learn most effectively from people they believe to be the best teachers, and these people are their parents. Since you want to be the best teacher for your children, there are three reasons why it is important that you become more actively involved with them.

First, effectively teaching young children in the home will increase their readiness to learn and improve their chances of succeeding in a large classroom. A few years ago a St. Louis school district decided to do something to help prepare preschool children to learn. Their approach was basic: they placed a dictionary in each child's home and raised funds to help families go on little excursions. Families went to supermarkets (where a child could feel a carrot, smell a head of cabbage, or see a banana), to zoos, to fire stations, to parks, or to the country—all to help their children learn. To those who have several dictionaries in their homes and whose children see fresh vegetables or take trips to the country or to the zoo often, this approach to helping children learn may seem very simple. But that's the point: for parents who will use the resources at hand— resources available in their own homes—teaching children *is* simple. The St. Louis study revealed that parents were instrumental in helping children to markedly increase their scores on tests measuring readiness to learn in schools. Think what you might accomplish if

5

you were to develop a better plan for teaching your children. But at the same time remember that the significant results of the St. Louis study were the consequence of parents who cared.

The second reason for you to teach your children is so you can bring them into contact with some of the bright and wonderful things in the world. Research examining the intellectual development of younger children indicates that when parents expose even a very young child to bright-colored objects of various shapes and textures, that child develops a sense of curiosity that helps him learn more about his environment. Bringing bright-colored things to young children is fairly simple; think of what even a little more effort will do for your children's sense of wonder.

A third reason for parents to be closely involved in teaching their children is that, through teaching, a close and long-lasting relationship can be established. With today's increased use of television and automobiles, the ideas and values that influence children come from many sources outside the home; so if you try to teach your children in the way you were taught by your parents, you will probably find your techniques incapable of meeting present challenges. But rather than doing nothing about the situation we face or throwing our hands up in despair, we need to develop a positive involvement with our children. A cooperative activity like teaching will very likely increase cohesiveness and trust among family members; parents as a result will retain more influence over the lives of their children.

If you will begin now to actively teach your child, you can discover a sense of closeness between you and your child that will last through the years and be a source of fulfillment for both of you.

Fortunately, children come into your family willing and ready to learn. Anything you do, then, can potentially promote their capability for learning. Talking to an infant or giving him a great amount of physical contact will help him learn things that the infant who is talked to very little or who receives little physical contact will not learn. Everything you do in the presence of your children has the effect of teaching, and, depending on what you do, the principles can be good or bad ones. Being a successful parent-teacher requires a general knowledge of how to teach, what to teach, and methods of motivating your children to learn. Through a regular and fairly easy approach, parents can teach their children many things. It is important that parents teach; children learn much from parents, and if nothing else they will acquire a positive attitude toward learning if parents spend the time learning how to teach.

Teaching is not as difficult as you may think, and it can add fun and enjoyment to your family. When learning becomes fun, even exciting, then you have started your children toward a lifetime of fulfillment.

ACTIVITY: WHY PARENTS SHOULD TEACH

Goals: List five specific behavior goals for each child. These might include honesty, confidence, table manners, respect for authority, etc.

Behavior: Using a scale of 0 to 10 describe the child's behavior in relationship to the goal ("0" being poor, "5" being average, and "10" being excellent).

Method: Suggest the method of teaching most likely to cause the behavior to improve (for instance, example, direct instruction, discipline, communication).

		Goal	Behavior Rating	Method
Child 1	1 2 3 4 5			
Child 2	1 2 3 4 5			
Child 3	1 2 3 4 5			

Implement the suggested methods for improvement of specific behaviors and chart each child's growth. If improvement is not noted, substitute another method of instruction. Further aid in the use of these methods can be found in subsequent units. Continue this process for each child until the desired goals are achieved.

UNIT I
ORGANIZING YOUR FAMILY

Every family has some form of organization, and, depending on the values of the parents, the organization may be loosely knit or tightly bonded together. This would be of little consequence if family organization made no difference to parents and children. But the evidence from family research clearly indicates that different types of family organizations produce different characteristics in children. In some cases, for example, methods of organizing a family tend to produce successful, happy children; other methods tend to produce children who are unhappy or unable to achieve.

The chapters in this section describe methods of organizing families that have been tested and that seem to work. We do not suggest that in order to be successful every family has to be the same; sameness is impossible, and it would be extremely boring even if it could happen. Instead, we have tried to outline basic principles that you can apply in a number of ways to your own family.

CHAPTER 2
WHAT FATHERS ARE FOR

Almost everyone will agree that fathers are important to their families, but too few know exactly why fathers are useful. The father's role in our society has been so neglected that many men don't know how to be effective fathers. This situation is critical, because mounting evidence indicates that fathers who fail to create certain conditions for their families can have marked negative effects on the lives of their children. In contrast, the effective father greatly increases the likelihood that his wife and children will live happier and more successful lives.

At the time in history when most men were self-employed on farms or in small businesses, fathers spent more time with their families than is possible for many men (or working mothers) to spend in this day and age. At that earlier time many facets of the father-child relationship developed as a natural consequence of working together; an added bonus for the child was the learning of a skill or craft. Today's complex and fragmented society, however, requires that one or both parents spend greater amounts of time away from home; generally this situation has negative impact on the children. But since parents are necessarily occupied outside the home, some adjustments need to be made, especially to retain the father as a prominent and positive figure in his family.

To be successful a father does not need to be more right or wise than a mother; he does not need to be more powerful, more knowledgeable, more competitive, or more successful. But he does need to be equally present in the minds of his family members and involved in his family's growing pains and achievements.

Father's Influence in the Home

Describing a father's influence in the home should not be taken as an indication that mothers are less important; mothers are equally important, but fathers do some things differently from the way mothers do. Furthermore, when fathers fail the effects can sometimes be worse than they are when mothers don't succeed. Researchers have recently found that fathers may have a more significant effect than do mothers on some facets of a child's development; for instance, fathers significantly influence the achievement attitudes of both male and female children. Studies have shown that most high-achieving men and women associated with fathers who had lofty expectations for their children, who were involved in actively teaching, who set an example of reading in the home, and who were perceived as being clearly involved in family decision-making and problem-solving. In contrast, children who had failed most often had fathers who tended to be aloof and distant in their relationships with their children, who consistently imposed their will on their children in an autocratic manner, who were absent from home for continuous lengthy periods, and who were ineffectual as parents because of a poor self-concept and the inability to make decisions. While there are certainly exceptions to this rule, the level of a child's achievement is directly affected by how a father acts in his family. Two significant implications of these findings are that a father can change his child's attitudes about learning and that children consider fathers to be extremely important and need active involvement with them.

A father also seems to influence the social behavior of his child. For example, children whose fathers were absent from the home for long periods or who were unsure in their roles as husbands and fathers tended to be quite withdrawn, made friends less readily, and/or exhibited inappropriate social behavior. Children who follow rules and adhere to customs and who are well-liked by friends tend to come from homes where the father actively participates in estab-

12

lishing family discipline, takes a meaningful part in family communication, and displays confidence in his role as a husband and father. Interestingly, both sons and daughters need these characteristics in their fathers—boys need someone to follow, and girls need an example of the way women associate with men.

Besides affecting achievement and social behavior, a father influences the moral and sexual development of his children. Fathers relating to mothers demonstrate the framework of boy-girl relationships, but some feel that it is the father who has the greater influence in determining how a boy or a girl feels about being male or female. For example, when a father treats his family so that others know he is a caring and a loving man, he helps his children feel good about themselves. On the other hand, fathers who are unduly harsh, unjust, and uncaring often make children uncomfortable about their sexuality.

Boys who do not grow close to their fathers tend to feel less confident about their own sexual identity. A girl who is unable to form a bond of closeness with her father sometimes receives fewer cues indicating that she is an attractive female; as a result she may doubt herself. Such maladjustment in a child doesn't usually manifest itself until puberty, and just when a child is most unsure of the appropriate sexual and moral roles he should adhere to, he finds that he still does not have a positive example to follow. The resultant trial-and-error learning process that he is forced to try only increases his confusion, and sometimes it establishes unsatisfactory values that remain through his entire lifetime.

While there are probably several other ways that fathers influence children, one other significant area of his influence revolves around his role as a husband. A man's behavior when he is with his wife affords his children the most realistic example of marriage that they will ever experience; what children expect in their forthcoming marriage is learned during the years of watching father and mother. Not only do children form specific attitudes from watching their parents, but they also decide whether or not marriage is a happy institution.

Fathers probably do not produce these results by themselves, but the influence of the father is always present. Even in his absence he can be a source of positive, happy, and constructive memories when he is effective or he can be a source of misery, despair, and hurt when he is irresponsible.

Probably the single most important step a man can take toward becoming an effective father is to solidify his own marriage. Evidence suggests that when a man strives to create a fulfilling relationship with his wife his children tend to be more stable and tend to become less anxious or upset.

While the father is extremely important to the family, most men who want to be good fathers face a difficult dilemma: most, if not all, education in parental skills is directed to women, so many men may not have the necessary skills and knowledge. A man's first task, then, is to learn what he needs; once he assesses his needs and meets them, then he can apply his learning in his home.

The Father's Role as an Initiator

Few things are as important for fathers as the skill of initiating. Some fathers hope that others will eventually do what is desired; a man who does not talk about important topics such as the family budget, for example, is playing a waiting game—he thinks that when the budget needs to be balanced his wife will just take care of it. And many women *do* take over, only to find that their husbands retreat even further from their responsibility in sharing duties in the home. A man's importance in the eyes of others, especially in the eyes of his children, stems partly from his ability to get things started—especially if the events he starts are helpful and happy ones. Initiating is not difficult, but it does require responsible involvement.

There are several important things a man may initiate, some of which exert great positive influence on his family members. Beginning with first things first, a father can initiate things that indicate he is interested in his marriage. He can, for instance, request that he and his wife have regular conferences where they discuss where they need to improve their relationship or what things both of them like or dislike. During these conferences the wife can also brief the husband on things he may not know about the children. The husband needs to make sure that he requests this conference as often as his wife does.

Another way a father can initiate is to begin a family discussion about family decisions. Asking for each family member's opinion on each issue, he can direct the discussion until a decision that is acceptable to everyone is reached. When a man acts in this way he shows involvement and interest in the family.

There are other everyday things a man can initiate. For example, a father can arrange when it is time for the family to depart for meetings or activities and when it is time for the family to take an outing. A father can also help children begin their own tasks. When he and his wife decide that a child is able to perform a household

14

chore, a father can give the assignment at least half of the time and he should consistently follow through when he makes the assignment.

A Father Needs to Be Informed

Too often fathers work away from home so much that they become ignorant of what is happening in the life of each family member. Most fathers depend on their wives to supply useful information about the children, but this procedure by itself is insufficient. To be effective a father must know about each family member, because if he acts or makes decisions based on inaccurate information a father soon becomes an autocrat in his child's eyes. By contrast, the man who sincerely collects information about his family members proves to them that he is interested in their lives; in addition, he'll be more secure and confident in his role as disciplinarian.

A father is a different person from his wife, and each has his or her own perception of the children. When a father adds his view to a mother's, then they as parents have a better basis for making decisions concerning their children. But if a man relies solely on his wife to supply him with information about the children, he will find himself responding to things he may not see, and as a result he may be caught between loyalty to his wife (and her viewpoint) and trust in his own perception. Although it is important for a father to maintain constant communication with his wife, he should seek other ways to obtain information about his children.

Besides getting information about family members from his wife, a father needs to spend time with each family member. Even if it is only an hour a week for each child or random snatches of time here and there, a father can use the minutes to listen, question, or tell stories. One father spends time each night at the bedside of each child. Another plans his weekends so that he spends some time alone with each person in the family. Many families have a "marriage night" when the children go to bed early, allowing the husband and wife to be alone, and a "family night" is scheduled at another time for fun activities that can be shared by parents and children. By working together in ways such as this a husband and wife can establish a cooperative family plan.

A Father's Relationship with His Children

Sometimes busy fathers try to compensate for their absence from the home by doing only those things while they *are* at home that can involve the entire family. While whole-family activities are

15

important some of the time, a father also needs to do some things with each child individually. Each child needs to know his father and needs to know that his father cares. All of us can remember when Dad sent us a personal letter or took just us with him for a ride or trip of some kind. Things are still the same today—children who have an individual association with their fathers feel a special glow inside and believe that they are quite important.

While the need for fathers to know their children is quite apparent, sometimes the father's need to be known by his children is not so obvious. Fathers are people; they have needs. Children should be made to realize that fathers need to be loved, to be respected, to be attended to, to be enjoyed, and to feel important, and that children can help fulfill these needs.

There is a lot of focus on a father's duties to his children, but emphasis also needs to be given to the rewards that a father can derive from his family. Most of these rewards stem from positive relationships with his children. These positive experiences can be more easily accomplished when a man recognizes that he must have his own relationship with each child. Part of developing that relationship is letting each family member know the father *personally* through his telling them openly about his interests, experiences, dreams, work, and many other things. One father whose son had a very poor attitude about school told his son about some success experiences he had had while a student, especially one when he was recognized as an outstanding math student in the sixth grade. It was not long before his son's attitude changed.

A father can also create a personal positive relationship through proper discipline. When a father knows the reason why he wants a child to do something and shares the reason openly with the child, he is involving himself in the life of his child. Additional involvement develops when a father helps enforce rules in the home.

Finally, men often believe that it is not manly to express emotions, especially affection for children. Yet a father's feelings about each child are vital to that child, and when affection is expressed it can create a great positive influence. Paying attention to a child, caressing him, spending time with him, and consistently enforcing rules that apply to him are effective ways of expressing love.

The Father's Role in Family Discipline

In many families, discipline is something parents use to stop children from doing things. Most often the mother, who is at home more frequently, establishes discipline so she can function as she believes she needs to. Usually the father somehow learns to fit in; instead, he should be a more integral part of family discipline and communication.

Every father should take an active part in shaping the values, social skills, and morality of his children. Some men believe that the lecture method is best, but unless constructive rules have first been established and enforced, lecturing only frustrates a child. Fathers who develop family rules have a greater influence and can more effectively organize the family, an experience that is both fulfilling and rewarding.

Among the ways a man can involve himself properly in family discipline is to ensure that he and his wife reach agreement about each rule that affects the children before that rule is implemented. During conversations the husband and wife can discuss what the rule should be, who will enforce it, how it will be enforced, and when it will be enforced. A father can then organize a family council when it is needed to discuss new rules or to explain changes in old rules. When he is at home, a father should act to enforce rules.

Probably the most important disciplinary thing a father can do is to organize and participate in a program designed to teach his children how to behave. Such a program simply consists of showing a child what to do, having the child practice the good behavior, and then having a discussion about it. When a good behavior is reinforced in this way it will strengthen. This is much more effective than waiting to see what happens and then punishing undesirable behavior. If a father continues to actively teach good behavior he will be esteemed in the minds and memories of his children.

There are numerous conclusive ways a father can act to become more effective in his family. Even though some suggestions have been given here, the most important thing is for a man to try in his own way to be a quality father for his children and to improve as he learns. Few children need a father who does everything correctly; most children blossom when they see that being a good father is important to the man they call Dad.

How To Be an Effective Father

1. Initiate family activities.
   Plan the family budget.
   Schedule maintenance of yard and house.
   Provide meetings for making family decisions.
2. Gather information about family members.
   Hold weekly conferences with wife.

17

Have mealtime talks.

Have school papers put by dinner plates.

3. Create a personal relationship with each child.

Spend time alone with each child.

Set and enforce family rules.

Listen attentively.

Do something special "from Dad."

4. Express affection.

Say "I love you" to each family member daily.

Touch and embrace each child often.

5. Establish family discipline.

Agree with your wife and child before establishing a rule.

Discuss family rules at a family council.

Actively enforce all rules.

Set guides for action instead of always saying "No."

ACTIVITY: WHAT FATHERS ARE FOR

The following activities are to be initiated by the father.

1. Request a time block of at least thirty minutes to talk to your wife about the children. Ask her point of view about each child, and ask her to discuss both their problems and strengths. Share your opinions about what you both need to do for and with each child.

2. Gather the family members together for thirty minutes to have a family council. Using the information collected from the conference with your wife, present a problem for the family to solve. Ask for each person's opinion. Avoid interruptions. Summarize the opinions of the group before giving your suggestion for the solution to the problem. Implement a program to solve the problem together.

3. Many projects, activities, or problems require families to make decisions. Effective decision-making, led by the father, is vital to effective fatherhood. Some important principles are involved:

A. Each person needs to voice his opinion; each person's views should be occasionally followed.

B. Family decisions will usually take longer than individual ones.

C. Each person needs to know what a decision means to him individually.

18

Discuss and practice with your wife the following decision-making steps:

A. Identify the alternatives that are open to the family.
B. Have each person declare which alternative he prefers.
C. Weigh the alternatives to find the advantages and disadvantages of each.
D. Specify the decision (one which the most prefer or the one which has the most advantages) in a way so that each person knows what to do.

Select a decision that could be made by the family. Gather the family together and state the purpose of the council as "needing to make a decision." Teach each family member the four decision-making steps listed above, giving examples of each. Guide the family through the decision-making steps until a firm decision is made.

NOTE: First trials are usually not completely successful. Praise any good behavior that you observe and ignore most of the bad. Remind the family that you and they will practice together again in the future.

CHAPTER 3
WHAT MOTHERS ARE FOR

We have sung, written, taught, and dreamed so much about what mothers do that most of us think we know what mothers are for. Yet in today's world women are faced with integrating their talents, family, marriage, and social relationships. Decisions need to be made concerning how much time is spent in the home, what should be accomplished during that time, and what role needs to be performed with children.

A successful mother does two things: she is responsible to herself and organizes her family and children so that she realizes her full creation as a woman; and she acquires and effectively implements constructive wife and parenting skills. Mothers who genuinely succeed are able to make these two parts of their role coincide.

Sacrifice and Self-Preservation

The ability mothers have to sacrifice themselves for their family has an early beginning. From the moment a woman conceives, the sole function of her body is to nurture the growing life within her. For example, if a woman doesn't have enough calcium to supply the needs of both her and her unborn child, her body gives all that is available to the child. In addition, her body provides a safe and secure environment for the fetus to grow in. Some knowledgeable mothers, realizing that any chemical taken into their bodies may affect the child's growth, also refuse to take medication or stimulants for themselves if there is any chance that the baby will be affected. Mothers then give babies birth at the expense of considerable pain and discomfort. All this, combined with the devoted care necessary to sustain life, usually forms an enduring attitude of sacrifice on the part of the mother. The desire to sacrifice is so strong that even mothers with adopted children display it. In most women sacrifice is the hallmark that brings satisfaction; in many, however, the sacrifice response is unbalanced with a mother's need to preserve herself as a woman. When this imbalance is too inordinate, it causes the woman to suffer low self-esteem, depression, and a sense of personal failure.

To be successful a woman must resolve the conflict between sacrifice for children and preservation of self. Unfortunately, most women are unaware of this conflict and consequently they don't know how to solve it. Feelings of guilt are associated with a woman's efforts to do something just for herself, while entrapped feelings are associated with efforts to spend her total time with and for her children.

The successful mother is one who strives to foster the best conditions for her children but who also achieves personal objectives if she wishes to. One of the first things a woman can do to realize this goal is to clarify what she values most and why. She needs to know and to be able to say what she wants for herself, how she wants to spend her time, and how she wants to develop her talents. Furthermore, she needs to carefully assess the boundaries of her emotional life and know how much stress she can tolerate, know what things renew her, and know how to assert her right to spend some time enhancing her own life.

To begin with, list the activities that uplift you. Some of those activities will be with your children, some of them will be with your spouse (unless you are a single parent), and some of them will be things you do alone. From the list select those activities that must occur regularly (weekly or biweekly) in order for you to maintain a good balance. These activities might range from social and religious functions to personal grooming or time with your husband. Realize that in order for you to give to your family, you must receive something for yourself. Communicate your need and desire to participate in these activities to all family members who are old enough to understand. By participating in these activities and by giving careful thought to your goals and values, you can be clear and definite about those things that will help you feel alive, real, and important to yourself.

A married woman needs a positive marriage in order to obtain those things that she values for herself as an individual. She and her husband as partners need to formulate a childrearing plan that will help her realize her personal goals. Emphasis should be given to developing a plan for child discipline and family organization; personal needs and desires should be included where they can be fit in. After the couple has come to a definite agreement about what they want for their children and how to get it, increased attention can be given to the individual desires of the wife. Formulating a program of family life and child care is a complex task that requires considerable trial and error combined with meaningful communication in order for each parent to realize individual responsibilities.

The Positive Marital Coalition

An increasing number of women are parents who do not have a partner. Single parents do not, of course, have to work as part of a marital team. But because a woman's role in her marriage relates so closely to what kind of a parent she is, we are describing how she can successfully combine the two to benefit both her and her children.

Some things are more important in families than are others. One of the important things is the marital relationship, and it should be a chief source of fulfillment for the two people in it. In fact, whatever it takes to maintain a good marriage is probably worth the effort. From the marital union a woman and a man can receive a significant part of what it takes to achieve satisfaction of self and can determine their own strategies for childrearing.

Getting Together

Children need and deserve a set of parents who work as a unit or team. When father and mother talk, decide, agree, and follow through together, the family environment tends to be more stable, positive, and growth-oriented for children. Conversely, when parents fail to agree on fundamental childrearing practices, children become the object of conflict and of a struggle for power between husband and wife. It takes two committed people who see the value of working as a team to achieve togetherness. Some people have partners who are not competent or who for some other reason neglect to work as an effective team member. In some cases one parent has to accept more of the responsibility for creating a positive childrearing plan. Whenever possible, however, sustained effort should be made to involve both parents as a team because the mental and emotional well-being of the family often depends on such teamwork.

A mother needs to learn about herself as an organizer and she needs to learn about her children so that she can decide what she wants for her family and the best methods of achieving what she wants. This learning usually comes from reading, taking classes, talking with more experienced parents, and trying different methods at home.

The important thing for a woman is to find a plan that works for her in helping her achieve her objectives as a parent and a family organizer. The plan should integrate home management and child-rearing with a woman's personal desires. When a good system is in effect, none of the three will dominate. Balance is crucial.

To be most constructive, a woman must be quite definite. Otherwise demands made on her time by her children, by her husband, or by outside interests will keep her so distracted that she will only inadequately provide her share of the organization that is needed by the family. A great deal of evidence suggests that only parents who systematically neglect or abuse their children are more harmful than those who are inconsistent and indefinite.

Once they have started to form an organizational plan for the family, the husband and wife need to decide how to maintain their own relationship. Ordinarily this evolves as they learn how often they want to talk, to date, to be intimately alone, or to work together on family activities. Too often insufficient time has been spent deciding these things, and both husband and wife feel alone. Marriage, the most important relationship of all, needs regular time and attention.

Mother's Discipline as a Way to Promote Growth

Successful mothers know that the absence of unpleasant things (such as quarrelling and arguing) is not the same thing as the presence of constructive behavior. There is a balance between letting a child freely unfold or grow and the need to actively teach children through discipline. Though it is often equated with punishment, discipline really should be considered consistent teaching.

Most parents have some definite ideas about the characteristics they desire in their children. Each child will have his or her own skills and abilities that will need parental respect, but mothers also want children to learn certain things. Discipline helps encourage children's natural abilities and teaches them what their parents desire for them.

Setting up an effective program of discipline requires that parents identify what they *want* their children to learn as well as what they *do not want* their children to learn. Enforcement techniques used by parents can generally be divided into two groupings: (a) those that promote a cohesive bond between parent and child, such as showing affection, talking, playing together, giving praise, bestowing rewards, and spending quality time together, and (b) those that promote action, such as establishing family rules and restrictions, teaching and showing what behavior is wanted, learning from logical consequences, assigning chores, instructing, evaluating, and helping a child control his or her own behavior. Because a woman is the mother and because she is part of the marital team, she is closely involved with both sets of disciplinary tools. It is most successful to strive for consistency and to develop an orientation toward personal growth of all family members.

Consistency

Consistency (unless we are consistently destructive) is the single most valuable factor in discipline. It means two things to the child. When a mother establishes a rule or teaches something, the child knows that she will follow through to see that it takes place. Secondly, consistency means that the child sees an emotionally stable, usually calm mother. When mothers remain calm and follow through, children generally accept direction, benefit from guidance, and value the mother's attention. A mother has then achieved status and influence with her children, and they will grow and progress as a result.

Orientation toward Child Development

Successful mothers have an attitude of encouraging and stimulating growth of what is best for the child. If a child needs to learn good work habits or cooperation skills, a good mother implements a plan to help him or her learn. Furthermore, such a mother anticipates the requirements that will be placed on a child in other social situations and helps him or her acquire the skills to avoid failure. Consider, for example, the parents who knew that a school play was planned for the coming year. To help their child prepare, the family organized some playlets where the child learned to say lines in front of people, dress in a costume, act out a role, and accept praise from others. The possibility of success for this child would be much greater than for a child whose parents did not have an orientation toward the child's growth.

Instead of interpreting misbehaviors as something to punish, a mother with a growth attitude will conclude that the child does not know something he needs to know, and she will create a learning plan. Two brothers who argue frequently and hit each other could be punished, but the mother could conclude that the boys were simply unable to talk over differences in a respectful way. One mother in this situation gave her boys a choice between being punished or trying to talk through their differences. They chose to practice talking over their differences. This mother focused on the development of her sons rather than on punishing them for bad behavior; this emphasis helps a mother succeed as a disciplinarian.

Enjoying, Loving, Cherishing

One of life's great lessons is that a time and a season exists for everything. This applies to mothers and children: we only have children once, and they are only young once. A mother owes it to herself to treasure the special moments she has with her family, both those moments that spontaneously happen and those times that can be arranged purely for the purpose of enjoyment.

One mother complained frequently of dirty hand prints on windows, pans pulled out of drawers, toys scattered around, and noisy voices. One day after she had voiced one of her complaints, her husband replied, "I'll bet someday we'll wish we could have a dirty hand print on the window." His simple statement jarred his wife's thinking. She had been thinking of her children as a dutiful burden and obligation; but now she began to find ways to enjoy them. She discovered that in order to be enjoyable, children had to be taught some correct behavior; she also learned that they could be enjoyed, loved, and cherished because they were there and they were hers. In that home considerable emphasis is now given to the making of pleasant and happy memories.

Too often the daily whirlwind of work, home management, or family life leaves barely enough energy to finish the day's duties. While trying to finish all that we need to get done we sometimes forget about loving and caring. On the other end of the spectrum, some of us organize our time and plan definite activities with our children. Mothers need to believe that enjoying and loving children is a valued end in itself. Hopefully, enough will happen in this loving process so that long after children are grown a mother can fill her memories with loved and cherished moments.

ACTIVITIES:
WHAT MOTHERS ARE FOR

1. Make a list of the ten things that are most important to you in your life; then write down why those things are important to you.

2. Make a list of what you would do next week if you could do whatever you *wanted* to do. Don't pay any attention to what it might cost or to whether you have enough time or any other hindrance. Now put an X by each of those *want to's* that you know you will get to do. Next, look at the remainder of the list and pick out two other *want to's* that you could do if you rearranged your schedule (it doesn't matter if it inconveniences some other family members). Write down a plan of how you are going to accomplish these two additional *want to's*. Follow through on your plan.

3. Make a list of the things that uplift you and raise your spirits the most. Make a plan of how you can experience one of these uplifting events each day.

4. Make a list of the three things you really want your children to accomplish in the next year (i.e., getting good grades in school, learning to play the piano better, learning to swim, keeping their rooms clean, etc.). Now decide what you can do to help them. Be specific: list such things as provide money for lessons, set aside fifteen minutes right after breakfast to give them time to practice, listen to them read each night, etc.

5. Do the activities listed under *What Fathers Are For.*

CHAPTER 4
FAMILY DISCIPLINE

The rules you establish and the ways you influence your child to behave properly help him learn such complex social attitudes as honesty, respect, responsibility, and independence.

Discipline deals with seven specific questions: (1) Who defines correct behavior? (2) Why do you get emotional about the way your child acts? (3) What does it take to establish rules to govern specific situations? (4) How are rules best enforced? (5) How can rules be adjusted? (6) How can every child be helped to develop responsible behavior? (7) What is the relationship between discipline and social behavior?

Defining Correct Behavior

Establishing an effective set of disciplinary procedures requires deciding which kinds of behavior are acceptable or desirable. Most people decide how their child should behave in very general terms, but you must be specific. How long should he sit and listen? Should he engage freely in play activity? How much time should he spend playing? Remember that *you* must decide these things, and you must decide how you want your child to act in a certain situation before that situation occurs.

Why Parents Get Emotional

The second principle of discipline relates to the first. Parents who do not decide how a child should behave in a given situation cause the child to be similarly indecisive; the child then behaves to test their response. Then, feeling powerless to control him, parents often get too emotional about the child's behavior. But establishing a program designed to help your child behave properly will help reduce the emotional part of discipline—parents will get less frustrated and less angry than they did prior to making a decision.

One set of parents tried to give a great deal of freedom to their children without setting any limits. Things went well for the most part until the second child began making excessive demands. He ordered a certain type of breakfast, teased, criticized, and broke other children's toys. His verbal outbursts and destructive acts made the parents so angry that they argued with him and screamed at him. He would sulk and throw tantrums as a result of these confrontations with his parents, but his behavior didn't change. Had these parents made a firmer decision about correct behaviors they would not have been so emotional, and they would not have had a harmful relationship with their son.

Family Rules

In *Child Management,* a book written by Smith and Smith, the authors state that any demand made on a child by his parents is a rule. Any task a child must perform is a rule. Any decision regarding what a child may or may not have, what he may or may not do, is a rule.

Many parents dislike establishing rules; they usually feel guilty, especially when they require some unpleasant behavior. But consistent enforcement of a rule makes the world safer and more comfortable for the child. Sometimes parents unconsciously disguise rules to ease their guilt. They ask a child, "Wouldn't you like to do the dishes?" or, "Do you want to take a nap?" If the only acceptable answer is "Yes," then the question, regardless of the way it is stated, is a rule. It would be much less confusing for the child if the parents would say, "Do the dishes now," or, "It's nap time." Long-term rules, which usually govern a chore or a family routine, must be enforced again and again. Short-term rules, or commands that are less easily recognized as rules, are the decisions parents make that

30

are peculiar to particular situations. Like long-term rules, these short-term rules require consistent enforcement, but they are often more difficult to enforce because they have not been carefully planned.

By increasing the consistency of your child's life you will make him more comfortable and will help him to develop positive attitudes. You can increase the consistency in your child's life by establishing rules. Establishing one long-term rule, usually a household chore, and enforcing it consistently is a good way to start. Whatever rule you decide to implement in your family should fulfill three requirements: it must be definable, it must be reasonable, and it must be enforceable. You must first decide the way you want your child to behave. Second, you must estimate whether or not your child can do what the rule would require. And third, you should anticipate that at times the rule will be broken. A healthy, normal child will need to test any rule, so if you cannot enforce it consistently you cannot expect him to follow it. If a rule is clearly defined and enforceable, and if you believe your child can follow it, you are ready to establish it.

To implement any rule you should first explain what the rule requires; then break the behavior into small parts and teach one part at a time. For example, if you want to establish the long-term rule of making a bed, first do the whole task for the child, indicating that what you have done is what the rule requires. Then break bedmaking into small parts: remove the pillow and put it on the chair, pull the bed out from the wall, throw back the covers, smooth the bottom sheet, and so on, until you have made the bed.

Establishing any rule to govern the way a child behaves requires the same procedure. Suppose you are interested in setting a rule to govern how your children greet people at the door because all of your children run to the door at the sound of a knock or doorbell and all of them want to speak at the same time. The first step is to break door greeting into small parts:

1. Approaching the door.
2. Opening the door and greeting the person who is known to the family.
3. Opening the door and greeting a stranger.
4. Inviting the person into the house.
5. Showing the person where he can be seated.

Each of these parts can be shown to a child and then the child can practice until he can perform the behavior on his own. This same procedure can be used for a multitude of situations like manners, mealtime behavior, sharing with friends, and so on. This procedure is fairly simple, yet it is effective and it is far better than criticizing children for things they do not do and probably don't understand.

Rule Enforcement

The next principle of effective family discipline is to enforce rules consistently. Establishing a rule to govern a task requires that you make sure the task is carried out. Enforcing a task such as bedmaking, for example, requires that you set a time by which the bed must be made. For younger children that usually means that they must make the bed before they can do something else, such as watch cartoons on television; for older children it means beds must be made before a specific time. Be sure to enforce the rule consistently. If children cry or throw a tantrum hoping to avoid the task, ignore the tantrum and respond only to the behavior that will accomplish the task.

Establishing a rule to govern behavior requires asking the child to restate the rule; irrelevant behavior should be ignored. For example, if you establish a rule to govern mealtime behavior that says a child must eat quietly, converse in a quiet voice, and avoid loud, emotional responses at the table, asking for a restatement of the rule whenever a child breaks the rule means asking him unemotionally, "What is the rule?" This procedure sounds so simple that it is hard to believe it works, but the experience of many parents indicates that it is more effective and easier to use than a system of punishment and penalties. If your child restates the rule but throws a tantrum and still fails to behave properly, ignore the tantrum. Respond only to behavior that is related to the way you want your child to act.

Enforcement of rules also requires that you know what your child likes to do. For example, most children love to have their parents read to them. With that knowledge parents may require that their children put on their pajamas—usually an undesirable requirement in the children's opinion—before the parents read to them. Having a story read then serves as an incentive. Parents can say, "Put your pajamas on so we can read a story." This method of establishing a routine or sequence of events requires that you identify activities that your child likes and doesn't like, and then that you put the liked things after the unliked things in a sequence.

Another way to enforce a rule is to praise desirable behavior. Catch your child when he is doing something right rather than when he is doing something wrong. Reward the child for each experience—be it positive or negative—by encouraging him to express his feelings and explain why he did what he did. Too often parents are so concerned about controlling children's behavior that they fail to establish a positive and a close relationship with them. Enforcement of rules is not effective when parents are hostile and cold. It is more effective to talk, to explain, to clarify, and to be affectionate. Parents who talk freely with children, who are affectionate with them, and who play with them have fewer disciplinary problems than parents who fail to do these things.

Finally, avoid arguments. Very often children argue to avoid following a rule. By arguing you are paying attention to disobedience and setting the stage for a poor relationship.

While some rules that you establish early will persist, others will not, and these will require an adjustment. There are some basic ways to adjust rules. First, establish only one rule at one time. Don't give your child a number of rules at the same time; add new rules one by one as each preceding rule is learned. Second, change rules that need to be changed. If, for example, you have had a rule that your children must take their shoes out of the living room, your growing child's increased ability to clean the entire living room will make a rule about picking up shoes too specific and, therefore, irrelevant. As a child grows older you will need to increase the flexibility of rules. When a child is young, he needs an environment in which rules are consistently enforced; but as he gets older his life becomes more complex and he requires more flexibility. One of the greatest sources of trouble between parents and an adolescent is the parents' attempt to enforce rules that they established during the adolescent's childhood, ignoring his need for increased flexibility.

Whenever you introduce a new rule or change an old one, discuss the change with your child. Invite him to tell you his point of view; try to arrive together at the basis for the new rule or the adjustment of the old one. When adjusting a rule, first state the present rule, and then have the child indicate the necessary change or adjustment. If you begin rule-change conversations with a child while he is at an early age, you'll discover that as he grows older he will feel increasingly free to discuss rule changes with you. He will see you as consistent but willing to negotiate, and you will see him as responsible and self-respecting.

One family moved to a new home, and the parents wanted to establish the boundaries within which the children could ride their bicycles. When asked to do so, the children identified where they thought the boundaries should be. It went so easily that the parents were happily surprised, and they turned the discussion to another topic. Interrupting, the oldest boy said, "I think we need some rules for going to other people's houses." Surprised, the parents responded to his request in an attitude of cooperation with their children. This example illustrates that children need rules, and that they will cooperate in creating new rules or in adjusting existing ones.

Building Responsibility

To become a truly responsible person, a child must have his own task that he is responsible for completing by a certain time and that he knows has a meaningful or worthwhile part in the family organization. In teaching a child responsibility, first make sure that the initial task you give him can and will be done successfully. Too often parents mistakenly assign a task that is either too difficult or too complex, and the child fails. In order for the child to learn to be responsible, he must believe that he can succeed. Responsibility is its own reward: when a child completes a task given him he has a fulfilling, rewarding feeling inside. Even though you assigned the child the task, by completing it on his own he feels responsible, and in the future he will complete and be thorough about other tasks assigned to him. A second way to help a child become responsible is to ask him to decide what he would like to do. Identify several tasks that are equal in difficulty but that are all likely to produce success. Then give your child an opportunity to decide which he will do. For example, bedmaking and dishwashing are probably equal in difficulty and can both be accomplished by children of four or five years of age. Suggest to your child that he may choose between them; because he was able to choose his own task he will have a feeling of increased responsibility.

The subject of responsibility can also be explained in your family discussions. Praise can be given when children complete tasks, take assignments, and follow through. One chief source of self-esteem for any person is the self-assurance gained by responsible productivity. Every child needs to experience authentic accomplishment; there is no substitute for the actual opportunities created by parents.

Discipline and Social Behavior

The rules you establish and the way you enforce them will be transferred from your home to your children's school, church, and other social situations. If you reserve the sole right to make rules in your family and if you do so without careful explanation to your children, they will have attitudes about people in authority that may be difficult for them to overcome. Children who are reared in these kinds of homes tend to see themselves as being acted upon by the people in their world. They either begin to overconform to rules or to avoid rules altogether. Neither style of living provides the constructive interchange that permits people to get along harmoniously. In contrast, if parents establish rules that children need and ask children to help in setting new rules or adjusting existing ones, children learn to discuss openly with people who affect their lives. They tend to be emotionally controlled and to believe they can affect their own destiny. When problems arise, their first impulse is to try for mutual discussion rather than to overreact or to comply, causing resentment or fear. Through effective discipline parents can teach their children to stay involved, to make mutual decisions, and to work cooperatively with other people.

Conclusion

Effective discipline results from deciding how you want your child to behave, establishing rules, enforcing rules, adjusting rules, helping your child to become responsible, and remembering the relationship between family discipline and social behavior. Decide what kind of parents you would like to be and work to accomplish your own standard of performance; don't make the mistake of evaluating yourself solely on the behavior of your children. It is important that you believe in yourself and believe that you are capable of providing those things your children need to become responsible adults.

Most of the time serious problems in families stem from parental reaction to an event rather than from the event itself. A child's early sexual exploration is probably no problem, but an extreme reaction by a parent can be a problem. When you decide about your own parenting goals, set rules, and enforce them you are less likely to react inappropriately. If you are able to establish rules, enforce them, and adjust them to fit your child's needs, you can count on his establishing positive attitudes towards other people and towards responsibility and honesty.

ACTIVITIES: TEACHING THROUGH FAMILY DISCIPLINE

1. Decide on Desirable Behavior
   Identify a task that you want your child to complete and write a description of the behavior you want him to exhibit while he completes the task.

2. Establish Rules
   A. Establish a task rule.
      1. With your child identify the task you'd like him to do.
      2. Break the task into small and specific parts and show your child how each part is done.
      3. Explain the task as you demonstrate it. Ask the child to tell you how he is to do it.
      4. Establish a time limit.
      5. Describe the consequences of completing the task.
      6. Enforce the rule and ignore behavior that is irrelevant to the accomplishment of the task.

   B. Establish a behavioral rule.
      1. Identify the desired behavior.
      2. Demonstrate that behavior.
      3. Discuss what was done.
      4. Describe the consequences of the behavior according to the rule.
      5. Do *not* set a time limit.
      6. Enforce the rule and ignore irrelevant behavior.

In the table below identify 3 rules that you have for your children and then tell whether you as parents agree on the rule, and then what each of you does when a child complies or doesn't comply with the rule.

Increasing Parental Consistency
Identify three rules you have established for your child.

	Rule 1	Rule 2	Rule 3
Do you, husband and wife, agree that each rule is really a rule?			
Father, identify how you act when the child complies with the rule.			
Mother, identify how you act when the child complies with the rule.			
Father, identify how you act when the child does not comply with the rule.			
Mother, identify how you act when the child does not comply with the rule.			
Together, how can you enforce each rule more consistently?			

CHAPTER 5
EFFECTIVE FAMILY
COMMUNICATION

Why are some families so close and others so distant? For what reason is the influence of the family so great and so long-lasting? Effective family communication can strengthen the bond that ties families together, and the way family members communicate with each other creates the influence that affects us all.

There are many reasons why good communication is important, but most important is the effect it can have on the self-esteem of each family member. It is largely through communication with other people, and especially with you, that your child learns about all the things he himself believes. If your child is to gain a positive concept, you must learn to communicate effectively. Good communication employs the following principles:

1. Parents must actively listen to their children. Listening means receiving what is sent in the same way the sender intends it. Listening is not easy.
2. Parents must consider each child's ideas as worthwhile even though parents may not always agree with the child's ideas. In many families, when a child's idea is disagreed with the child also

believes the idea was stupid or inadequate. It takes skill to consider an idea as worthwhile even though you don't agree with it.

3. Speech and action must correspond. For example, if you express words of love, your actions must communicate the same thing.

4. Family communication needs to be filled with humor, needs to emphasize the positive, and needs to give more suggestions of what children can do rather than what they cannot or should not do.

5. Parents must learn what their actions mean to their children. Every act is a form of communication, whether or not you intend it to be, and every act will have meaning for your children.

Active listening, the first principle of communication, does not mean merely being silent; it means hearing what your child says, seeing what he sees, and feeling with your heart what he feels. Specifically, it means stopping what you are doing, asking to be told more, clarifying what is said by repeating it to make sure you understand clearly, and reflecting the same emotion the other person is experiencing by sincerely saying, "You seem to be really happy [or excited, upset, or discouraged] now." When you listen to your child this way, he will begin to believe that what he feels and thinks is important, and he will develop self-confidence and assurance based on the idea and the belief that his parents really do understand him. There is evidence that often the message a sender sends is not the message the receiver receives. Why? We don't always say what we really mean; as listeners our brains work much faster than our ears do, so we frequently "tune out" the speaker. It is probably not too harmful to miscommunicate some of the time, but in families members tend to be inaccurate about the same things and with the same people. Once a cycle of poor communication begins it is difficult to reverse. One way to ensure good communication is to learn to listen. It requires work, but it can be a rewarding experience. It will surprise you to learn how many terrific things your children are saying.

The second principle of effective communication is to consider each child's ideas as worthwhile. This is not easy: children do not always have thoughtful and helpful ideas; instead they tend to ramble and say unconnected, illogical things. But within every family each child needs to have his ideas considered as useful some of the time. The following techniques may help:

1. When you make a family decision, ask each child his opinion.
2. Tell each child that you like to hear his opinions.

40

3. Praise each child when he expresses an idea, and try to put some of his ideas to use. When you use your child's ideas, he will begin to believe that he has something to offer and will develop a sense of worth.

Matching your words with your actions is the third principle of effective communication; although it is probably the most difficult principle, it is also one of the most important. In an attempt to disguise their true feelings, many people say things that are very different from the things that they feel inside. Because this inconsistency can create serious emotional and mental problems in families, it is very important that you make your words match your feelings. You can improve your ability to do this by practicing some elementary principles:

1. Several times during the day try to identify how you are feeling. Then verbalize your feelings by saying, "I am feeling happy," "I am feeling angry," and so forth. This will bring you in tune with your feelings and teach you a better emotion-word vocabulary.
2. Express your real feelings to people in your family. Most of the time it is better to say "I am angry" than to act angry and make people guess how you feel.
3. Ask other family members how they feel. Your children will be good at this, but often adults will have problems expressing their emotions.

One purpose of family life is for parents and children to become emotionally kindred, and this purpose is accomplished when parents and children share emotional experiences. While sharing emotions is important, it will occur only when your children can read your behavior correctly. If your words and actions are not congruent, your children will become suspicious of you and afraid of what you really mean. Because they will acquire the same ineffective form of communication that you exhibit, they will very likely have difficulty communicating with their friends and with other people throughout their lives. However, when your words match your actions, your child learns that what he believes about himself is correct. Mirroring the self-assurance that you exhibit, your child will acquire self-esteem and will develop confidence and an inner calm.

Fourth, include humor and emphasize the positive aspects of your child's behavior. Far too many parents regard rearing children as such a serious matter that they fail to laugh about themselves and their children. Similarly, they allow too little time for the enjoyment of family jokes. Under such conditions, parents begin emphasizing what children cannot or should not do rather than helping them identify what they can and should do. Such parents often tend to overreact emotionally. Humor and fun in family life can be cultivated if you do the following:

1. Try to catch your child doing something right. Instead of concentrating on controlling deviant behavior, pay attention to and focus on catching your child doing something you approve of.
2. For two hours each day avoid saying the word *don't*. You will discover that there are numerous ways to correct behavior without saying that particular word.
3. Ask your child to tell you a funny story, and then tell him one of the same kind. You will discover that even young children have a creative sense of humor and all that is needed to cultivate it is a little encouragement and reinforcement.
4. Tell your child about a funny experience you have had recently. He will learn that when you can laugh at yourselves he, too, can laugh at you.
5. Parents, laugh at each other—not in a harmful or painful way, but at the funny things each of you do; children feel calm when they see their parents laughing and enjoying each other.
6. Teach your child what *sense of humor* means, and help him practice using it.

All of the ways that you act have meaning for your child. Often small gestures, facial expressions, body postures, or voice tones may mean something to him. To improve your communication with him you need to learn what your actions mean to him. One way of learning is to ask your husband or wife to tell you about a specific action of yours and what it may mean; then ask your child. You will discover that he is very observant, and he will be able to tell you what some of the things you do mean to him. Another way of learning is to set your child on your lap and ask him to make a happy face, a sad face, a surprised face, and so on. If he does well in expressing these emotions accurately, you are probably doing well, too.

The role of the father is particularly closely related to his child's ability to learn: the effectiveness of their communication can have a marked effect on the child's classroom performance. But when one PTA group of 150 was asked how many had spent five minutes that day alone with each of their children, only twenty raised their hands; and only two of those were men. In our fast-moving way of life, it seems, the fathers are unfortunately pushed out of a close associ-

42

ation with their children. Solid communication cannot be created during a two-week vacation once a year; communication is a day-to-day process. Take it as a challenge to spend five minutes alone each day with each child. You will find it to be as rewarding and helpful to you as it is to them.

ACTIVITIES: TEACHING THROUGH EFFECTIVE COMMUNICATION

1. One night each week select one child and organize an evening to honor him. Let him help in selecting the games and refreshments. During the evening identify and share with the child reasons why he is special to your family. Emphasize that he, like all of your children, is very special to you. Activities for the evening might include looking at pictures, slides, or movies of the child, talking about things he has done, or just enjoying his company. Afterwards ask each child how he felt being the special child of the evening.

2. Take ten minutes to talk with your child. Ask him to tell you about an exciting thing that has happened to him. After he has finished speaking say, "Please tell me some more about it," or "Let me see if I understand what you are saying." As he continues speaking look directly at him. Attempt to describe the emotion he has expressed by saying something similar to, "You seem to be feeling . . .". Most of all, listen actively.

3. Select a time period of one to two hours during the day. During this time do not say the word *don't,* and avoid being negative or critical about your child's behavior. When he exhibits undesirable behavior, describe to him the more desirable behavior instead of just criticizing the negative behavior. For example, if he asks for something in a whining voice, respond by saying, "I would rather you ask in a calm voice." If he jumps on the furniture, tell him what else he can do instead of what not to do. Always emphasize the positive.

4. Ask your child to make a happy face, a sad face, a sleepy face, an angry face, a fearful face. Next, have him identify similar expressions as you make them.

On the following page are several faces. Ask your child to point to each face as he names the emotion it is expressing. After he has

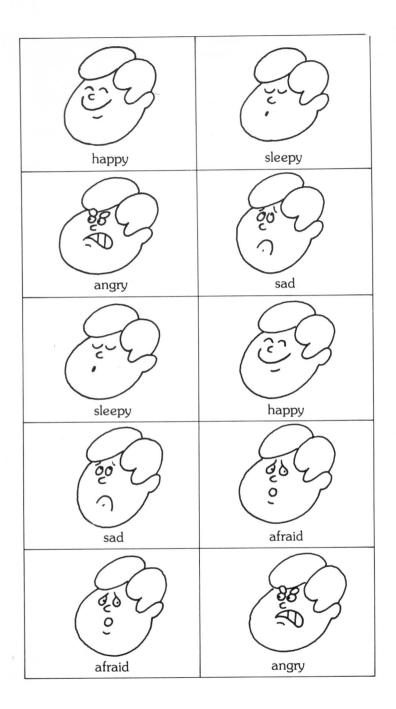

happy

sleepy

angry

sad

sleepy

happy

sad

afraid

afraid

angry

44

completed this, help him cut out the sections on the page. Mix them up carefully and assist him when necessary as he matches each face with one expressing the same emotion.

CHAPTER 6
TEACHING YOUR CHILDREN THROUGH DIRECT INSTRUCTION

Being a teacher may be a new and unfamiliar role for you; it is unfamiliar for many of us. You may feel uncomfortable in this role, and you may even be unsuccessful at first. But try—you will find you can probably be successful. To teach children requires that you establish a quality learning relationship and include certain specific activities.

Creating a Learning Relationship

To be a good teacher you must establish a trusting, close, and open relationship with your child. There are some specific things that will help. First, be consistent. If possible, have a regular time for teaching; if that is not possible, establish a time that the child can look forward to occasionally. If you set up a regular schedule but don't feel like teaching at the appointed time, say so and indicate that you would prefer to wait until the next appointed time.

As you begin the actual process of teaching, share yourself with your child; make sure you touch the child affectionately, show praise and encouragement, remain calm, and let the child decide how long each learning session will be. Let your child know that you enjoy spending time, that you feel close to him, and that when he gets excited you are excited, too. This sharing is what produces cohesion. As you share, your child will also learn to share.

After you and your child have completed an exercise or activity, ask your child what was good or bad about it, letting him know that you're willing to listen. Then share your opinions and reactions as well. This evaluation will help produce openness.

You may think that a young child is not capable of establishing a good learning relationship with an adult, but usually by the time a child is three or four he not only can function in this kind of relationship, but he usually strongly desires one. Older children are even better at it. Most often, though, a good learning relationship develops over a period of time, so don't be too discouraged if at the beginning you don't have as good a relationship as you would like. Anticipate, instead, that at first you will have some good experiences, some frustrating ones, and some negative ones. But keep applying the principles, and your learning experiences will improve.

Creating Learning Procedures

After you have established the learning relationship, practice the specific things you must do to help your child learn. Here are eight:

1. Find out what your child already knows and the way he or she likes to learn best.
2. Set a goal or objective that you would like to reach.
3. Give your child ideas to think about.
4. Give directions.
5. Ask questions.
6. Encourage cooperative activities.
7. Reward desirable performance.
8. Evaluate your child's performance.

Preassessment

Before you begin teaching, you must discover some of the things your child already knows and some of the ways he learns best. You will need to discover such things as what he likes to do in his free time, how long he can sit and do one thing, how well he follows directions, and the best way to give directions.

You must learn the kinds of things your child does well. Can he listen? How well can he draw? Can she identify the subjects in pictures in books? Can he speak clearly? Is she adventurous?

48

You must also learn some of the best ways for your child to learn. Does she prefer doing things or seeing things? Most of the time children like to do and see rather than to listen.

Last, during preassessment you must learn about yourself. How long can you be patient? When is a good time in your daily schedule for you—father, mother, and child—to spend time together? Answers to all of these questions will help you preassess yourself and your child and will help you make the most of the teaching situation.

Setting a Learning Goal

Establishing a goal of what the child is to learn is essential if you are to accomplish all you can. Your child must understand and agree with the goal. Tell your child in simple words what will be learned in an activity. Then ask your child what he is supposed to learn. Express your confidence in his ability to achieve the established goals.

Presenting Ideas

When you begin to teach, use examples and stories to illustrate a point. As you tell a story incorporate the child into the illustrations, because a child likes to learn and hear about himself more than he likes to hear about any other person.

Ideas and explanations should be given in short sessions using simple examples and brief sentences.

Giving Directions and Asking Questions

While talking to a child, simplicity is the key. Playing games with pretend people and telling a story is a good approach; it is important to make sure that a discussion, rather than a lecture, exists. Generally it is best to avoid talking for any great length of time unless you are telling a story. Suppose, for example, you want to teach an older child an idea about the Civil War and you want to teach about General Grant and General Lee; instead of telling about them right at first, ask how much the child already knows. Once you begin teaching, say a few things and then ask the child to repeat. Then tell the child a few more things and make up a story or game. A child can absorb a lot of information in short bursts, but in long bursts boredom sets in.

In addition to teaching the child ideas you will need to give him directions and ask him questions. Both are important and easy. Make directions short and simple, repeat the directions you give your child, and ask your child if he understands the directions. In asking questions, use the following techniques:

1. Vary your questions. Once in a while ask a memory question, such as, "What was the name of that animal?" At other times ask a leading question. Ask your child for his opinion about anything that interests him.
2. Make your questions brief: "Who was that?" "What did he do?" "How does this work?" "Why is that important?"
3. Avoid saying "right" or "wrong" all of the time. Occasionally say, "That's a helpful idea. Can you think of some more?" To give your child an opportunity to express himself fully he must not feel the need to be right all of the time.

Developing Cooperation

Direct instruction requires cooperative activities. Often the child would much rather do something *with* you than for you, so keep these things in mind:

1. Let your child take the lead. Sit back; let him be first to draw the circle or give an idea about a picture. Then you can draw your circle or give your opinion. Occasionally it will be important for you to take the lead, but you should avoid doing it all the time.
2. Let your child tell you what he thinks must be done. This will help you know how well he understands the instructions for the activity.
3. Show some enthusiasm. Drawing a circle may not be a lot of fun for you, but a child needs to know that you enjoy participating with him.
4. Take turns doing things.
5. Sometimes you should let your child's work be better than yours. If yours is always better, he will get discouraged.
6. Praise what your child does to help him overcome the fear of making mistakes. Every child needs to learn that it's all right to make mistakes, and he can learn this best if parents freely and openly admit to making a mistake themselves.

Rewarding Your Child

Always remember to reward your child for a good performance. Praise and encourage him for such things as sitting down and participating with you. Freely praise his part in some of the activities. Praise him for having a new or different idea. Make sure he understands that it's important for him to think by himself. Use different kinds of rewards. A reward may be praise and encouragement, it may be a piece of candy, it may be doing something fun, or it might be a special television program. It can be anything the child likes to do.

Some react negatively to setting up rewards for a specific behavior, but remember that a child thrives on recognition. Getting a reward does not mean manipulation or bribery to the child; the child usually feels justified in light of his effort.

Evaluating

Evaluating your child doesn't mean deciding whether your child is a success or a failure or whether he is good or bad. It means finding out whether or not he has learned specific things. You know the importance of setting a goal; evaluating simply means finding out whether or not you and your child have achieved that goal. It will be helpful during evaluation for you to answer the following questions: Did your child follow the directions? How well do you think something has been learned? Did you reach the goal? Were the activities interesting? Did you both get involved? Did you both enjoy the learning activities? Rather than answering these questions on a piece of paper, discuss them with your child. Effective evaluation consists of a discussion between the two of you.

ACTIVITIES: TEACHING YOUR CHILDREN THROUGH DIRECT INSTRUCTION

1. Gather information to answer the following questions:
   A. How long will your child sit and participate in an activity with you?
   B. Does your child like to listen to stories in order to learn?
   C. Does your child like to see things in order to learn?
   D. Describe four things your child likes to do.
   E. Will your child follow directions?
   F. How often do you praise and encourage your child?
   ___Often ___Sometimes ___Seldom ___Rarely
   G. Would your child rather learn by himself or with other children?

2. Select from the following list three things that are difficult for your child to do:

_____counting   _____naming pictures in books
_____drawing   _____pasting
_____cutting   _____saying words clearly
_____writing   _____tying his shoe

Establish a thirty-minute teaching period for each of the above tasks that your child has difficulty accomplishing. Referring to the steps for teaching through direction instruction (listed below), prepare and implement a teaching plan. Be sure to evaluate your teaching/learning experience.

3. Ask your child if you can play with him. Allow him to take the lead and tell you what to do. Express enthusiasm at being able to do things with him. Disappointments should be handled cheerfully. After completing one activity with him, ask him what he liked best about what both of you did.

Teaching through Direction Instruction
    1. Preassess
    2. Set goals
    3. Present information
    4. Give directions
    5. Ask questions
    6. Encourage cooperative activities
    7. Reward desirable performances
    8. Evaluate

CHAPTER 7
HELPING CHILDREN
LOVE TO LEARN

The family plays a major role in determining not only what children learn, but also how fast they learn it. This influence begins when the child is born and continues throughout his entire educational experience. Research suggests that even college students who learn while away from home may be influenced by the family environment. Most parents are anxious—sometimes too anxious—to help each child do well in school. They buy educational toys, repeat the alphabet over and over, and fuss about a child's ability to identify colors. But while a child's ability to learn in school and in the world is affected by parental teaching, research about families indicates that the child's achievement will depend on many things.

To help your child love to learn you can start while he is young, increase the amount of information you share, arrange tasks so a child can work independently, develop a variety of ways to converse with and express affection for your child as he tells you his thoughts, and work to build your child's self-esteem and social confidence.

Beginning When a Child Is Young

Much of a person's attitude about the world is formed during the early months of his life. To foster your child's curiosity and his willingness to learn, you can introduce him to objects that have a variety of bright colors, textures, shapes, and sizes. Permitting a child freedom of physical movement by allowing him to crawl, feel things, and explore helps him develop a positive attitude toward learning. If you place the crib in the middle of the room away from the walls, a child can see out on all sides instead of only one or two. When your child is learning words, you should pronounce them clearly and help him to follow your example. Listen to the sounds of words and letters. A child who is beginning to speak listens to sounds and watches the shape of the mouth as other people talk. When you say words clearly instead of using "baby talk," the child will pronounce the words more clearly. As your child tries to say words, gently nudge his mouth into the shape necessary for him to create a given sound. The mouth must, for instance, be shaped differently to sound an L than it does for an O sound; when a child hears accurately and speaks clearly and correctly, reading, speaking, and writing will be easier for him.

Most parents know that children will respond to pictures before they respond to stories. This means that you can help your children get interested in learning by asking them to point out certain animals, plants, or other objects from pictures in books. Later, when you read to them—an important part of achievement—they will recognize these pictures and will correlate the words you say.

Family Information Exchange

A child needs to have something to think about, and much of what he considers comes from his family. This is probably true because family relationships are among the most intense and important relationships a person will ever experience. Consequently, what parents tell children and how they share information cannot be treated lightly—even though children of all ages usually act like they are not paying attention.

Learning in school and in other places in life occurs when children are able to absorb and share different kinds of information. For example, they must be able to listen to and follow instructions, which means that they must be able to hear and understand words. They also need to memorize such things as names and dates and they must be able to analyze problems and integrate elements, showing how one thing relates to another. To be a good achiever, a child must learn to think about many different kinds of information, and his ability to do so depends on how he communicates with his parents and his brothers and sisters.

To help children achieve well, a family needs to organize itself so that parents and children have access to the most possible information. For example, when some parents are using the telephone, they tell a noisy child, "Be quiet." Others say, "Be quiet; I am using the telephone and I can't hear"; the second remark shares more information. When parents give short commands or instructions such as "Be quiet," "Shut up," "Get off," and "Move away," children learn to act out of fear of punishment rather than with an understanding of the reason for their actions. Sometimes, too, when parents tell about a new situation such as going to school, they give only brief explanations of how the child should act and what he can expect. For example, a parent may say only, "School is a place where you go to learn things and do everything the teacher says."

To help children love to learn it is important that parents share information with their children. Children whose parents are abrupt and uninformative will not hear much of what a teacher says; they will simply stop listening—even though the teacher may be sharing some very interesting ideas. Some children have actually been trained to not listen past the first few words they hear because of the low quantity and quality of information that is available to them in their homes.

You can practice sharing more information with your child. First, try explaining why you want him or her to do what you have asked. For example, instead of just saying "Get off the couch," explain, "When you walk on furniture it gets dirty and wears out faster." Second, read stories or other articles and then tell them to your children. When you tell your child about something you have thought about, you are teaching your children to listen. Third, before you give instructions think about all of the things you want your child to know, and then attempt to share enough ideas to teach your child those things. Fourth, share an activity, such as visiting a zoo, so that each of you can talk about the same things. Children can receive more information if they already know something about the subject being discussed.

Some families fail to bring much information into the family from the outside by curbing family discussion or by limiting the number of newspapers, books, and magazines found in the home. Families who want to help children love to learn will encourage their children to talk about what they see around them, will help their children listen to others, and will bring each child into contact with as many good and beautiful things as possible.

Independent Work

To be successful, any child must learn to begin projects on his own initiative and to work without a great deal of help. Many parents mistakenly believe that they must always work with their children in order to help them learn. But while it may be true that a child needs to see his parents working while he is working, it is not correct that parents should *always* work closely with a child or that they should work on the same projects. Instead, parents must help each child work independently. When parents get too involved, children can fail to be independent workers and can fail to learn that they must complete the tasks that they begin. There are a number of ways that independent working habits can be achieved:

1. Give a child a small task. Explain the task to him, carefully teach him each step in the task, and express your confidence in his ability. Then *leave him alone*. Return a short while later to check on his progress; show a bit of interest, and then leave. When the child has finished, report his progress to the family. This way a child learns to accept the responsibility for projects assigned to him.
2. Children like independent play. Arrange a box of crayons, papers, small scissors, and other tools. Then when one child wishes to play, give him the box, show him where to play, and *leave him alone*. Return only enough to help him maintain order and to ensure that he helps clean up.
3. After the age of three, a child can be directly taught the concept of working independently. Occasionally use the words, "You have done this work independently" when you praise your child's efforts. Foster independent work as something that is very worthwhile.
4. Ask a child which of two or three small tasks he would like to do; ask when he will do the task he has selected, and then let him proceed on his own. Be sure to praise any efforts he makes.

Many children fail in life because parents are present too much and take too much responsibility for children, and this is particularly true of eldest children because parents have more time to dote. But success in our society depends on the ability to work independent of a great deal of help from others. For most children there is a

56

balance between working with or for parents and doing things for or by themselves. Successful children achieve this balance.

Developing Self-Esteem about Learning

Children need to believe positive things about themselves; when they believe positive things, they acquire self-esteem and confidence. A child who has self-esteem believes he is worthwhile and valuable; the confident child believes that, given opportunities, he can try new things and succeed a reasonable amount of the time. Family communication is essential in developing self-esteem, and real accomplishment is essential to gaining confidence.

Most parents, wishing to help their children gain confidence and self-esteem, tell them loving things, praise them, and give them encouragement. While these techniques are certainly necessary, they are not enough: children develop beliefs about themselves more from what they themselves think and say than from what they hear their parents or others say about them. So the task is to help children think and say positive things about themselves. There are several ways to accomplish this.

1. Make sure that every family member has a chance to express his ideas. To facilitate this, establish the rule that everyone listens to a speaker's ideas without interrupting. It is the primary responsibility of parents to make sure that every family member follows the rule.

2. When a child colors a picture, builds with blocks, or accomplishes anything, he wants his parents' approval. But once you have given him your attention and have praised him, find out what he thinks about his work. You can say, "How do you feel about what you have done?" or "Do you think you can do this again?" or "I'll bet you are really excited about this." The important thing is that the child be given a chance to say how he feels about his accomplishments.

3. It will be helpful if you remember that what children often say is what they think you want to hear. One mother praised her son profusely but ignored him when he said positive things about himself. On the other hand, when he criticized his ability to do things she responded by disagreeing and by praising him. The son soon learned that to get praise from his mother he had to say something critical about himself.

4. You can help your children be successful by organizing tasks for them. Real accomplishment is the best way to foster confidence, and opportunities for such accomplishment come

from everyday family life. It will help, for example, to make sure that your young children (ages three or four) dress themselves most of the time, have responsibility for a few simple chores around the house, and otherwise contribute to the family. In one family the youngest prepare the table for one meal a day. The four-year-old sets the table, the six-year-old clears the table after the meal, and the three-year-old is responsible for putting the salt and pepper shakers on the table and putting them away again. While it may be easier and quicker for the parents to do that work themselves, they are building confidence in their children by letting them experience real accomplishment.

By using these suggestions, parents can increase the probability that their children will develop self-esteem and confidence. It is probably not as important to be right as it is to be able to weather failures and solve problems. The optimism and hope needed to carry a person through to achievement stem from self-esteem and confidence; they are gifts any parents can give to their children.

ACTIVITIES: HELPING YOUR CHILD LOVE TO LEARN

Listening

1. *Simon Says* is a game that makes learning to listen enjoyable for young children. The leader acts out each command he gives to the child, prefacing most of the commands with "Simon says." Unless these words are used before a command, the child must not obey what he hears. Instead, he must keep the position he had before he heard the command. When a group of children are playing the game, if one follows a command that is not preceded by "Simon says," he is out and must sit down until a winner is determined. Suggested commands are such things as close your eyes, touch your toes, touch your elbow to the floor, wiggle your nose.

Following Directions

2. Issue a series of simple directions for your child to follow such as "touch your toes, crawl under the chair, sit on the stairs," or "wiggle your nose, turn around, sit down." As he improves in his ability to follow directions in a series the tasks can be made more difficult or the number of tasks can be increased.

Storing and Recalling Information

3. Read a familiar story to your child and afterward allow him to review it while you check for proper sequence of events and details. Encourage him by asking questions like, "Which happened first? Which happened last? How did he feel? What color of dress was she wearing?"

4. Play a variation of the game *I Went to China.* Begin it by saying, "I went to Grandma's house and in my suitcase I took my toothbrush." The child then needs to repeat what the leader said and add one item, for example, "I went to Grandma's house and in my suitcase I took my toothbrush and my nightgown." The game continues back and forth two or three times until it becomes frustrating for the child. Then a new series can be started by using a new sentence such as, "I went to the moon and in my pocket I took a . . .".

Solving Problems

5. On a tray organize several objects made of wood, glass, and/or metal. Give your child a magnet and assist him in categorizing the objects into those that are attracted to the magnet and those that are not. Help him discover the common quality of those objects that are attracted to the magnet.

Independent Thinking

6. *Do as I Do, Not as I Say* is a game that requires the child to think and act independently of what he hears. Similar to what is done in *Simon Says,* the leader gives a command for the child to follow. However, if the leader does not follow the command, the child must not. Instead, the child must always do exactly what the leader does.

Social Skills

7. Social skills are best acquired by imitation. Given an opportunity to act out the roles of others, a child is given the chance to clarify and create his own roles and understandings of social behavior. One interesting situation that will bring a great deal of insight to the parent is to allow the child to be the parent and the parent to be the child in a pretend situation. The problem to be portrayed might be that of the child doing something wrong and the parent discovering it and taking care of it. Other problems and situations can be created as the circumstances suggest.

Working Independently

8. Have your child help bring materials that you select to a table or central place in the room. These materials might include blocks, paper, crayons, paste, scissors, and scraps of fabric. Let the child decide what he will do with these materials, and then leave him on his own to work on his project. After about ten minutes return to see how he is doing, but make your visit brief. Return only to ask if he has done what he wanted and then praise him for doing the work by himself. This same set of procedures should be followed both when your child has a task to do or when he is playing by himself.

Creating a Positive Self-Image

9. Spend five to ten minutes alone with your child in a quiet situation where disruptions are minimized. Use this time to listen to your child and to discover just what he thinks about things—what makes him happy, sad, afraid, and so on. Ideally this listening time should take place daily. As the child learns to express himself more effectively he will also gain in his feeling of importance because he knows that you care enough to listen and to spend this time with him.

10. Posing for a picture always delights a child. Spend a few minutes taking snapshots and letting the child choose his pose. If you have previously taken pictures of him, sit for ten to fifteen minutes looking at the pictures and telling the child how special he is.

Building Confidence

11. Choose an activity or skill that your child has not yet experienced and assist him as he develops it. This might include learning a new song or poem, doing a somersault, or jumping a rope. Remember, however, to keep the level of difficulty adjusted to the child's needs. Praise, encouragement, and positive reinforcement are necessary in helping the child accomplish the desired goal.

Developing Family Communication Patterns

12. Parents must learn three communication rules:
   A. Clarify what others say: "Let's see if I understand you."
   B. Establish a rule of not interrupting when someone else speaks.
   C. Help everyone express his opinion: "What do you think?"

Call a family council to demonstrate and explain the three rules of communication to the children. Then present a topic to the family to discuss. Examples could include the following: "I would like to talk about what we are going to do this weekend," or, "We are not spending enough time together and I would like to know what to do about it." While the topic is being discussed practice the three communication rules.

UNIT II
UNDERSTANDING
YOUR CHILDREN

Throughout history people have looked at children in a number of different ways. Some viewed them as adults with little bodies. Others have seen children as annoyances until they were old enough to make a contribution to their family or an employer. Still others believed that a child comes to the world like a blank sheet of paper and that his environment dictated what became of him. Then there was the view that many parents still have: a view of perplexity, confusion, and frustration. Sometimes it seems that children cannot be understood at all.

If a parent doesn't understand at least a little about children, there is a substantial risk that the parent will respond incorrectly, despite good intentions; this goes on all too frequently in far too many homes. So what can parents do? In striving to learn about a child's nature, to learn about his development, and to analyze his actions, a parent can begin to understand the child himself.

CHAPTER 8
EACH CHILD IS UNIQUE

The viewpoint in America today concerning the nature of children is quite different from what it has been in the past. In fact, the concept of childhood as a separate and distinct stage of development has only existed for about 150 to 200 years. Before the nineteenth century having twelve to fifteen children in a family was common—but because of high infant mortality, many of these children never lived past the age of five. As a result children were often raised in an unaffectionate, businesslike, no-nonsense atmosphere; it was often difficult for parents to get emotionally attached to a child and to give much of themselves in training him. Oftentimes just as parents started to get involved with and attached to a child he would contract a disease or get injured and die, leaving the parents broken-hearted.

Because of the difficult lifestyle, children usually had little time to play with their friends or to participate in any of the other activities children enjoy today. Those children who survived illness and injury were apprenticed out to learn a trade, or they began working around the house in rudimentary on-the-job training. Children became economic necessities, and the man with a lot of children who could help him with his business or work for his neighbor had an advantage over his friends who had fewer children. Because children were thus involved in adult work, nobody thought that they were innocent or needed to be protected from physical and psychological harm; they were exposed to every aspect of adult living.

When large pools of cheap labor were needed during the Industrial Revolution children were exploited terribly, especially in the mining and textile industries. Because children were small they could often crawl into narrow, dark holes to dig coal from small seams that a man couldn't reach, or they could crawl beneath the large textile looms to thread the treadles, and so on. Before child labor laws were enacted to protect them, children of five and six years of age were working a full day in mines and factories. For most children childhood was a grim experience.

In the middle 1800s the death rate in western Europe dropped because of improved sanitation, awareness of some basic health laws, and rudimentary nutritional knowledge. When that happened parents became more involved with their children, became attached to them, and started to care about their welfare. Some people proposed that childhood was a stage of innocence which was qualitatively different from adulthood, and that children ought to be protected from adult pressures, concerns, and activities. Eventually the birth rate also dropped; and with fewer children to care for, parents devoted themselves more to the task of rearing their children properly. Parents actually began to instruct their children in both moral and intellectual pursuits. Most parents had grown up in impoverished conditions, and therefore they dreamed of rearing their children so that they would attain a higher station in life; most parents were willing to sacrifice many things to ensure such improvement. And when parents realized that the best way to facilitate this upward mobility was through public education, there began to be a strong emphasis on getting children to attend and to stay in school. In the last forty years a subtrend in child development seems to have appeared: the child has become the main focus of the home. He is as important as is anyone else in the family.

The Child as a Unique Human Being

Current theory, and that advocated in this book, is that every child is a unique person and that parents need a different set of expectations for each child. There are probably three causes of our uniqueness. First of all, we each have a unique biological or genetic makeup (unless we happen to be an identical twin or triplet). We don't know all the traits that genes control in the body, but we do know that genes influence things such as hair color, eye color, size of nose, height, and the age at which we enter puberty; even brothers and sisters differ in appearance and are programmed to mature at different times. Similarly, we know a little about how genes influence intelligence and creativity, and we are just beginning to find out how genes may predispose us to some forms of disease or to certain emotional states.

A second source of uniqueness is our environment. Every person who has ever lived has had a unique environment, even children who have been born very close together in time (like twins). Some parents make the decision to rear twins in as near the same environment as possible, giving them names that sound alike (such as Rob and Bob), dressing them alike, placing them in a playpen so that they have to play together, and buying two-seat strollers so that when the children are wheeled down the street they see the same things. But it is impossible to raise children identically because they won't have identical experiences. Over a long period of time they may act roughly the same: both may get angry at their mother at some point in time and both may scream or throw a temper tantrum, or both may experiment with their food by putting bowls of cereal on their heads or throwing some of the cereal on the floor. Most normal children experience these activities, but while both children do similar things over a long period of time, parental attitude toward those children will not be identical. One child may get angry at his parents when they are rested and have a lot of time on their hands and when they can take time to analyze what is frustrating him. A second child may get angry with his parents when they are very harrassed; having less patience, they will respond quite differently from the way they did when they had fewer pressures. Both children did the same thing, but because the parents responded differently, each child's environment became different. The parents saw only one child's behavior in an understanding light. Often parents interpret the behavior of one child positively and the same behavior on the part of another negatively. Once that happens, it's easy for a parent to get the notion that this child is good while that one is bad. Think back in your own family. Maybe you will remember that each child had a label. Your parents might have referred to one child as the funny one, the smart one, the cute one, the musical one, the good one, or maybe even the bad one. But while they may have been saying it half-jokingly, the child may have believed that he was that kind of person and tried to fulfill his role.

If parents think a child is funny, he's going to practice being funny. He'll achieve status by being the funniest child. Or if he's known as bad, he will practice being the worst because he knows that that's what you expect, and he wants to please you.

A third source of variation, something that's born within us and that isn't part of our genetic makeup, a phenomenon that pushes us to seek certain experiences or to perform certain actions, was described by Freud as the *Id*. Poets have also noticed this third source of uniqueness. In fact they sometimes seem to have greater insight than professional people do. For example, William Wordsworth wrote:

Our birth is but a sleep and a forgetting:
The soul that rises with us, our life's Star,
  Hath had elsewhere its setting,
    And cometh from afar;
  Not in entire forgetfulness,
    And not in utter nakedness,
But trailing clouds of glory do we come
  From God, who is our home. . . .

The assertion is that each person has a spirit that existed before it entered his body. During a preearth existence the spirit had a distinct lifestyle, a personality that carried over into this life and that contributes to a person's uniqueness. Any mother who has had two or more children has noticed that even in the first day of life each child behaved uniquely.

The first task for parents is to have clearly in mind what we believe the nature of children to be and, then, once we have determined that, to make our actions consistent with our beliefs.

ACTIVITIES: EACH CHILD IS UNIQUE

1. Write a *brief* statement about what you believe regarding each of the following issues. There are no right or wrong answers. Throughout history many good and wise people have embraced nearly all possible positions on each question; it is important that you write down what *you* believe.

A. Is a child born good, bad, or neutral? Why do you think so?

B. Is a child mostly a product of his hereditary qualities (traits that he was given at conception and can't change) or is he mostly the product of his environment?

C. Who knows what is best for, and therefore makes most of the decisions concerning, a developing child: the child himself (in which case parents let their child take the lead and they support the child in the things he wants to do), the parents of the child, or a specially trained adult (i.e., doctor, counselor, teacher, minister, etc.)?

D. Once a child has developed a habit or a personality trait, is it easy or difficult to change the child's behavior?

E. Is a child able to control his own life and be a free agent, or is he controlled by forces outside himself (i.e., his environment, the sign of the zodiac he was born under, etc.)?

F. What is the ultimate goal for human beings to accomplish?

2. Now ask your spouse to answer the same questions. Compare your feelings. In those areas where you disagree it will be important for you to try and come to some agreement so that you have a united philosophy about rearing children.

3. Try and decide if the way you respond to your children is consistent with what you have written down as your beliefs. If your actions and beliefs are not consistent, make a plan so that they will be

consistent. For example, if you said that you believed children know what is best for their lives *but* you are always telling them what to do with their free time, you are not being consistent. Try to change.

4. Across the top of a sheet of paper list the name of each of your children. Next list all the traits or skills that you can think of for each of your children. Notice how each child is unique from each other child. Now put an *H, E,* or *S* by each of the qualities listed to indicate whether you think they are caused by heredity, environment, or the spirit.

CHAPTER 9
UNDERSTANDING CHILD
DEVELOPMENT

Parents familiar with the critical periods in a child's physical, emotional, and social development can help him accomplish certain developmental tasks when he ought to. With that knowledge, parents will know better when to give a child challenges and when to restrict him.

Trusting the World

Erik Erikson, a psychologist at Harvard University, believes that in the first year of life a child develops an opinion as to whether or not the world is a trustworthy place. An infant's world is not very extensive; it probably ends ten or twelve feet away from him at a point beyond which his eyes stop focusing on objects. As far as he knows, he is the center of the world. If he is frightened or becomes hungry or cold, he will signal the world that he needs to be soothed, fed, or warmed. As those needs are regularly satisfied, the child comes to believe that the world is a good place.

A child's trust of the world develops in his first year of life as his physiological needs are met. So smart parents take care of any need their young child has at the earliest possible moment. They may even try to predict when a child will have a particular need—such as when he will be hungry—and to take care of that need before it becomes too strong. Unfortunately, some parents believe it's best for their child to learn what the "real world" is like. For some parents, the "real world" is not a place where needs are cared for quickly, so they make their child wait. They let him cry for a couple of hours because "that will develop his lungs." It may develop his lungs, but it also teaches him not to trust in the world: we all agree that an unpredictable environment is not to be trusted.

If a child doesn't gain a sense of trust in his first year of life, he will develop a generalized feeling that the world is untrustworthy. Such a child can be spotted very easily at age four or ten or twenty. On his first day of school he refuses to let go of his mother's leg; he holds on tightly because he is convinced that this new experience will not be good. At the playground he refuses to try a teeter-totter or a swing, even after great coaxing or threats from his parents. The playground is a new situation, and he can't feel safe with it.

On the other hand, a child who has learned to trust the world runs out eagerly to meet life. Not everything is great for him, but when he trips and falls, figuratively skinning his nose, he jumps right back up and takes off again. He is willing to meet the world head on.

Developing Self-Trust

After developing a sense of trust in the world, Erikson tells us, a child ought to gain a sense of trust in his own self. This *I can do* feeling should develop between the ages of one and two and a half. There is a reason why children need to do things by themselves. Imagine how it would be to have some person make every decision for you: decisions about when you went to bed, when you could get up, when and what you could eat, when you had to be dried, whether you went to the store or stayed home, and what clothes you wore (or even whether you wore clothes or not). It seems like a tremendously degrading situation—yet that is what happens to every young child: parents and other adults make all those decisions for him.

Because the spirit of man strives for self-expression, a child will rebel against attempts his parents make to usurp his free will. So as soon as he gains some control over his body he begins to assert himself, wanting to do things on his own. The push to be a free agent, to be independent, is a child's motive for learning to walk, to feed himself, to become toilet trained, and so on. Thus smart parents will provide a number of opportunities for their child to have success experiences. They will buy some clothes that he can put on by himself: not a narrow-necked shirt that he can't pull on, a pair of pants with a tricky zipper, or a pair of shoes that lace; but instead they would get pants with elastic tops, shirts with wide neckbands, and slip-on shoes. And they would give him some choices in life, such as what he would like for dinner; then they'd let him take the responsibility of serving himself and feeding himself. Parents who can do these kinds of things will satisfy a child's need to be able to trust his own ability.

When helping a child do something on his own, parents ought to be prepared to allow him enough time to do the job properly. If he's going to dress himself, he'll need a lot more time than if his parents dress him. A parent who doesn't allow his child opportunities to do things himself is saying to the child in a subtle but real way, "You're no good. Let me do that because you're too slow. You're incompetent." As a child hears that refrain over and over he begins to believe it; instead of learning to trust his abilities, he begins to doubt them.

Many students, even those of college age, have basic doubts about their ability to accomplish things. A student's roommates may try to talk her into trying out to be a cheerleader or auditioning for a school play or trying out for an athletic team; but her response is always something like, "Aw, gee. I don't know if I could do that. I just don't think I'm up to it." Much of a person's self-doubt stems back to his second or third year of life.

Developing Initiative

Children ought to accomplish what Erikson calls the task of initiative. At about age three to six a child begins to experience social interaction outside of his home for the first time. His social world expands to include people besides the members of his family. There are little friends down the street who become important to him. When he and his friends get together, all sorts of opportunities for leading and following evolve. Two can't play with the same toy at the same time, and there can be only one boss at a time, so arguments will arise. When that happens, the easiest thing for one of them to do is to run to his parents and say, "Johnny won't let me play with the toys." Most parents are inclined to try to settle the argument on the spot by figuring out some wise compromise, but the effect of the best decision that a parent can make is going to be

73

inferior to the effect of any decision that two children can work out by themselves. One of the tasks of this stage of initiative is for children to learn to be good followers and good leaders. The child whose parents are always resolving differences arbitrarily isn't learning to lead or to negotiate. Parents who respond by settling arguments are training children to be "tattle tales." As long as children aren't physically harming one another, stay out of the argument. You can help your children learn to lead and follow by telling them to go into a bedroom or into the garage and work on the problem together until both of them feel good about the solution—and tell them to stay until they have a solution.

Another way the child develops his initiative is by expanding his horizons. He moves outside the home. He becomes very curious about things. He intrudes into other people's lifestyles. You may know a preschool child who is interested in what everybody is doing, but that doesn't mean that he'll grow up to be the neighborhood busybody. It is normal for a child between the ages of three and six to be curious about other people, but because this is also the age at which conscience really begins to form and develop, a child's curiosity sometimes makes him feel ashamed or guilty. The child who is constantly made to feel dirty or nasty will be bound up with this guilt and withdraw instead of using his initiative to build his capacity for making friends, leading, or exploring new areas.

Learning Industry

From six to twelve years of age children ought to learn industry. By that time they know that they have some control over their bodies and that they are developing skills, and they want to be recognized for those skills. You may have had a young child in kindergarten or the first grade who told you, "I'm in the best reading group," or, "I'm the fastest runner." He told you that because he needs recognition. A wise parent or teacher will look for opportunities to praise him legitimately ("Gee, you are a great ballplayer." "You certainly are a good speller." "You're the best cook I've ever seen.") and to help him develop the skills in which he can excel. Such a parent will spend a little bit of money to give the child lessons so he can develop those skills, or a parent will help the child get started in activities such as stamp or coin collecting.

Unfortunately, some parents feel that intellectual skills are the only ones worth developing or recognizing. But in fairness to a child the parents need to recognize that his area of excellence might be in another area, such as social relationships. A child might be the most compassionate or loving person in the family, and if that's true, he should receive recognition for that skill.

If a child feels that he doesn't excel in any activity, he feels inferior to some degree in all activities. One thing you can do to help build a child's sense of accomplishment is to give him opportunities to compete with and beat significant people in his life—teachers or parents. The easiest and fairest way to do this is to have them compete in games, especially games of chance where the child is as likely to win as is the adult.

Forming an Identity

During early adolescence a child should gain a sense of identity; he should find out who he really is and commit himself to a value system. All children probably absorb their parents' value system in some form or other from infancy, but it seems to be normal for children to question that value system when they are in junior high and early high school. It isn't normal for a child to exhibit the excessive rebellious hostility that supposedly characterizes adolescents, but parents can prevent that rebelliousness by acknowledging and satisfying their child's need. Wanting to look around at other value systems is not wrong, because out of this searching comes the internalization of the value system. When a child comes home interested in somebody else's church or in reading a book on some other religion or value system, a parent should accept that. It's much better to talk with a child about a value that he wants to explore than to shut off all discussion of the topic at home; doing so simply forces him to discuss it with outside sources, a situation where you are unable to put in a pitch for your own value system. If parents live their value system and try to show its applications instead of being arbitrary and dictatorial, their children will most likely adopt their value system.

A person who doesn't internalize a value by searching and deciding on his own doesn't have any roots to anchor him morally. He tries to be all things to all people: with a group of his church friends he'll try to look like a good faithful church member, but when he's with a group of rowdy high school friends he'll be one of the rowdiest. He changes personalities, lifestyles, and value systems just as readily as some of us change coats—a real Dr. Jekyll and Mr. Hyde. The parents' task is to teach the child their value system in a meaningful way.

Establishing Intimacy

Late-adolescent and college-age youth ought to be developing a sense of intimacy, which leads to the ability to get along with people of the opposite sex. In elementary school children learn to get along with people of the same sex—boys play with boys and girls play with girls. Some children achieve excellence in dealing with same-sexed peers in elementary school but are very inadequate later in dealing with members of the opposite sex. High school activities, dating, and church parties provide the kind of physical setting that helps people make smooth transitions to heterosexual activities and a setting that helps them learn about, and become friends with, members of the opposite sex. An adolescent who ties himself down in his dating to just one person is cheating himself, and parents who try to influence their children to date a variety of people and to have social contacts with several members of the opposite sex are doing the right thing.

Some people never develop a sense of intimacy. They never feel entirely comfortable with members of the opposite sex, and so they never get around to picking out someone to marry. Most of these people eventually feel lonely and isolated because they do not have a productive lifestyle; because of the same problem, though, some people feel isolated even within a marriage relationship because they haven't learned to feel comfortable and trusting around others.

Parents can help children develop intimacy. As their child begins to be interested in, and talks about, members of the opposite sex, smart parents won't make fun of, belittle, or laugh at their child's clumsy attempts to relate to his peers. Parents need only recall the pain they endured as they struggled into this stage of adolescent development to help them be understanding and kind to their children.

Conclusion

Recognize and treat each child as a unique human being. Learn that each child develops differently, and that one child may stay at one stage longer than another. Adjust your parental behavior to the stage of development that your child is experiencing. Realize that you and your child are both marvelous creations worthy of respect and confidence.

ACTIVITY: UNDERSTANDING CHILD DEVELOPMENT

In the following chart list each of your children's names in the left-hand column. In the next column put the developmental task each child should be accomplishing. Finally, make a plan with your spouse and list five specific things you can do to help each child accomplish the task he is working on.

Name of Child	Age	Task he should be accomplishing	How I'm going to help
1.			1. 2. 3. 4. 5
2.			1. 2. 3. 4. 5.
3.			1. 2. 3. 4. 5.
4.			1. 2. 3. 4. 5.
5.			1. 2. 3. 4. 5.

Expand this chart as necessary to meet your specific needs.

CHAPTER 10
YOUR CHILD'S
PHYSICAL GROWTH

Have you ever heard a parent say, "I can't understand why this child is such an active, involved child while my other child is not active. I try to do everything the same way for both of these children. I try to give them both the same amount of love and the same amount of attention; why are they so very different?"

Such parents must learn that a child's physical development has a marked influence upon his behavior. The child who is a victim of malnutrition, for instance, is slower in his actions, doesn't participate as much, seems more sluggish and lazy, and seems more unhappy than a child who eats properly. The quality and the quantity of his behavior are definitely reduced. Similarly, genetic characteristics have a marked effect upon a child's behavior. For example, a child who is small or subject to certain hereditary illnesses will exhibit behavior unlike that of most other children.

Each child is unique, with an individual pattern of growth and development that he follows at his own unique rate. Even within the same family no two children are quite alike; there are differences in size, in shape, and in personality attributes. Each child must follow his own unique rate of growth. It's important for parents to recognize that there are unique rates and patterns of development.

Because behavior is related to growth rate, it should be apparent that until a child reaches a certain maturational level he will not be able to do certain things. A child who cannot be toilet trained as early as others probably can't control his sphincter muscle. A child cannot grasp or pick up objects until his muscles are mature enough and until there is coordination between the eyes that see the object and the fingers that grasp it.

It is also important to know that none of the child's physical needs can be met satisfactorily if his other needs are not satisfied. For example, if a child is worried, tired, and hungry, it is essential to attend to all three of those needs. It would be very difficult, if not impossible, to satisfy only one.

Each child is part of a unique family, one with a special way of living, unique habits and traditions, and fundamental beliefs—all of which determine how his physical and other needs are met. It's awesome to recognize the influence that the family and its traditions have upon the child's physical development.

Physical Growth of an Average Child

To understand the interaction between physical development and behavior, we must be familiar with normal patterns of growth and development. Knowing these and being able to predict behavior in your own children will help you work with them.

After the rapid growth that occurs during infancy, the child's growth slows considerably. While the average child increases in height by fourteen to fifteen inches during the first two years of his life, he will grow only nine to ten inches during the next three years, reaching half of his adult height when he is about two years old. Although the average child gains fifteen pounds in his first year, he gains only five pounds annually until he is five years old.

During the years of early childhood the child's body proportions change considerably. By age six they will begin to resemble those of an adult. Although his head growth is somewhat slow, his head will almost have reached adult proportion by age five. Because his leg and arm growth is rapid, the child will lose the unbalanced or top-heavy look of a toddler. Gains in height may be counter-balanced by loss of baby fat, although children tend to keep a protruding abdomen until about age six. During this period of physical change, as his fat pads dwindle and the cartilage and bones of his face mature, the child's face becomes more well defined and individualized. Skeletal growth is less rapid than it was during the first one and a half years of life. Instead, because the bones are not completely calcified, the process of ossification continues. This helps the child's skeletal system keep flexible and helps prevent his bones from breaking easily. By age three, the child's set of twenty deciduous (or baby) teeth is usually complete. Loss of the first temporary tooth occurs at about five years of age; by this time, the child is eating all types of food.

Muscular development occurs mainly in the large muscles. Muscles of the three-year-old are still largely undeveloped and uncoordinated, and until age four his muscle development is roughly proportional to his general body growth. But between ages four and five, muscle tissue comprises seventy-five percent of the child's weight increase.

In addition to the physical traits of children of preschool age, some characteristics and abilities generally typify the three-year-old, the four-year-old, and the five-year-old. The three-year-old who is experiencing growth and development of the large muscles is gaining good motor control; he is developing coordination that is increasing his competence and balance, and he is more sure on his feet. He has learned to dress and undress himself fairly well, although he may need help with tasks that require coordination and control of smaller muscles; he may be able to button and unbutton his clothes if the buttons are large. He has almost completely mastered bowel and bladder control, although he may have occasional accidents. He is usually quite independent in feeding himself, and he especially enjoys finger foods that he can control by himself. He stands erect, he alternates feet, and he can stand on one foot. He can usually run rapidly or slowly, can turn sharp corners, and can make sudden stops. He may roll a ball and may throw it underhanded; he may move his body to different rhythms when he hears music. He usually likes to use peg boards and can handle crayons fairly skillfully. He climbs with ease. He usually likes jumping from low heights, but he is not too sure of jumping fom higher places—in fact, he finds it frightening. It can be very fascinating—at times funny—to watch him trying to get down from a high place.

The four-year-old is more independent and sophisticated. With his increased motor control, he can saw and cut on a straight line as well as throw a ball overhanded. He climbs easily and he runs, jumps, and hops with more vigor than previously. He moves fast, but he has great ability to control sudden stops and starts. Besides the locomotive play, he enjoys more manipulative play—the kind re-

81

quired for such things as puzzles, small toys, and intricate block designs. He likes cutting, pasting, finger painting, and other activities that improve his motor control and provide an outlet for his creativity and, sometimes, his aggression.

The five-year-old's growth rate is somewhat slower, but he is more vigorous and noisy and is full of energy for all types of activity that allow freedom of body movement. He is more capable than four-year-olds in many things: he runs faster and climbs higher and with more confidence; his better balance and muscle control ensure him more success in reaching, grasping, and jumping; he sits longer; and he has mastered lacing his shoes and buttoning his clothes. He stands on one foot and he hops and skips; he keeps time to music, and he can bounce and catch a ball. Freedom of movement and opportunity for vigorous movement are essential in all five-year-old activities.

The ages of three, four, and five are spent improving muscular control and acquiring skills in fundamental physical activities. Each child's rate of growth and development will determine when he learns each new skill and how quickly he perfects old skills.

Physical Growth of Older Children

In summary, the preschool child's physical needs must be satisfied if he is to grow and progress satisfactorily. The child needs to eat when he's hungry, drink when he's thirsty, and use the bathroom when that is necessary. He also needs proper rest and nutrition—and the opportunity to feed himself and to dress himself whenever possible. In short, he must learn to do things for himself and by himself.

Conclusion

Being aware of your child's physical growth can help you properly adjust your expectations of what he can do. Observe what skills your child can easily perform; this can tell you what tasks you can reasonably hope he will do. If your child's performance is very different from that described for an average child, you may wish to consult a physician to determine if his growth is within healthy limits.

In addition to knowing about the physical development of your child, it is useful for you to develop a view about his nature by learning the stages of mental and emotional growth most children experience. From this knowledge you will be able to further expand your ability to be a successful parent.

ACTIVITIES: YOUR CHILD'S PHYSICAL GROWTH

1. Hold a rope tight and close to the ground while your child jumps over it. Raise the rope a small distance and have him jump over it again. Continue to raise the rope about one inch between jumps.

Next, have your child move under the rope in some creative way. (Suggestions for creative movement include sliding, rolling, crawling on knees and elbows, etc.) As you begin the rope should be about three feet off the ground; as you continue, however, the rope can be lowered after each attempt.

Swing the rope slowly and close to the ground. Encourage your child to jump over it as it swings. Raise it a few inches after each successful attempt. As it gets too high for him to jump over he may move under the swinging rope in any creative way.

2. Forward roll: instruct your child to crouch on his knees and to place his hands on the ground in front of him. Guide him as he rolls forward so that he rolls on his shoulders rather than on his head.

Backward roll: have the child squat on the ground. As he begins to roll backwards, tucking his chin to his chest, assist in boosting his legs over his head.

3. Select music of various rhythms and speeds. Encourage your child to move in response to this music by hopping, skipping, jumping, running, or other appropriate movements. Suggest a direction in which he should move. Rhythm instruments can be used in place of music; scarves and streamers will add to his creative enjoyment. Participate with him.

4. Instruct your child in the safe use of a hammer, saw, and nails, and allow him to use them when he builds or creates objects.

5. Stretch a wooden plank on the floor and ask your child to walk, slide, or skip on it. Direct him to move forward, backward, or sideways. Make it even more of a challenge by having him move with his eyes closed.

6. Give your child a series of rapid directions which he is to follow as he hears them. Suggestions include "Run, twirl, hop, roll, rest" or "Spin, skip, jump, freeze, run" and so on.

CHAPTER 11
WHY CHILDREN DO
WHAT THEY DO

Many times you may not understand why your child acts a certain way, but there are reasons. It is important to understand these different reasons; you as parents can be more successful with a given child if your approach towards him is consistent with the reason for his action.

One set of parents had a son who frequently wet his pants even though he was six and a half years old. They tried to be patient, but eventually they gave in to shaming him, spanking him, or grounding him. Nothing seemed to work. Seeking help from a counselor, they were asked to subject the child to a physical examination. Results showed that the child had a very small bladder—so small, in fact, that he could not retain urine for any appreciable amount of time. Had the parents known the reason for the behavior they could have been more successful and would not have been so destructive to their child.

Behavior Due to a Stage of Development

First, behavior may be attributed to a *stage of development.* Certain cues help identify behavior caused by a developmental stage.

First, you can remember behaving similarly at that stage of your own life; if you can remember, you can be sure that your child's behavior isn't peculiar to him. It might really be behavior that is prompted by a stage of growth common to all children.

A second cue is if you have seen the same behavior in other children of the same age. A scoutmaster who was having problems of rowdiness with his twelve- and thirteen-year-old scouts came home from a scout meeting and told his wife, "I just don't understand these boys. And the funny thing is that the boys I had last year were the same. And the scouts I had five years ago were doing the same things." This scoutmaster should probably attribute the rowdiness to a stage of growth. But if you're going to use this cue you need to have seen a lot of behavior. You can get fouled up by thinking, "Okay, I saw such-and-such once, so I know that's what all children are like." Imagine, for example, a student teacher who goes to a junior high to do some teaching and gets into an eighth-grade classroom where the fulltime teacher is a regular dictator. The students come in, sit at their desks, place their hands on the top of the desk, and sit looking straight ahead. They do not chew gum, talk to their neighbors, or leave their seat until the bell rings. The children, because they are frightened of their teacher, are models of good behavior. The student teacher might come back from his experience of a week and say, "Boy, eighth-graders are at the greatest age in the world! I can't believe how well-mannered, polite, and quiet they are." If so, this student teacher has made two mistakes. First, he has not observed enough eighth-graders to make a valid judgment about what *all* of them are like. Most eighth-grade children are much more active; in fact, they are at one of the most difficult ages for growing children: they are pushing limits and trying to tell the world that they are not children any more. Second, the student teacher had never observed the behavior of those same eighth-graders under less restricted conditions. Children who are coerced, who live in fear, or who have a poor environment probably will not act like children who live in normal conditions.

Recognizing the third cue requires that you have read about child behavior. Taking courses in child development and reading about what is expected in normal children helps you establish norms and helps you know what kinds of behavior you can expect from your child at certain ages.

The fourth cue is that the behavior may simply feel right to you. You may not remember it in your own life and might not have seen it happen or read about it, but instinct tells you that the behavior is appropriate for the child's age.

At various ages different types of behavior appear, dominate for a while, and then disappear. Consequently, when you have decided that your child's behavior is caused by a stage of growth you should not blame yourself for it. You didn't cause it; the cause lies within the child. The best thing you can do is to wait the behavior out until growth changes it. Be patient and know that the behavior won't last forever; realize that it will be there for a while and that it will then go away. And know, too, that most parents will experience the same thing, or something very similar, with their own children.

Although children sometimes pass through good stages, parents are often unaware of them, attending instead only to those stages that they think are negative. Many times parents aren't even aware that their child is going through a "good" stage.

Parents often demand good behavior out of their children; some feel that it is their God-given right to have good children. For example, parents get nervous about overdependency in the young child: at the age of one and a half, a child may start clinging and hanging onto his mother or his father, not wanting them to be out of sight. What happens then? Parents use their "common sense" and push the child toward independence. If instead the parents would just wait a couple of years, that same "overly dependent" child would be out in the neighborhood playing with his friends.

At about the age of six or seven the highest incidence of lying, cheating, and sneaking behavior occurs in children. Children at this age have a strong need to be accepted and to be better than others, and because all of them have limited success experience, they often make up stories to make themselves look better or more powerful. What should parents do? If the behavior is part of a stage of growth, try to tolerate it. If you can't tolerate it, try to help the child channel his actions in a way that is acceptable to you but not stifling for the child.

Suppose you have a child that steals and that tells lies to make him appear stronger, neater, and greater; but suppose that lying really disturbs you and that despite your attempts to be patient you have a strong reaction to lies. You have several options: when a child tells a lie you can ignore it, if you are able to; or, you can try and channel it. By channeling such behavior you could ask the child to make up stories where he is an important person. You could say, "I cannot let you tell lies. You must tell the truth." You could then proceed to make the child feel important and powerful, thus partly eliminating the causes behind the child's lying.

If you do stop a particular behavior, you ought to make it clear that you are stopping it because of factors within *you:* if an action is a result of a developmental stage, the action is not bad; the child is not bad; it is just that you cannot let your child act that way. If the action is a result of a stage of growth, try to be patient; the behavior will change by itself.

A Child's Needs

Needs are a second cause of behavior; needs that are both innate and learned have to be fulfilled. When the child's needs are not fulfilled, an internal mechanism pushes him to seek fulfillment.

Of course, the first need of all human beings is to stay alive. When denied anything essential to maintaining life (e.g., air or water), they will do just about anything to overcome the deficit. Almost everyone has heard the story of the man who was lost in the desert. He became so thirsty that when he found a spring, even though he realized it was poisoned, he drank its water and died. When people are hungry enough they will steal for food or will sell their most valuable possessions. The story of Esau and Jacob in the Bible is a great example of this: Esau got hungry enough to sell his brother his greatest gift, his birthright.

But while we're all aware of the need to maintain life—to resist dying before our time, so to speak—parents might be less aware that there is another need as great as the need for food: the need to be close to others. All animals have the need to be close, and in this respect human beings are no different. If you watch animals you'll see mothers lick, nuzzle, fondle, cuddle, tweak, bite, kiss, and paw their young. Cats do it with kittens, dogs do it with pups, and human mothers should do it with human babies. We never outgrow that need. But suppose a child is deprived of this contact comfort. Suppose that his parents reject him, or suppose he only *thinks* his parents are hostile or angry towards him. He will feel pushed and will do things to get attention and to try to get close; sometimes his need for attention will be so strong that his behavior will be anti-social.

Another need we all have is to feel that we are worthwhile. If a person has lived in a hostile environment long enough, he will learn not to value himself and will stop seeking experiences that communicate, "You are a good person." But this is abnormal, and would probably indicate that the child is quite disturbed. People want to know that they are worthwhile; when a child is not getting that message, he is going to be hungry for it.

We all have a need for new experiences to satisfy our curiosity. To fulfill this need, people take vacations to see new places and read new books for new ideas. When a young or an old person is trapped in an unchanging situation, boredom sets in; when that happens, the person looks for new experiences, and the experiences the person chooses don't always promote healthy emotional and moral development. When a parent or society denies a child opportunities for wholesome new experiences, he may turn in desperation to those that are undesirable.

Another need is to have order in our lives, to make sense out of our experiences. This need is apparent in the teenager's struggle to find a value system that pulls all the facets of his life into one meaningful whole. Consequently, whenever a religious philosophy satisfies a person with its answers to life's questions—and especially when it answers more questions than does a person's own value system—that religion has a convert. For some people life has so little meaning that any philosophy looks good; such people use a trial and error approach, and they may get desperate and resort to extreme measures such as taking drugs to try to find meaning in their lives. Young children also seek order, trying to make experiences in their lives fit into a pattern; if their lives are chaotic, they respond accordingly. In the home there ought to be harmony and consistency. When family discipline is unstable or inconsistent, it reduces the order for a child.

Finally, everybody needs to feel that he is in control of his life. The person who feels that outside forces totally control his life feels helpless, and feels that he might just as well lie down and die (and people sometimes do just that). We all have a need to control our own destiny, to be free, and to *feel* that we're free from too much external control.

When their needs are not met, children struggle to fulfill them. And just as there are cues for behavior caused by stages of growth, so there are cues for behavior caused by a desire to fulfill needs. The first cue, and possibly the most important, is that the behavior seems inappropriate for the age of the child. A nine-year-old child who is dragging a teddy bear around is an example of this. The child is waving a red flag, saying, "Help! I need some kind of nourishment."

Second, his behavior has an electric, supercharged quality to it. You may have known children who were so tense and anxious that whenever you touched them you almost expected an electric shock. Unless they have physical problems, children who are overly active, who run or jump excessively, or who are unable to concentrate may be struggling to fulfill a need.

A third cue of unfilled needs is when the behavior doesn't occur in just one environment—when the behavior manifests itself at home, at school, or at play. The child is going to try to satisfy his needs everywhere. School counselors, for example, often find that a child who disrupts school also has problems at home, with his friends, at church, and so forth. A fourth cue is when bad behaviors keep popping up. Even though you may be able to train the child to discontinue one behavior, another behavior will take its place if the basic need is still there. In much the same way, when a person has an infection that manifests itself as a boil on his neck, he can put salve on the boil and clear it up; but another one may appear on his knee. And when he clears that one up, it breaks out again on his elbow, and so on until the infection—the *cause* of the boil—is removed. Similarly, when there is an unfilled need inside prompting bad behavior, the behavior will *not* go away until the need is filled. When the cues indicate an unfulfilled need, you must ask yourself, "What's my child trying to tell me? What isn't he getting out of life?" And when you have the answer, you must then satisfy his need. Sometimes this may appear to go against the grain of common sense. Suppose, for example, that your older children want to be close to you all the time. And suppose that you have decided they are acting that way because they feel displaced by the new baby that occupies so much of your time. If you shove the other children away, saying, "Get out of here. Go to your own room! I told you not to hang around," you'll simply increase their need, and so their behavior of staying by your side will get stronger. The better thing to do to correct the behavior is to hold each one on your lap for fifteen minutes as often as possible. This will fill their emptiness, and after a few days or weeks each child will become full of love again and will think, "Ah, I haven't been displaced. I still do have my mom." Such a child will get off your knee and will go about his own business.

A Child's Environment

The third cause of behavior is the *present environment*. If your child suddenly begins acting strangely and if none of the above cues explain the behavior, you may need to examine the present environment of your child. Who is present? How are they acting? Or ask yourself, "Has anything unusual happened? Did my child move into a new school? Did a parent die? Was there a divorce in the home? Did he lose a best friend, or was there a fight with somebody at school?" If you can pinpoint things that happened very suddenly at about the time that the child's behavior changed or that questionable behavior appeared, you've probably found the cause. In this case, a child didn't cause the situation; forces outside him probably did. And so, instead of growling, "That's a dumb way to behave," a better approach is to alter the situation if you can. In this case, your role as a parent is to be a forerunner for your child, to sweep the stones and the stumbling blocks out of his way. If there is trouble with somebody at school, go and be his advocate. Learn about the situation, and then communicate your support to the child. Maybe it means that you will even need to change. But one thing to be careful about is not to allow a child to be irresponsible. If the child brought about something in his environment, he must learn to pay the consequence.

Many of us get caught up in our own business, and we fail to really concentrate on the reasons behind a child's actions. Rather than think, we react and punish. When a child's behavior is due to an environmental condition, punishing the child thoughtlessly will only make the situation worse. Consider the example of the boy who gets in fights at school. Wishing to be helpful, the school principal calls the boy's father and explains what is going on. Hearing the news about his child, the father gets angry and punishes his son. Instead of helping, the father has probably failed to smooth the way for his son. A better way for this father (and any parent in a similar situation) to react would have been (1) to hear all he could about the situation before he reacted; (2) to talk to his child and to other people who were involved; (3) to identify the cause of the child's behavior; and (4) to help the child to work out a plan to alter or solve the problem. (In some situations the parents themselves may need to solve the problem for the child.)

A Lack of Knowledge

The fourth cause of behavior is simply that *the child doesn't know any better*. Particularly in families with many children, parents can lose track of which lessons they've taught each child; as a result, they may have forgotten to teach a child a particular lesson. If none of the other listed causes seem to account for the child's behavior, you might decide, "Maybe I'm to blame for this because I didn't teach my child." If you *are* to blame, don't nag the child; sit down and teach him what he should do instead. By instilling good behavior, you help the child conquer the undesirable behavior.

There are many reasons why parents may fail to teach a child. Work demands, too many children, and tension in the family are some of the hindrances to teaching that are most commonly reported by parents. But, as we stated elsewhere, parents cannot *not* teach. Parents need to either take the effort to help a child learn correct behavior or they risk having to deal with undesirable behavior. Even a few minutes of teaching each week can make a great difference in a child's behavior.

Conclusion

There are four causes of behavior: developmental stages, needs of the child, something in his environment, and the child's lack of knowledge. Of the four causes of behavior, only the first is determined by the child—and he isn't aware of the developmental stages he is going through. The other three causes are beyond a child's control: a child doesn't create a hunger inside, manipulate his environment, or play hooky from a lesson that you didn't give him. If he didn't bring the causes about, you shouldn't be angry with the child. Knowing the different causes of behavior and using the cues to identify them can help you to relax, to know how to best provide help, and to enjoy your child more.

ACTIVITIES: WHY CHILDREN DO WHAT THEY DO

1. In the following list, study each of the behaviors and then list the reason why you think the behavior occurred. Then compare your answers with those of your spouse.
   A. Two five-year-old children are out in the garage playing "doctor and nurse."
   B. In the past, several children have dug holes in the sandpile and have urinated in them. You have told them not to do it, but one day you see them doing it again. You go out to the backyard and very angrily say, "I told you not to pee in that hole!" Your child answers, "We're not, Mom, we're peeing in this little cup."
   C. A father has taken his son fishing for the first time. The boy keeps snagging his hook and getting mixed up about what he should do.

D. A three-year-old insists on riding his big brother's bicycle but keeps falling off.
E. Your five-year-old child usually goes to bed without any fuss. However, tonight you are having a party and your child comes out of the bedroom several times demanding your attention.

2. Discuss with your spouse what you would do to change each of the above behaviors.

3. Observe one of your children several times during the course of one week. What reason do you think he has for each of the activities he participated in? Record here the behaviors and what you think the reasons are for the behaviors.

Behavior	Reason

Activity	Need

Now, determine the number of behaviors that seem to be caused by a stage of growth, by a hunger inside, or by either of the other two causes. Is there a pattern to the way your child does things? What can you do to help your child as a result of what you have found out?

4. With your partner select three behaviors of your child that bother you. Determine the cause of each behavior and create a plan of action, outlining how you will deal with each of the problem behaviors. Finally, implement your plan of action and record your results.

Behavior	Cause of Behavior	Plan of Action	Results
1.			
2.			
3.			

CHAPTER 12
HELPING YOUR CHILD
GROW SOCIALLY

As far as science can tell, no individual is born social; he *learns* social behavior, and most of that learning is done as a child. In fact, it has been suggested that by age six a child has acquired the attitude toward people and social experiences that will characterize him for the remainder of his life.

Three essential principles of socialization are (1) opportunity, (2) motivation, and (3) methods found to be adequate for interaction with others.

In examining opportunities, it is important to remember that the child benefits from social experiences not only in the home, but also outside the home. Restricting his opportunities for social experience may have detrimental effects on him. Without the foundation of social experience during his early years, a child will be hampered in his overall social development. Again, though, the quality of social contacts in early life is as important as the quantity. A child needs opportunities to communicate with members of his family, to converse with his parents face to face. And he needs to associate with other people in good activities—as well as in activities that might be classified as poor; he needs to see some positive reactions and some negative reactions as he interacts with others. He needs to see success, and he needs to be allowed to fail. Parents should not, however, arrange specific failures for a child; they just need to provide opportunities for him to participate in many experiences, and failure is bound to be a natural part of some experiences.

Motivation is another essential factor in the socialization process. The kinds of experiences the child encounters largely determine whether or not he desires to repeat them. If he feels happy and secure in his social activity and contacts, he will likely strive for further encounters. On the other hand, if his social experiences leave him feeling fearful and insecure, he is less likely to want to repeat them. The satisfaction he gains from working and playing with others will strongly influence his future sociability. If, for example, he feels good about talking with his parents or with his teachers, he will be motivated to talk to other adults. Similarly, if his parents make him feel that what he says is not worthy of adult attention, he will not likely seek opportunities to talk with other adults, or perhaps even with his peers.

Third, as a child has various experiences with others, he learns that certain types of behavior bring satisfaction and success. He adopts these behavior patterns and uses them as his own.

As with other facets of child behavior, social behavior develops in stages. The three-year-old is beginning to cooperate with other people and he enjoys playing with other children; he is learning to share and to take turns. He may have difficulty sharing toys and may not be able to share his work and play space with others, but he is interested in and sensitive to other people and tries to please them and to conform. The three-year-old enjoys dressup and dramatic play. He enjoys activity and tends to act while he talks. He may begin to be interested in the opposite sex, but such interest at this age is probably minor. He wants very much to be accepted, but he wants to be accepted as he is: he doesn't want to have to pretend to be five, and if he acts like a two-year-old, he wants someone to understand. When he is angry or upset, he wants to be allowed the privilege of honestly expressing himself, and yet he hopes someone will help him identify and overcome the cause of his unpleasant feelings.

A three-year-old is both affectionate and hostile toward others—both playmates *and* adults. He makes little effort to control his emotions and he makes no effort to conceal them. He is curious, honest, and sometimes frightened—of bees or of sleeping or of being left without his mother. Sometimes he is hurt and just wants someone to be near. Whatever his behavior, he needs understanding. Whenever his behavior is socially acceptable, he needs reinforcement.

The four-year-old is sociable, but even though he likes companionship he may be boastful, bossy, or very talkative. Name-calling may be a common practice, because he enjoys inventing and using names. ("You're nothing but a stupid dumb." "You're a therry therry"—or a "threeder threeder" or a "sevener sevener.") Remember that these nonsense words—whether used for fun or other purposes—all have meaning for him.

The four-year-old may develop friendships with children of his own age very quickly and may play with them very well; he may also sever such ties equally rapidly and firmly. But while sometimes it may seem that former friends are going to be enemies forever, suddenly the four-year-old and his enemy are back together with arms interlocked once again. At this age he is learning to express sympathy and to recognize that others share his feelings, or simply that others have feelings of their own. Remember: all these events are essential to learning social behavior.

The four-year-old is sensitive to others and is beginning to cooperate with other children in important associative play and in dramatic play activities. He will dress up and play mailman, house, or car. Play is his prime way of becoming socialized. Acting as he sees a mailman or a car act, he is learning to experience the world from another point of view. It should be apparent, then, that by making fun of him or his play at this stage, an adult can do real damage.

Although the four-year-old enjoys associative or group play, he still likes to be independent, and he enjoys playing by himself. He constantly tries and tests his new-found abilities: "Can I do this for myself?" "No, Dad, don't do that. Let me do it. I can do it." When a child expresses this interest and desire, he needs opportunities to do things for himself. And when he feels his independence, he will want to test his new abilities and quite often will experience a change of behavior. Sometimes his behavior is confusing—when he's very quarrelsome, he will suddenly become very cooperative and charming.

Generally he dislikes isolation unless he chooses to isolate himself to get attention.

The four-year-old's idea of important people usually centers around his own parents and family, not the president of the United States or some important leader in the community. Father and

Mother are unquestionably the most important people in his world, and he is frequently found quoting them as authorities.

The five-year-old is more self-confident, stable, and cooperative. Although he plays best with one child, he can give and take in groups for a short period of time. A five-year-old's cooperative play with age-mates, or sometimes with older children, to plan and carry out group projects is a sign of his movement toward maturity. Usually preferring friends of his own age and development, he will be heard to say, "No. I don't want to play with those *little* kids."

The five-year-old is growing in his ability to share songs, pictures, toys, and stories with the group and sometimes with individuals. He is finding that words are better than fists for settling disagreements: nobody needs to be socked or hurt.

During the age range from three to six, the child learns to adjust to others and to cooperate in group activities. He learns what is expected of him and chooses either to conform or to misbehave. Early social contacts, generally within the home, lay the foundation for such encounters. And, of course, the number of social experiences he has will influence his social development—although it is the *quality* rather than the *quantity* of social experiences that has the greatest effect. At this early stage, since he is unable to determine what is socially desirable and what is not, he will imitate both "good" and "bad" behaviors of people around him, so it is crucial that he be exposed to people who exhibit desirable behavior patterns. Of course, the most effective way of helping a child learn is to teach him specifically, but if he does not receive such guidance in his home, it becomes much more important that he learn through appropriate experiences with people outside the home.

An obvious example of guidance in the home is that of teaching a child manners. People often believe that a child should be taught to say "please" and "thank you." If, when asking for something at the table, a child does not ask properly, the parent will say, "You can't have it," or, "What do you say? Pass the butter, what?" The adult would do better to set a proper example to be imitated, such as, "Pass the butter, please." The child then recognizes that using manners is an important way to get the job accomplished. When an adult responds with, "What do you say?" or, "As soon as you ask properly, I'll give you what you want," the child learns that adults have power to grant his request, but he does not achieve the desired goal—good table manners.

The significance of family influence cannot be overemphasized: the child's social behavior and attitudes reflect the treatment he receives in the home. In fact, child-rearing practices in the home are the principal factor influencing the child's social development. Children from democratic homes are usually better adjusted socially than are children from either indulgent or authoritarian homes. Children who enjoy social experiences with others outside the home most often have had satisfying and happy experiences with their own family members in the home.

In conclusion, socialization is the process by which the values and customs of a culture are transmitted from one generation to the next. As he is socialized, the child learns to behave acceptably, adapting to his society in ways that are fulfilling to him and not harmful to society. But before he can be effectively socialized, he must attach meaning and importance to people and must acknowledge and accept their rules.

Usually the well-socialized individual has a positive attitude toward people and sees rules as necessary for functioning in society; he is willing to modify his own behavior to meet the needs of society. But, of course, the very young child (the preschooler) will have difficulty in understanding all the rules, and that is why parents have the great responsibility of assisting their children in the home.

ACTIVITIES: HELPING YOUR CHILD GROW SOCIALLY

In doing the following activities with your child it is important to remember the principles of socialization—opportunity, motivation, and methods of interaction. Keeping these in mind will aid you in reaching the goals of this unit.

1. Make stew for dinner. Prepare ahead of time slips of paper with written instructions for each member of the family concerning the process of making the stew. Each member should have a task which, if not done, will disrupt the whole program. Cook the meat ahead of time to reduce the actual preparation time. Emphasis should be on courtesy, willingness to share, and table manners.

2. Identify three things you would like to do with your child for fifteen or twenty minutes. Allow your child to select the activity he wants to do most and become actively involved with him. Above all, be sure to have fun.

3. Invite some children to your home who are about the same age as your child. Before they arrive, show your child how to do the following and allow him to practice them:

1) Open the door and invite friends in.

2) Ask the friends to sit down or to go to a play area.

3) Ask the friends to choose which toy they would like to play with.

4) Behave well when a friend doesn't do what he wants them to do.

Watch your child as he goes through the above steps and praise his desired behavior. When he is playing with his friends, leave them alone.

4. Dramatic play is an important part of the socialization process because it helps a child look at the world from many points of view. It teaches him what it is like to be a postman, a doctor, or a teacher.

Think of an occupation you know something about. Describe this occupation to your child and provide him with a few props. A teacher might need a bell with which to call the class to order, a book to read, a flag to salute, and so on. Given encouragement, the child will proceed to develop his own understanding of the role of a teacher as he is allowed to be that person for a short while.

5. The use of puppets is helpful in getting an otherwise shy and withdrawn child to become active in role playing. As a child is able to hide behind a puppet stage, he is able to forget about himself and become involved in the characters of his puppets. In acting out a pretend situation, such as a child who has gotten in a fight with a friend, he is able to form more concrete understandings of social behavior. A simple puppet stage for use in this activity can be made from a cardboard box. Puppets can be made from stockings, paper bags, popsicle sticks, and other inexpensive materials.

6. Refer to the Evaluation Sheet on the following page. Considering the age of each child, rate each according to how well he is developing the social skills listed. (Use a scale of 0 to 10: "0" meaning no development of the skill, "5" being average, and "10" being very high in development.) When this is completed, make suggestions as to what can be done to help each child develop and improve those skills in which he is deficient. Make a conscientious effort to follow through with those suggestions made.

Evaluation Sheet—Social Skills	Your Children		
Social Skills	Child 1	Child 2	Child 3
How well are they being developed in each child?			
Affection: the ability to give and receive love			
Communication: the ability to transmit and receive ideas			
Concern: an interest to serve and care for the well-being of others			
Cooperation: working well with others			
Friendliness: the ability to make and keep close friends			
Self-Control: the ability to hold in check impulses, emotions, desires			
Sharing: helping and doing things for others			
Recommendations			
What can you do to help each child develop or improve the skills listed?			

UNIT III
CHILDREN'S FEELINGS

Most parents do a very poor job of providing their children with guidelines for emotional development. Everyone agrees that our emotions are an important part of us, but we don't usually help our children to recognize and cope with their emotions. One of the reasons may be that parents aren't really sure what emotions are; there is also a great deal of confusion over whether emotions are good or bad. If some emotions are bad, we're not sure how to go about eliminating them in our children. Parents need to understand the nature of emotions, whether emotions are good or bad, and how to teach children to be emotionally honest. It is also critical that parents understand how three important emotions—love, anger, and fear—are developed and that they learn how to help children cope with these emotions in a mature way.

A child's feelings for himself are of vital importance. A child's self-esteem is most important in determining how he develops socially and intellectually. A child with low self-esteem gives up, withdraws, and does not take advantage of opportunities in the real world. On the other hand, a child with high self-esteem can meet many disappointments in life and does not become discouraged, but continues to move ahead undaunted. Parents need to know how they can build up self-esteem in their children and also in themselves.

CHAPTER 13
EMOTIONAL DEVELOPMENT
IN CHILDREN

What are emotions, and how do they operate in a child's life? Which are innately good or bad? How can we develop emotional honesty in children?

Many parents make the mistake of trying to equate emotional activities with intellectual activities. While both activities center in the brain, they are different.

First of all, intellectual activities involve voluntary movements that we can control, and they center in the higher areas of the brain; but emotional activities, although they may have some components that center in the higher areas of the brain, are also directly involved with our autonomic nervous system, over which we have very little control.

Second, intellectual activities can be measured against some standard of truth. Thus, we can say, "That was a great way to solve the problem! That was really clear thinking." But it's more difficult to say, "That was an inappropriate feeling that you had." What a child or an adult feels is valid for him. When someone is angry, he is angry, and that's all there is to it; it is hopeless to try to talk him out of it.

A third difference is that intellectual activities can be recreated very accurately. It is easy to recall the chain of events that led us to the solution of a physical or technical problem we struggled with; the process is just as clear days or months later as it was when we first solved the problem. But it is more difficult to relive emotional events. We might be able to recall the situation and the circumstances, but to recall the feelings, the pounding heart, and the sweaty palms is difficult. Try to relive an emotional experience right now: can you remember the first time that somebody you really care for gave you a kiss? Do you feel the same as you felt then?

Last, inappropriate intellectual activities can be corrected. A feedback system lets us know when we have taken the wrong approach to solving a problem, and it helps us change very quickly to a different approach. But when an emotion that has been aroused may be inappropriate at that moment, it is difficult to say right then, "Hey, wait a minute. This is an inappropriate emotion, and so I'm going to switch to another one." Usually there has to be a cooling-off period before a person can assume a different emotional state.

When parents recognize the difference between a child's voluntary thought processes and his emotions, they will not demand that he control his emotional life in the way that he controls his intellectual life.

Just what is an emotion? Is it something we feel inside? Or is it a response to a feeling? Many people believe that observable behavior is an emotion, but emotions are the feelings that lead us to certain kinds of behavior. Although we do attribute emotions to people on the basis of their external responses or behaviors, the *emotion* is an internal feeling or state.

Are emotions innately good or bad? What about feelings of hatred, for example? Most people would categorize hatred as a bad emotion, but to hate sin wouldn't be inappropriate, would it? Or you could hate disease or ugliness or poverty. If you can accept the notion that very few emotions are innately bad, you won't feel the need to train out your child's emotions; rather, you will teach him to be emotionally honest—to have the ability to recognize his own feelings.

A newborn child doesn't have a wide range of emotions; at least he doesn't employ a wide range of behaviors in responding to emotional states. Usually infants have a generalized response to pleasure—they lie in the crib and look pleasant—and a generalized response to frustration—they thrash around and get agitated. As the child grows older, the number of ways he responds to emotional states increases, as does the variety of emotions that he feels.

Emotions in children are usually aroused when their needs are not being met, or when they are being inappropriately met. For instance, a child who wants to run outside and play but whose mother is holding him on her lap probably will become angry. And he will manifest that anger by struggling, fighting, and maybe even crying. But when he is feeling dependent or hurt, he will snuggle up close to her. In one instance she denied his needs by holding him on her lap; in the other, she fulfilled them by exactly the same behavior.

It is difficult for parents to realize that their child's interpretation of a situation may differ from theirs. When we interpret an event or a situation in one way, we expect our children to interpret it in the same way, forgetting that because their background and skills are different from ours, they won't see things the same. For instance, you might send a young child into the basement to get a jar of fruit. You wouldn't be frightened of going down into the basement, but he might. You find yourself telling your child, "Shape up. Don't be such a big boob. Get on down there. There's no such thing as a boogie man." Well, that's not going to get rid of his fears. He's operating within a frame of reference far different from yours.

This brings us back to the bad practice of training children to deny their emotions. We do a lot of such training in our society, especially with our young boys. Specifically, we teach them to suppress grief and affection by telling them that such emotions are not appropriate: "Little boys don't cry." Or, "Kissing is sissy stuff. That's what girls do." Then wives have to pay the price: they marry men who don't know how to *show* affection or who may not even *feel* love and affection because they have been trained not to. The result? A pretty dull existence.

Imagine that you are holding a yardstick right now. Let's say that the end with the number *one* represents a very low, depressed emotional state, and the other end represents a high, positive emotional state. The middle represents an everyday, calm emotional state. If we were to use that yardstick to record people's feelings, we would find many men operating within very narrow bands at the middle of the yardstick. In fact, some men take pride in not deviating from the calm middle. Such a man will say, "Boy, you know, I'm just as stable as a rock. I never get too excited and I never get too depressed." When his wife comes home with some really exciting news, he responds with, "Big deal," cooling her enthusiasm completely. On the other hand, some women fluctuate widely and maybe even wildly from one end of the yardstick to the other. Generally women are more emotionally honest than men. It's much more exciting to live with somebody who is like that.

When we recognize that a child's emotion at a given time might be inappropriate, rather than teaching him to deny that emotion, let's teach him to recognize what he's feeling and own up to it. Perhaps at a later time we can teach him to feel a different emotion in a similar situation. You may want to teach a child who has been wronged to turn the other cheek—that is, to feel love or compassion instead of anger. You can train a child to feel such an emotion of love or compassion, but that is not the same thing as teaching him to deny anger by saying, "No, you're not feeling angry. What you're feeling is love for that person." That is teaching him to be emotionally dishonest. Teaching him emotional honesty means teaching him to face up to his feelings. It has nothing to do with teaching the right response for a given emotion. In fact, there is no *right* response for any given emotional state.

After you have taught a child to recognize his emotion, saying something like, "I can tell that you are very angry because I wouldn't let you go outside and play," you might also tell him what he is allowed to do while he is angry. You might say, "You cannot sit here and kick the furniture. You cannot yell bad names at me. What you can do is to go downstairs and bounce the ball or go out in the garage and yell or go and hit a punching bag or run around the block." You can teach him a set of acceptable responses to anger—responses that you and the rest of society could live with.

A child taught to deny his emotions may respond to the world with a defense mechanism that Sigmund Freud called a *reaction formation.* It operates in this way: suppose a parent has some hostility toward one of his children. Because society has taught him that good parents aren't supposed to be angry towards their children, he goes around saying, "Oh, I really love this child," or, "My child is really dear to me." But his actions always give him away. While he is talking a good game of loving he is repressing the child, harming him, or getting even with him in many subtle ways. For example, as he prevents his child from doing things, he usually does so beneath the guise of, "No, I love you too much to let you do that." If a parent could learn to be honest with himself and say, "I know that I really feel some hostility toward this child," he could begin to change those feelings. But as long as he keeps denying what he really feels, pretending to feel the opposite, he'll never be able to make that necessary change.

ACTIVITIES: EMOTIONAL DEVELOPMENT IN CHILDREN

1. Once there was a girl who was attractive but who had been on only three or four dates in the three years that she had been at college. For some reason she just kept getting passed up. She was very shy and sensitive. Finally, when she was a junior, her roommates talked her into preferring a certain fellow for the Girl's Preference Ball. She was so nervous about choosing a fellow that all of her roommates had to go and stand with her in line, hold her hand, and give her constant encouragement. She finally made the big step and actually preferred a boy.

The rules for this particular dance went something like this: after a girl had preferred a boy the girls' association sent a card to the boy in the mail saying that so-and-so had preferred him for the dance. The fellow then had a certain amount of time in which to call the girl and confirm the date. The deadline for accepting the date was Thursday night. This fellow had not called this girl by Thursday night. Finally at the last hour, eleven or twelve o'clock in the evening, he called her and accepted. She was elated. She made an appointment to have her hair done and bought a new dress. Everything was ready.

The boy was supposed to come by for her at eight o'clock. Eight o'clock came, but he was not there. Nine o'clock passed, and then ten o'clock, and he hadn't shown up. Here this girl sat all dressed up with no place to go. It wouldn't have been so bad except that one of her roommates wasn't going to the dance that night and was sitting in the apartment with her. Someone else knew that she had been stood up.

At ten-thirty what emotion do you think this girl was feeling? Write your answer on line A. Below this answer write the behavior that might have been appropriate in that situation.

A. _____

Appropriate behavior for the girl would be_____

_____

At ten-forty-five the boy's roommate called the girl and told her that her date would not be coming. On his way to pick up a flower for her he was involved in a car accident that had paralyzed him from the waist down. He was at that very hour in the emergency room of the hospital.

Now what do you think the girl's emotion was? Write your answer on line B.

B. _____

If lines A and B are different it is because of the girl's knowledge and perception of the situation. What had happened was the same—the boy had not appeared—but she had more information at ten-forty-five than she did at ten-thirty, which changed her perception, as it did yours.

2. Write down how you would teach your child to be emotionally honest and to recognize the real feelings he is having. Next, make a list of appropriate behaviors to express those feelings.

3. For a week make a conscious effort to recognize every time you feel a "tender" emotion. When you have such feelings mention it to your children and then do something to express that emotion.

CHAPTER 14
DEVELOPING LOVE

A definition of love includes concern for, attachments to, and desire to be near another person. When those three elements characterize a relationship, we can call it a love relationship. But how is it developed?

Children aren't born into the world with innate love feelings. They don't care about other people; they are very self-centered; they don't necessarily enjoy being near other people. They have to learn that it is good to be close to other human beings.

Love develops in the context of having a relationship in which a young child's needs are taken care of. A very young child can take care of only about one-half of the needs that maintain his life. He can't get his own food or water, nor can he maintain his own body temperature. So he depends for those things on caretakers who are around him. If somebody feeds him when he's hungry and warms him when he's cold, he will begin to develop an attachment for that person. But children do not instinctively attach themselves to humans. For example, if an adult always wore a tiger suit when he took care of the needs of a child, the child would grow up with an attachment to tiger suits. The person we love and have feelings of closeness for and want to be near is the one who took care of our needs when we were little. Few of us—probably none of us—had our needs fulfilled by a human being dressed in a tiger suit. So we have learned to respond favorably not to tiger suits, but to humans.

Dr. Harry Harlow has conducted several experiments at the University of Wisconsin to see just what aspects of child care help children form attachments. The children he used were baby monkeys. In one ingenious set of experiments each baby monkey was given free access to two mechanical mothers. One mother was a piece of chicken wire with a head on the top. The other one was also a wire mother, but she was covered with terry cloth. Other than the difference in covering, both mothers were essentially identical. The wire mother fed some babies, and the cloth mother fed the others. Dr. Harlow found that the baby monkeys spent most of their time on the cloth mother. Even when they were being fed by the wire mother, they went to her for only an hour a day—long enough to eat. They spent the rest of their time with the cloth mother, hanging on to the terry cloth covering, cuddling, and rubbing up and down against that mother's body. They seemed to be satisfying a need for contact comfort.

Many people believe that the fulfillment of this need in human babies is also important. The cuddling, fondling, and nuzzling that go on between a mother or a father and their child helps develop an attachment, a feeling of closeness, the forerunner of the kind of love we know.

There is a critical period between thirty and ninety days of life in which baby monkeys can best form this attachment. If in that time he doesn't have a mother, either real or cloth, with which to develop that attachment, he may never learn to form attachments or to love. The critical period for human babies to form attachments seems to be between six months and a year. If a human baby doesn't have a meaningful relationship with an adult in his life during that time, he may have a difficult time later learning to form attachments and to feel close to other people.

Similarly, mothering does not seem to be instinctive. When we are very young, we learn mothering behavior by having someone care for us and do for us the duties of mothering such as feeding and so on. If we don't experience this when we are young, we probably will not make good mothers. Some monkeys in Harlow's lab were raised with no mothers. From birth they saw neither a real nor a mechanical mother. Monkeys raised in this kind of environment

112

who later had babies always rejected and refused to take responsibility for their own babies. And there is reason to believe that the same thing happens with humans: a girl who has been rejected by her mother or who has been institutionalized and has therefore seen no good example of mothering will, in her turn, be a poor mother. She will not know how to be warm and affectionate. A child who grows up thus deprived is going to grow up lacking some ability to give of himself or to have concern for others.

We must teach children several kinds of love. They need, first of all, to love themselves. Each child needs to know that he is worthwhile and that he has great potential; parents can teach that kind of love by accepting each child and telling him things such as, "I really love you. You are a great person. I find you good." Once a parent has said this, he must act as if that were true: a parent can do this by holding a child close, by seeking him out to put an arm around him, and by having close physical contact with him. However, healthy self-love doesn't mean that a child should pour his energy into self-fulfillment, satisfying his own goals exclusively. But part of his energy ought to be directed toward achieving his highest potential. A healthy person loves himself and looks out for himself.

Second, we have to teach people to be able to love members of the same sex. Boys ought to learn to love their fathers and other boys. Learning to love members of the same sex is bad only when people introduce physical sexual love into the relationship and when they don't learn the third type of love: love for people of the opposite sex. Normally, people's emotional love for members of the same sex becomes a springboard for learning how to love members of the opposite sex both physically and emotionally.

Within the third kind of love it is possible to have many love relationships. One of the myths we perpetuate in our society is that a grown person can love only one other person of the opposite sex. While you were dating you may have learned a lot about two or three of those people whom you were dating, and consequently you may have come to love them. It's foolish to think that such love would be suddenly eliminated when you became engaged or married to another person. A healthy person can love many people, and marriage partners ought not to get defensive about that.

Next we must teach our children behavior appropriate to expressing love for themselves, love for same-sexed friends and parents, and love for opposite-sexed parents and friends. We don't express our love for nor accept love from a child in the same way that we do from our marriage partner, although we love both. In some ways we severely limit our children's—especially our boys'—avenues for expressing love. Many people teach boys at a very early age not to cuddle and not to seek close physical contact—especially not with their fathers. But this is a real mistake. There is nothing wrong with reaching out, touching, and hugging people of the same sex. You may have seen French generals or Russians giving each other an embrace on television; other cultures are much healthier than Americans in this respect. Furthermore, when we teach a boy that it's "unhealthy" to want to be close to his father or brother, we are teaching him to curtail those feelings for people of the opposite sex. We should teach instead the difference between emotional and sexual love.

Once there was a young boy who helped his father raise sheep. One spring there was a large number of lambs who had lost their mothers; this boy fed these lambs from a bottle. One of those lambs fell in love with him and followed him everywhere. And the boy loved the lamb. As a result, it didn't have to go out into the field with the others; instead it played with the boy all summer long. But then autumn came, and it was time to market the lambs. As the boy stood on the tailgate of the truck, his father handed the lambs up to him, and he lifted them over the side and gently put them into the bottom of the truck. The last lamb was his lamb, the lamb that he loved. As the boy took that lamb, instead of gently lifting it over the side, he threw it into the bottom of the truck, where it landed on its head and lay bleating painfully. The boy jumped from the truck and ran to the house.

If you had driven into the farm yard at that very moment, you would have found his hostile behavior toward that lamb very puzzling. The boy's mother saw the behavior, and as he came running through the yard where she was hanging out clothes, she stopped him, put her arm around his shoulder, and said, "It was hard to say goodbye to the lamb, wasn't it? It's always hard to say goodbye to somebody you love." And the boy broke down and cried.

His mother had discerned his true feelings. He wasn't cruel. But because he was being separated from something he loved, he was afraid that he would break down and cry in front of his father if he was tender to his lamb. So, because he didn't know what else to do, he acted cruelly. And then he fled the scene.

When we raise young boys without showing them how to express affection towards others, we train them to act aggressively instead of tenderly. This love is disguised in the child who bangs his friends on the arm or fights with them instead of acting tenderly or telling them that he cares for them. Similarly, some adults mask their love for their marriage partners and their children by teasing them or by acting rough.

Love is a difficult emotion for children to deal with. And as we grow older, it exacts a terrible price: an honest expression of love exposes us many times to hurt. It makes us vulnerable. The antidote for injuries incurred in love relationships is not to hide our feelings of love, but to develop self-love. We should teach children to be honest and open about their feelings even though somebody may wound them. If they feel good about themselves, if they have some real self-love, they'll be able to endure the times when other people turn against them or break their hearts. To love and be hurt is a chance we all have to take. The more that people are willing to do this, the better the world and society will be.

ACTIVITIES: DEVELOPING LOVE

1. Learn about different kinds of love.
    A. List the different love relationships that you have.
    B. List the ways you could express love for three of the categories of people you listed above.
    C. Identify a couple of outstanding loving episodes from your life. What made them memorable?

2. To help your children develop love for each other encourage the following activities:
    A. Gather the family together for an evening of love. Taking turns, each family member should tell two good things about each other member of the family. This will foster understanding as well as increase each person's awareness of the love that is held for him by others.
    B. Have each person write one note a day for a week telling something good about one other family member, and leave the note lying around where the other person can find it, i.e., under a plate, taped around a toothbrush, and so on. A young child should be encouraged to dictate a note for this same purpose.
    C. Play Pixie. Every day each family member should do something extra nice for another member of the family without

115

being caught doing it. The whole purpose of this activity is to be a secret pixie. Care should be taken so that during the week one pixie visits every member of the family each day. To assure this you might put each person's name in a hat to be drawn by the family members. Each person whose name is drawn will receive treats from the person who draws his name for the entire week. Surprises might include making a bed, setting the table, a love note on a mirror, and so on.

D. Have a "Love of the Day" award to be given at dinner time to that person who most openly demonstrated love during the day.

3. Make a conscientious effort to say "I love you" to each child three times each day. Accompany each saying with some nonverbal love gesture, i.e., pat their head, squeeze their arm, wink at them, and so on. Be a good model and be emotionally honest.

CHAPTER 15
CHANNELING ANGER

Anger in children is a great source of concern to parents. For one thing, it usually leads a child to aggressive, destructive behavior. Thus, because anger most generally arises from frustration, parents should learn to identify sources of frustration in their children's lives and then try to eliminate those sources.

One source of a child's frustration is his inability to reach some goal. When he wants a cookie but can't reach the jar because the cupboard is too high, his frustration may lead him to attack the cupboard by kicking it. Frequently the barrier is physical, but sometimes goals become inaccessible to him because of his own inability to do things. For instance, as he matures and gains some degree of control over his body, he starts wanting to do all the things that he sees other children doing. Unfortunately, though, because his intellect has developed more rapidly than his motor skills, his body isn't capable. And, meeting with failure after failure, he will thus be constantly frustrated. For example, when a child learns to ride a bike, his younger brothers and sisters will also want to learn. But, lacking the necessary coordination, they are certain to meet with failure and frustration while the older child meets with success.

A second source of a child's frustration is the pressure adults put on him to excel in some activity. Recurrent in parents' conversation with their children is the theme of speed: "Hurry up. Do this quickly. Right now ... immediately!" But the fact is that children usually can't do things "immediately" or "right now." Unable to meet the time schedule or to perform at the level of quality that parents expect is frustrating for the child. And the typical response to frustration is anger—to lash out at the world.

It's unhealthy for a child to be fighting the world continually. First, people that he lashes out at may retaliate. And because adults are bigger and stronger than a child, they can always have the last blow or can isolate him or can send him off to bed.

Second, a child preoccupied with anger doesn't have much room left for happiness or contentment. It won't do any good to say, "Don't be angry," or to try convincing him that he doesn't feel angry. When a child is angry, he's angry, and it's best for parents to accept the emotion, trying first to interpret it to him and second to define for him why he feels that way: "I know that you're angry and this is why. . . ." This is especially true when a child does not act out his angry feelings directly on the source of his frustration. Then if there's some way to eliminate the cause of the anger, do it. Or, if it's caused by something that the child is going to have to live with, teach him some socially acceptable responses to his aggressive feelings.

Finally, it's always possible that a child can be taught not to feel angry every time a goal is blocked. But the child who displaces his anger towards an object or person other than the source of his anger will be difficult to help.

Some know the story of the father who was angry at his employer but who, instead of letting his employer see his anger, yelled and nagged at his wife about a late dinner and a dirty house. The wife, in turn, approached the children, who were helping to set the table, and yelled at them for being slow and for leaving their coats on the floor. The oldest children then acted out their hostilities on the younger ones. Finally, the youngest child, the baby, went in and kicked the dog. If the dog had gone outside and barked at a tree, the chain of displacement would have been complete. Not one person in the family faced up directly to the source of his frustration. Unable to deal with the emotion, the family simply whitewashed it.

Sometimes children turn their anger inward toward themselves. Temper tantrums are a form of aggression directed towards the self. There is nothing pleasurable in them for the child: holding his breath, squirming on the floor, and rubbing his elbows on the rug are painful practices for the child. The best he could hope for is a rug burn. He doesn't act that way because he finds it rewarding. Rather, he does it to dispel his anger. Other evidence of anger directed towards the self is scratching, head banging, and hair pulling. Furthermore, some research indicates that accident-prone children are not just careless, but are inflicting pain upon themselves because they're angry with themselves. Such a displacement of anger is called scapegoating. Displacing feelings isn't necessarily bad; in fact, it might be the wise course to follow. But when a child displaces his anger, it's going to be difficult for his parents to determine what is bothering him and thus help him deal with his anger.

A parent must be able to deal with a child's anger on a day-by-day basis. He can do so using either a short-term or a long-term approach. The short-term method focuses on undesirable behavior caused by anger. For example, parents can effectively divert a child's attention from the source of frustration to something pleasant for him—get him channeled into a pleasant activity. When two children are fighting for the same toy, for instance, the parents might give one child another toy. Another short-term technique would be to separate a child from the source of his frustration, to physically remove him, to put him into another room. Of course these short-term "first-aid" approaches don't deal with the child's feelings; they simply make life temporarily easier for your child—and you—by removing the source of his frustration and thereby encouraging acceptable behavior.

An ineffective short-term way to deal with aggressive responses is to punish a child. Then you're teaching a lesson in hypocrisy: on one hand you tell him, "When you're feeling angry you can't go around hitting other people"; on the other hand, you punish him because you're angry with him. Using punishment to control aggressive behavior will usually intensify a child's feelings of aggression or hostility. Consequently, the more he is punished for aggressive behavior, the more frustrated, hostile, and aggressive he becomes. He may not display it in your presence, and he may not attack the object of his frustration directly, but he will experience increased anger. He may release it verbally in a bad way by nagging, teasing, and fighting with his brothers and sisters. But severe physical punishment may repress his anger completely, may in fact break his spirit. That is a terrible price to pay to get him to behave properly. Have you seen a child whose spirit is broken? Perhaps that is what ails autistic children: they completely withdraw themselves from society, sitting alone, staring into space, pacing back and forth, and seldom if ever speaking to anyone.

Short-term techniques may make us feel better, or may make our lives more bearable, but we should be more concerned with the long-range effects of discipline. We can achieve these long-range effects by eliminating entirely the sources of our children's frustration. The first way to do that is to set down the rules that you're going to live by in your family and then to enforce them in a consistent way. If a rule proves meaningless, however, eliminate it. Knowing the area of the ball park that he can play in gives a child security. He may want to test the rules you've set up; he may wander right up to the edge of a rule and push it a little. He may even break it. But there's a certain security that comes in knowing the safety of the ball park and that rules will be enforced.

A second thing that will eliminate frustration is to set realistic goals for children. Parents who plan for their child to be the brightest in school or to be the best in skill areas like piano playing or dancing may be putting unbearable pressure on him. Rather, they should honestly evaluate what he can do in school and in extracurricular activities, and then they should set goals consistent both with the time he can devote to each activity and with his mental and physical ability.

Third, make sure that he has proper nutrition, rest, and general good health. Small things become big things in the mind of a child who is either undernourished or fatigued.

A fourth point: don't reward a child for his angry responses. When you give in to your child each time he has an outburst of anger, you are teaching him that anger will help him get his way. Consequently, the next time he is frustrated, there will be another outburst.

Fifth, avoid becoming a model of aggression yourself. When a child happens to love his parents—which most of us hope our children do—he'll identify with them and will want to imitate their behavior. So if they strike him when they're angry, that's the behavior he will think is good and that he will try to duplicate.

The sixth point is that you *can* increase a child's tolerance for ambiguous or frustrating situations. A few years ago child development experts advocated letting children act out any emotion they felt. This was supposed to help the children get these feelings out of their systems. If, for example, a child were feeling angry toward a parent, it was thought that the honest thing would be to let that child be aggressive toward his parent. But this attitude will never help a child learn to deal with frustrating situations or handle his anger. It's not mature to always act out in haste the emotions that we feel, and when a child can learn that blocked goals needn't necessarily give rise to aggressive feelings, he'll be much happier.

Finally, it is impractical to tell a child that there is no way for him to express his anger. Rather, we ought to think of things he *can* do that will help drain off his strong emotions. If we don't provide that, if we block every avenue that he tries to use to get rid of his anger, he may develop an ulcer, colitis, asthma, or any of a number of similar physical ailments. A good way to help him work out his feelings is to let him pound a punching bag or hammer nails or dig up weeds in the garden—or participate in some other vigorous physical activity.

A teacher in a midwestern graduate school found his work to be really frustrating: while his job depended on his ability to publish the results of his research, he wasn't a good researcher and so he was never quite able to meet his deadlines. Consequently, he bought a home on three or four acres of scrub oak and made it his practice to chop down one or two trees each evening before going in to meet his wife. That way he drained out all the anger that had built up in him during the day. When he bought that land he thought he had a lifetime supply of trees, but in about two and a half years he had cut them all down. Then instead of cutting down a tree each night he would loosen up the ground around its root system and try to take it out. He had a good plan: because there was no other alternative for him so long as he wanted to stay at that university, he couldn't have made his life less frustrating, so he worked out his anger in a way that didn't harm anyone else. In fact, he turned his anger to a profit, increasing the value of his land.

In another family, school pressures—probably student competition—brought the children a lot of frustration. Wisely the parents insisted that the children not get into carpools with neighborhood children, but that they walk home from school each day. The exhaustive walk—uphill over a mile—drained the children of all the hostility that had built up during the school day. The parents could tell with about ninety percent accuracy when one of the daughters had ridden home from school with a friend: she was still angry. But because the parents insisted that they walk home, the children were not only less angry, but were also a lot healthier.

ACTIVITIES: CHANNELING ANGER

1. Answer the following questions:
    A. What does it mean to be emotionally honest?
    B. What is the typical kind of anger response?
    C. How do you respond when you are angry?
    D. How closely do your child's responses to frustrating situations match your own?

2. List the names of three of your children and their ages. Next, identify three sources of anger for each of them as well as their method of dealing with each anger. Finally, record how you would deal with each anger on both a short-term and a long-term basis.

3. With each child create a list of appropriate behaviors he can engage in when he is angry.

Points to Remember
   Help your children to be emotionally honest with their angry feelings by allowing them to verbalize what they feel and by using an appropriate outlet for the release of that anger. This can be done by:
    1. Accepting the emotion.
    2. Interpreting and defining the emotion.
    3. Providing consistent discipline and rules.
    4. Setting up realistic goals.
    5. Insuring proper nutrition, rest, and general good health.
    6. Avoiding rewarding angry responses.
    7. Avoiding becoming an aggressive model.
    8. Training your child not to feel angry in particular situations.
    9. Teaching your child socially acceptable responses for his anger.

Name of Child	Age	Source of Anger	Child's Pattern of Dealing with the Anger	Parent's Pattern of Dealing with the Anger	
				Short-Term	Long-Term
1.		a.			
		b.			
		c.			
2.		a.			
		b.			
		c.			
3.		a.			
		b.			
		c.			

CHAPTER 16
OVERCOMING FEAR

Fear is an emotional state that we attribute to people who exhibit rapid breathing, increased heart rate, and increased perspiration and who attempt to avoid a certain situation. From the time a person is born, some situations inspire fear in him; he doesn't have to be taught to fear them.

One such situation is a sudden change in the environment. A sudden change in an infant's environment will most likely evoke a *startle reflex:* he'll arch his head and back, he'll suck in his breath rapidly, and his arms and legs will flail out from his body and he will cry. If he is sitting in a relatively quiet room and if somebody makes a loud noise, that sudden change (the noise) will produce the startle reflex. If he is lying peacefully in a crib and his grandmother comes up and snaps his picture with a flash bulb, the sudden bright light will cause a startle. If you are holding him in your arms and you suddenly drop your arms six inches, leaving him momentarily without support, that sudden change will bring about a startle. It isn't the change that causes the startle response; it seems to be the suddenness of the change. You can *gradually* increase the noise level in a room without causing the startle reflex. So, to a class of events called *sudden changes in the environment,* even a very young child will give a startle response.

The sudden change also brings about several internal changes in a child's autonomic nervous system: his breathing rate increases, his heart pumps faster, and his body perspires more freely. More adrenalin circulates through his body, and more sugar is expelled from the liver, where sugar is stored. All of these events serve to arouse him.

But it is more pleasant to have the body in a resting state. When we are very tired, the body goes to sleep so that it can return to a relaxed, refreshed state. When we are hungry, the body seeks food to relieve itself of that unpleasant sensation of hunger, and thereby regain *homeostasis* (equilibrium). And likewise, after the autonomic nervous system is aroused—producing the increased heart rate, increased metabolism, and so on—it's very pleasant to get rid of that response, to have the body return to its normal or resting state. One way of regaining that balance is to get away from whatever is arousing the autonomic nervous system—and that is the usual response.

In one significant classical experiment conducted forty or fifty years ago a little boy about a year old was conditioned to fear his pet rat. Albert played every day with his little animal, petting it as he held it on his lap. Then, one day while he was playing with the rat, someone came up behind him and hit a loud gong—a terrible noise—which evoked the startle reflex. The next day when he was playing with his rat, someone hit the gong again, and again he had the startle reflex. After only two or three days of hearing the loud noise while in the presence of the rat, Albert came to fear his rat. As soon as the rat was brought in, Albert showed the startle reflex and made strong attempts to avoid his former pet. Albert was frightened of his rat.

Unfortunately, though, that wasn't the only thing Albert learned to fear: all things that were similar to that rat also elicited the startle reflex and aroused his autonomic nervous system. Apparently the characteristics that stood for ratness in Albert's mind were whiteness and furriness: cotton balls, his mother's fur muff, and Santa Claus's beard—all objects that were white and furry—elicited the startle reflex in Albert. Before the experiment, Albert had never seen a Santa Claus beard. Several months after the experiment he went with his father to see Santa Claus; as he approached Santa Claus and saw the beard, he became frightened and agitated. He held onto his father's leg, trying to avoid having to see Santa Claus. However, his father, not understanding the cause of this behavior, began to browbeat his child, saying, "Now stop being silly! It's just Santa Claus."

But Albert wasn't being silly, was he? He had *learned* to fear all things that were white and furry. Because the Santa Claus beard was similar enough in appearance to the white rat, Albert responded just as he had *learned* to respond to the white rat.

Sometimes it is very hard for parents to understand their child's fear of certain objects or events, but, knowing the principle, you might—by looking back into your child's past—be able to determine the cause of the fear. Albert's father couldn't understand the boy's fear of Santa Claus. He thought that because Albert had never seen a Santa Claus before, the boy was being irrational.

When we're young, this classical process of conditioning and generalization is probably the main way we develop fear. But as children get older, another source of learning fear develops: imitation. A child at home with his mother during a storm with a lot of thunder and lightning will, if the mother becomes nervous and frightened, notice her fear and imitate it. He will learn to be frightened of storms. Through the process of imitation or modeling, children acquire many of the fears that their parents have.

A third source of fear that may be innate, but unobservable until a child is older, surfaces when a child can compare new or novel events with events that are familiar. Up to a certain point, human beings seek for new experiences, situations that they can fit into the framework of previous experience. All of us like to do new things, go new places. When we have a *relatively* new experience—going to a party, trying a new dish at dinnertime—the experience is very rewarding, and we seek after that. However, when we experience something *totally* new, the experience is no longer positive but becomes negative or frightening, and we try to avoid that. For example, many people who have taken hallucinogenic drugs have had bad experiences—seeing undulating walls, giant insects, and so on. Such an experience is so new that nothing in their past lives has equipped them to handle it, so they find the whole situation very frightening.

This third source of fear occurs only after we have a notion of the familiar, a standard by which to measure the new. This behavior is first noticeable in children who are about eight or nine months old. At about this age, children seem to be able to distinguish their parents from other adults. When you try to get a child at this age to go to his grandmother or to an unfamiliar neighbor, he will cry, become agitated, and cling very tightly to the familiar—that is, to his parents. This happens with nearly all children, and it's called *stranger anxiety.* (However, at six months of age this behavior doesn't occur, because a child at that age doesn't yet have a stable concept of the familiar. He doesn't recognize that his parents are different from other people, or he may simply believe that adults in general are taking care of him.)

We experience this phenomenon when we move to a new city where everything we see is unfamiliar. We feel uneasy until we have a chance to drive around and find out where the shopping centers, church, schools, and downtown stores are. Then, as the city becomes familiar, it becomes exciting. Some of you will have experienced this if you've flown into a town in the middle of the night, rented a car, and driven off not even knowing which direction was north. You will have felt disoriented, possibly even frightened.

Suppose a child has developed several fears in his life. Obviously, many situations, such as a Santa Claus beard or a fur muff, have in them no real cause for fear, and it would be good to teach him not to fear them. But how can we help a child? It doesn't do any good to say, "You shouldn't be frightened of this," or to sit back and think that he'll outgrow it. Fear is a peculiar kind of behavior. The closer a person gets to the source of his fear, the stronger is his tendency to avoid it. So he usually removes himself physically from the thing that was frightening. But as he does this over and over, never coming into direct contact with the frightening situation, he may never learn that he needn't have feared the object in the first place. Some of us have maintained fears for years simply because we've never faced up to them.

When you try to help a child face up to his fear, do you do it all at once? If he is genuinely frightened of a situation, carrying him bodily into that situation wouldn't be very productive. Suppose a child is afraid of horses. You could saddle a horse and force the child onto the horse, but that might be too much. Sometimes when people can't physically withdraw themselves from a situation they will withdraw psychologically: they may pass out or exhibit schizophrenic behavior. Their body has to be there, but their mind doesn't have to be.

An example of this process occurs during wartime, when soldiers know they cannot physically escape from their foxholes during a battle siege, so they withdraw mentally. This phenomenon is called *battlefield psychosis.*

128

There are some ways you can train fears out of children. First, though, let's go back to Albert and the rat. Several months after Albert had been conditioned to fear the rat, he was trained not to fear it. When he was doing something that he really liked, such as eating ice cream, the researchers put the rat in a far corner of the room. The rat was so far away—maybe twenty to thirty feet—that Albert wasn't nervous. And while he was having his good experience that rat was just there, existing on the edge of his consciousness. The next day, when he was again experiencing something pleasant, the rat was brought a little closer, and the next day a little closer. After a couple of weeks of bringing the rat steadily closer, the researchers had Albert holding it on his lap. Notice that this wasn't a direct confrontation between the fear stimulus and the child; it was gradual.

Similarly, you may be able to control or eliminate a lot of your children's fears by taking this gradual approach. The first step is to think of something rewarding enough to overpower the fear. Perhaps your child is afraid of the dark and likes to have the light left on when he goes to bed. The light is a reward. You could gradually reduce his fear by using a dimmer switch on the bedroom light. One night he might go to bed with the light on bright, the next night you could make the room a little darker, the next night a little more dark, and so on. In a couple of weeks you could have the light totally off. It's important during this deconditioning that nothing frightens him, or he will once again be afraid of the dark. The dark will really come to stand for something that is frightening.

If a child is afraid of being alone in his room at night, you should begin by sitting on the edge of his bed. Then you tell him you are going to get up and walk to the other side of the room for a minute. As you walk over, be sure he can see you all the time. Then come back and sit on the bed. A little while later, go over to the door—always making certain that he can see you. Come back once again, and then go to the door and step outside for five seconds and come back. You might be talking all the time. He hears your voice even though he can't see you. In that brief time he didn't even have a chance to become frightened. Next you go out for ten seconds and then come back. Gradually you increase the amount of time away from him—until one night you give him a kiss goodnight and leave until you see him the next morning.

However, if you try to use this technique with a stimulus that really is unsafe or frightening, it won't work and may make the child even more frightened. Suppose you have an unsafe horse who throws riders half of the time. It would be very unwise to put the

129

child on that horse in the hope that he will learn not to fear it: half of the times you put him on, he will be thrown off. The horse is a legitimate fear stimulus.

If a child has just been frightened for the first time in a particular situation, it is probably a good idea to put him back into the situation as soon as you can. If he falls off a horse while riding one for the first time, the best thing is to get him back on that horse immediately—but only if you know that the horse is safe and that the first fall was only a fluke. The child will then have an immediate good experience with that horse, and the good experience will stick in his mind.

If you force your child into a genuinely unsafe or frightening situation, he may withdraw psychologically. But if it is not unsafe—like the cotton balls, the fur muff, and the rat for Albert—then the more he goes into the situation—either gradually (if he already has fear) or rapidly (if his fear is just building up)—the more likely he will be to grow up unafraid.

ACTIVITIES: OVERCOMING FEAR

1. Read Matthew 26 from the Bible and discuss the following:
   A. What was the fear-like situation?
   B. Which incidences indicated an arousal of the autonomic nervous system?
   C. Which incidences that you identified show withdrawal symptoms?

2. Record for each child the following information as it pertains to a minimum of two fears. Commit yourself to assisting each child in overcoming their fears.

Name of Child	Fear—What is he afraid of?	Symptoms—How do you know he is afraid?	Source—Why is he afraid?	Plan of Action— How will you recondition your child's fear?

3. Identify three of your personal fears that could possibly be imitated by your children. How are you going to overcome these fears?

Fear	Plan of Action
1.	
2.	
3.	

Never hesitate to ask for help from someone else in overcoming a fear. Hesitation itself indicates fear and should be overcome.

CHAPTER 17
YOUR CHILD'S SELF-ESTEEM

Everyone has certain feelings and beliefs about himself. These feelings and beliefs constitute what is known as self-concept. A person's self-concept is composed of many perceptions one has about himself; about how others feel and act toward him; about who he is, what he stands for, where he lives, and about what he does or does not do.

Some concepts are less important than others, but all concepts about self are significant. For instance, Sandra Lewis might see herself as a wife, mother, parttime secretary, and a fairly good swimmer. Her self-concept as a parttime secretary is transitory—that is, it may change. Her self-concept as a good swimmer may be rather unimportant in the overall view. Her concept of how she performs as a wife and mother is probably of greater importance to her. Basic descriptions of Sandra Lewis serve to distinguish her as unique from all other people. More important than basic descriptions (who she is or her self-concept) are the values she places on them. These values concerning her self-concept are based on personal feelings about who she is and her response or reactions to others' attitudes toward her. All these factors determine her self-esteem. She not only regards herself as a mother, but as a *good* or *bad* mother. She does not see herself simply as a person, but as attractive or ugly, pleasant or unpleasant, fat or thin, adequate or inadequate. Her self-concept can be either positive (she feels good and likes who she is), or it can be negative (she is unhappy, feels dissatisfied with herself, inferior, insecure, etc.).

The development of self-concept begins when a child recognizes that he is someone separate and distinct from his mother and the environment. The infant's waking hours are spent in exploration—tasting, smelling, feeling, listening to, and looking at. Very early in life he begins to distinguish between what is "me" and what is not "me." He begins to perceive his body—his arms, legs, hands, and feet—as being part of him. He perceives his voice as coming from himself. He recognizes his name as being a representation of him. Through continued exploration, perceptions become increasingly differentiated, and before long the child is in possession of a large number of perceptions about himself and his world. Eventually a sense of identity or a sense of who he is emerges. He becomes aware that he is a unique person with many qualities and values (how he feels about who he is and what he can do). Self-esteem comes into focus, and self-esteem plays an influential part in each consequential behavior throughout the rest of the individual's life.

A child's interaction with his environment is of great importance in establishing his self-concept, but his self-esteem is based largely on how he *interprets* these interactions. Mother and father, siblings, playmates, and all significant others in the child's life greatly affect his self-esteem. He is very dependent on interactions with family members and is dependent on their appraisals of him. Parents and family are daily contributors to the beliefs that children are forming about themselves. What they see and what they hear greatly affects their developing self-concept.

Responsibility lies with parents to start in these early years to build positive self-esteem in their children. A good self-concept and high self-esteem are essential to a child's proper growth and development to promote personal happiness and effective functioning. Research indicates that certain specific traits tend to be correlated with favorable and unfavorable self-concepts. Some of these traits are:

1. *Good overall adjustment and free utilization of abilities.* People who are not well adjusted usually perceive themselves as helpless and inferior, and they usually have difficulty in giving and

receiving love. They usually feel anxious, guilty or ashamed, and depressed. They are self-conscious and preoccupied with their own problems and difficulties. A person who is in conflict and who is dissatisfied with himself cannot reach his potentials. On the other hand, people who believe they *can* are more likely to succeed. They approach tasks and people with the expectation that they will succeed.

Dr. Abraham H. Maslow, professor of psychology at Brandeis University, studied the happiest people he could find. He selected people who were successful in their lives, and he watched them work and play. These people had no special genius, and they were not endowed with any particular gifts. They were somehow able to use themselves fully to achieve their capabilities. Dr. Maslow found his study subjects had a number of things in common: among the most important was the ability to accept themselves and their own natures without feeling threatened. They had very high self-esteem. They saw themselves as liked, wanted, acceptable, able, dignified, and worthy. Success is analyzed with positive self-concept much as is owning a stout ship: with a sturdy vessel underfoot, one may go sailing far from shore. When one has doubts about his ship and concern about his seaworthiness, he must play it safe and stay close to harbor.

2. *Honesty with self and acceptance of others, which promotes less defensive behavior.* A lack of a sense of self-worth causes a child to feel the need to defend his behavior. The child may begin bragging to cover up or bolster his feelings of inadequacy, or he may start searching for faults in others. The child who believes nobody likes, wants, or cares about him often concludes that people are his enemies. His attitude or defense mechanism becomes, "I don't care about anybody, either!" In an attempt to outwardly exhibit independence or "show" people that he doesn't "need" them, he becomes very defensive and defiant and ofttimes displays contempt for others.

A positive self-concept provides its possessor with a firm platform from which to deal with life and provides him with the means for efficient and effective interaction with people. He can accept his own faults, and can accept others' criticisms of him. He can express opinions and views without feeling threatened. He has an objective view of the behavior of others and the ability to "live outside himself" and be actively involved in helping other people.

3. *Effectiveness in groups and popularity.* The most popular children have moderate self-acceptance and good acceptance of

others, while the least popular are those children who have a low self-acceptance or an unrealistic view of their "superiority." Insecure people are apprehensive about expressing ideas. They do not want to expose themselves to possible ridicule, so they are listeners and bystanders rather than participators. People with good self-esteem trust themselves and their opinions and views, and they aren't afraid to express these opinions, even when they meet an opposing view. They are more likely participants and leaders in groups, thus increasing their popularity.

4. *Good achievement in school.* Here are some examples of how people affect others' self-concept in academic ways. A high school student received a ninety-eight percentile on a college entrance examination. He interpreted this score as being his IQ and thought that he was just an average kid, so he was sure he wouldn't do well in college. When he entered school he almost failed and at the end of the first term he came home and told his parents that he just wasn't college material. His concerned parents went to the high school counselor who had encouraged him to go to college in the first place. In talking with him they learned that the ninety-eight percentile their son had received on the test indicated that his IQ was 140. He went back to college and was able to do A work before the end of the school year.

A child with a self-concept that dictates that he is not good at reading will avoid reading—the very thing which would be most helpful for him. Since he avoids reading he does not practice, and consequently he does not read very well. The teacher can reaffirm his "poor reader concept" when he does not read well with, "My, Joe, you don't read very well." Additionally, the teacher sends home a report card which indicates that Joe is not a good reader, and parents join with the teacher to confirm Joe's beliefs that he is not a good reader.

Sheila's parents encourage her reading and comment on her progress. She feels that she is a good reader and she enjoys reading. She does well and the teacher encourages her by telling her, "Sheila, you are doing very well in reading." Encouragements of this sort assist Sheila's self-concept and aid her in continuing to improve her reading skills. Student's beliefs about their abilities are important in determining academic success.

By knowing the impact parents have on their children's self-concept development, how can you assist your child's development of good self-concept? Ask yourself these questions. What can I do today to help my child feel happy? How can I let my child know I really care about him? What can I do to help my child feel good about himself? What success experiences can I provide for my child today?

Positive self-concept is influenced first by expressions of warmth and love. Parental love is a basic element of self-esteem. There must be *love* in the family, not just the hugging and kissing or the verbal manifestations of love. Although these manifestations are important, children need the love that expresses real respect and concern for the child—the love that can be shown through a smile, a touch, a wink, or a compliment and approval. When the child sees that he is an object of deep interest and pride and that he is respected, he begins to feel that he is a person of some worth. As his feelings of personal worth develop, his ability to develop adequate relationships with others will increase. Manifestations of love and concern among parents and brothers and sisters is important, too. This provides the child with a feeling of stability and security. A child who feels that he is a worthwhile part of a family generally has little trouble loving himself and others.

Second, children need and want rules and guidelines. The child with permissive parents is likely to be alarmed and insecure. He is forced into making decisions that he has neither the knowledge nor the experience to make. Wrong decisions tend to lower self-esteem. The undisciplined child suspects that his parents don't enforce rules simply because they don't much care what happens to him. On the other hand, it's important to remember that guidance can bring about resistance and promote feelings of inferiority and can be interpreted as a desire to think and act for the child. The optional choice is to define standards and limits on behavior for children, but at the same time to consider the rights and opinions of the child as worthwhile and noteworthy. Children's views should be sought and respected. This gives them the opportunity to enter into discussions and gain confidence from the assertion of their own views.

As parents, work together to enforce and assist one another, and be consistent in your rules and discipline. When you reinforce one another, children learn that their game of playing parent versus parent won't work. Don't be wishy-washy. Make rules and then abide by them as much as possible. Lack of consistency hampers the development of self-concept because the child is placed in a situation where he must constantly reinterpret his actions and the actions of others. Inconsistent discipline may lead to lack of self-control. Consistency increases a feeling of security, which gives the child a sense of worth and belonging and permits many problems encountered outside the home to be handled more effectively. This is necessary for developing a feeling of adequacy.

Be firm but not harsh. Firmness shows respect for the self, which is the next step to helping your child develop good self-esteem. Studies show that children who display high self-esteem tend to have parents who are high in self-esteem. These parents also tend to be more emotionally stable and more self-reliant.

Third, children need the regular application of encouragement. Encouragement consists of a faith in the individual that gives him the freedom either to fail or to succeed and still be loved, valued, and accepted. Provide opportunities that promote feelings of success rather than those that are too difficult and often result in failure experiences. When a child tries something too difficult and makes a wrong decision or mistake, don't treat it as a failure; treat it instead as a stepping stone to learning. Wrong decisions tend to lower self-esteem, and they need to be handled properly. The child should be encouraged to make a series of small decisions (and they should be decisions that don't have a *right-wrong* option). For example, let him select from two or three choices an acceptable choice, such as the food for dinner, his clothes for school, or a family activity. This helps the child have success experiences and helps him develop the belief that he can make decisions of value to others. Be sure to freely but sincerely commend tasks that are well done.

Fourth, children need to feel that they are important. The following story serves to illustrate this important principle:

"Yes," said Mrs. Smith into the cold, black telephone receiver, "I guess she's been gone about 3, maybe 3½ hours. . . . You see, with five other children in the family . . ." her voice trailed off as the sergeant at the other end of the receiver said, somewhat impatiently, "Could you please describe her to me?" "Well," said Mrs. Smith, "Tammy is five years old, she's rather a plain little girl, with brown hair and big blue eyes. She's a little short for her age. Her movements are somewhat uncoordinated, not at all like her older sister . . . What does she like to do? . . . Well she is such a quiet child, and, . . . you see with five other children . . ." Panic now began to creep into her voice, "Officer, I've looked everywhere for her. . . ." She was thinking of how, just yesterday, Tammy was trying to show her that picture she had drawn. "Why didn't I stop my work long enough to notice, and she was so proud of that birthday present she wrapped for me last week, and all I could think of was how

much scotch tape she had wasted in wrapping it. This morning, when she broke that egg, she was only trying to be helpful, and I yelled at her . . . needlessly, and when she asked me to help her tie her shoe, I scolded her and told her she could do it herself. She only wanted some attention from me. Why didn't I take the few minutes to let her know that we really care about her? Last week she was trying so hard to learn to ride her bike. Why didn't we encourage her instead of comparing her to her brother?"

As Mrs. Smith's mind raced, the picture began to unfold of a shy, quiet, unassuming little girl who felt like nothing . . . because she had always been treated like a nothing. And now, this shy, quiet, unassuming child had gone away.

You must show your children that they are important to you. Do you really know them? Do you call each child by name? Is each child special to you? Do you know each child's favorite food, game, dress, or shirt?

Let's see what could have happened in Tammy Smith's life that day if her mother had taken time to use some of the principles we've discussed.

Mrs. Smith: "Come on, children. You'll need to hurry or you're going to be late for school."
Tammy: "Momma, tie my shoe."
Mrs. Smith: "I'll be glad to help you with your shoes, Tammy, but you'll have to be patient until I get your brothers and sisters off to school. . . . Tammy, please put the egg down. . . . Tammy, it makes me feel angry inside that you have broken that egg. You may clean it up. . . . Children, I'm afraid I failed to get you up early enough this morning. I'm sorry that you have to be so rushed . . . Thanks, Tammy. I appreciate your help. You've done a good job cleaning that up. Later this morning I'm going to bake a cake. You can help me and I'll show you how to handle the eggs so they won't get dropped and broken."

Later in the morning . . . Mrs. Smith is up to her elbows in dish soap and a million miles away in thought. Tammy annoyingly brings her back to reality with:

"Momma. Look at my picture. . . . Momma . . . Look at my picture."
Mrs. Smith: "Yes, honey. You've done a really good job. Why don't you tell me about what you've drawn while I finish these dishes; and then we'll bake that cake."

Comments of this type required the same amount of time as those in the first story, but they can make a whole world of difference in a child's life. This positive approach comes with a positive attitude on the part of the parent, and if used consistently, it creates in the child the positive self-concept that is so vital in his development.

ACTIVITIES: DEVELOPING SELF-ESTEEM

1. As parents you should make a list of twenty-five reasons why God could like you. You need not show the list to anyone, but you do need to write it down to commit yourself. If parents can see how they are worthwhile in some areas, then they can reflect that feeling of worthwhileness to their children, and it will begin to rub off on their children.

2. Make a list of twenty-five reasons why you can love and value each child. Make the list separate for each child. You ought to show this list to the children involved. Often we do not let children know that there are things about them that we really like.

3. Provide opportunities every day for each child to do something he excels in. It is important that you let him be successful in front of his brothers and sisters.

4. Keep a chart on a child and keep track of how many times people say positive or negative things to the child in the course of an hour. Dinnertime is an excellent time to record this. Then use the record as the basis of a discussion in your family for the need to be supportive in the family.

5. In nearly all families there are one or more members who are systematically ignored. When they speak no one answers, no one asks their opinion, and so on. See if you can tell who this person is in your family, and make an effort to include him in.

6. Write down five adjectives for each child in your family that you think best describe him. Circle the one that is the most descriptive. See if there is agreement between you and your partner. Do you see your children the same?

7. Start each child on a new activity or hobby. Let the child decide what it will be. You provide the lessons or raw materials for

him to get started. Every day or so sit down and ask how the child is progressing. Really be interested. Don't let all of the children do the same thing. Each child should strive for excellence in a different area from his brothers and sisters.

8. Go back to activity number six. Can you really classify a child in five words? Obviously not! Look at your list and see if your children are starting to do a self-fulfilling prophecy on you. Are they starting to act like you are telling them you expect them to act?

9. Spend at least ten minutes a day in a one-to-one relationship with each child. During this time, get close to your child. Find out what makes him tick. It is important that you reach out and touch your child on the arm or shoulder while you are talking to him.

10. Make a realistic assessment of your child's skills and readjust your expectations so that your child can have a more relaxed, pressure-free life. You'll also enjoy life more.

UNIT IV
MENTAL GROWTH

Probably no area of child development captures a parent's attention to the extent that intellectual development does. Parents realize that success and happiness generally come to those who are bright, so they stress intellectual activities with their children. In this unit, several topics dealing with the fostering of a child's intellect will be discussed.

As a child grows it is important for him to learn these intellectual skills: to notice the world around him and gather information about it, to organize and store the information he has gathered in some orderly way, and to use or retrieve the stored information in order to solve problems. Language acts as a tool to help the child perform each of these operations more easily.

The most appropriate time to help a child develop these skills is in his preschool years, through simple, gamelike activities.

CHAPTER 18
DEVELOPING YOUR
CHILD'S INTELLECT

Adults often have a tendency to invalidate childhood. We say, "As soon as you get big enough, you can do this," or, "When you grow up you will be able to do that," or, "Be Daddy's big boy," or, "Why don't you grow up!" or, "Don't act like a child." Statements like these suggest that childhood is not a legitimate part of human growth. It seems like we are saying, "As soon as we get you past this part in your life, you will be able to be a real, legitimate person."

Actually, a child digests more information in his early formative years than in any comparable period of time during the rest of his life. He learns as he interacts with friends, families, and peer groups and with his environment, his home, the facilities around his home, his toys, and other things not classified as toys: garbage cans, worms, ropes, dead rabbits. These stimuli help him perceive and understand his world.

Jean Piaget, an outstanding observer of children, classifies their development in terms of growth, maturation, and learning. As we observe the child, we see him increasing in size, which is *growth*. We see him becoming more adept, increasing the quality of his behavior, which is *maturation.* And we see him utilizing certain new behaviors and extinguishing old ones that no longer fit into his life, which is *learning.*

The growth of intelligence can be pictured as a flight of stairs. As a person mentally mounts these stairs, he continually interprets his environment from the standpoint of his previous experiences, and he changes his ideas and knowledge to fit the view from the step he is on. Piaget calls these two parts of the learning process *assimilation* and *accommodation,* terms we can use in considering intellectual development.

Assimilation means taking in new information. If a child who has never known the sound of a slamming door is told, while a door slams, "That is a door slamming," he receives this information through the process of *assimilation.* Relating this new information to past experience, making it a part of his repertoire so that he may act upon it, is the process of *accommodation.*

Sometimes, however, new information refutes information that the child has already accommodated. But accommodation also allows the individual to extract past information as he adds new information. This addition of new information "jars" the child. As the information is accommodated, however, the intelligence again reaches a state of equilibrium, a process that Piaget terms *equilibration.* Thus, the learning process is one of movement, or of acquiring new information and thus achieving a new level of understanding.

A child is not a stagnant bystander. He is always learning, not by passive observation of, but by active involvement with, his environment. His earliest means of gaining information (during what Piaget calls the *sensory-motor stage*) are his five senses.

We have all seen young babies who grasp things and immediately put them in their mouths. Parents may think, "My child must be pretty hungry—I'd better feed him," or, "He's always hungry; he's always putting things in his mouth. He must be starving." If we observe carefully, though, we will see that the child is using his mouth as an exploratory organ, a way of gaining information. This oral exploration, along with the use of other senses, helps him learn what he needs to know.

The child is not thinking in abstract concepts. He understands only concrete perceptions: the world that he can touch, taste, hear, smell, and see. While he cannot understand that two plus two equals four (an abstract concept), he *can* understand that if he pushes a truck into a wall it makes a bang (a concrete activity that he is experiencing at the moment). He cannot comprehend objects that are out of his sight. For example, in the game of peek-a-boo when the child cannot see the game object, it ceases to exist for him, and he loses interest. In the game of hide and seek he covers his eyes, believing that if he cannot see you, you cannot see him. The sensory-motor approach to learning is particularly effective until the child develops a more organized and systematic way to gain information, usually at about three years of age.

The second stage of intellectual development is referred to by Piaget as the *preoperational stage.* This stage includes children from age three or four to approximately age seven, children who do not yet think abstractly. Now, as in the sensory-motor stage, the child relates to the world in a very concrete way. He deals with the here and now in the real world. He cannot understand some things he cannot see, nor can he deal with perceptions he cannot associate with one of his five senses. He cannot yet understand the *idea* of a lady wearing a black hat in an elevator in a large building, or that there is a building called the Empire State Building in the state of New York if he has not seen it. Because he cannot see, touch, taste, smell, or hear these things, they do not exist for him. He probably cannot understand that two plus two equals four, either; he is not able to deal with things abstractly during this stage of his intellectual development.

However, as the child nears the end of the preoperational stage, he begins to comprehend a few abstract terms and their meanings.

A good example of this is the child who is starting to read. At first he finds reading very difficult, because he cannot associate the abstractness of the printed word with the things he is reading or with the object labeled. He can mimic the words, but his ability to associate the words with their meanings is very limited.

Piaget has demonstrated that a child at this stage can grasp such an abstract principle as the conservation of mass. By *conservation* Piaget means the maintenance of the basic properties of an object that undergoes a physical change. For example, even though a ball of clay might be changed from a round ball to a flat pancake, it still retains the same amount of clay, and it is still made of the same substance (clay). Unless something has been taken away or added to the original mass, it is the same regardless of shape, and the child can understand this. This is one of Piaget's principal techniques for determining whether a child really understands an abstract concept.

Even though a child near the end of the preoperational stage still derives most of his understanding from experience with his concrete world, he is beginning to comprehend a few abstract terms and their meanings.

Around the age of seven, according to Piaget, the child actively employs abstract terms and thinking. Age seven to eleven is termed the *concrete operations stage.* The child begins to comprehend increasingly complex thoughts: he comes to understand that two plus two equals four; he learns to read. He begins to put things together and understand their relationships; he can solve problems. He can visualize causes and determine effects; he understands that if he does such and such, he must be prepared for certain predictable consequences. Even though a child can deal with abstract thoughts, he still learns through assimilation and accommodation, a process that continues throughout life.

Piaget's final stage in intellectual development, the stage of *formal operations,* begins at about age eleven and continues through adulthood. Although much of the concrete world still plays a big part, the individual now thinks mainly in abstractions. He can visualize an Empire State Building in the city of New York in the state of New York even though he has never been there. He can also understand the idea of a large building that contains an elevator that is carrying a woman who is wearing a black hat.

The child can devise theories. For example, if *a* is combined with *b,* we can be assured that *c* will be the outcome; or if we put *this* together and add *this* portion, we can be assured that *this* will occur. The increased ability for abstraction is made possible by vast experience and by an intellectual repertoire built up since birth.

You may wonder what advantage there is in knowing the stages of your child's intellectual development. The advantage is your understanding, which will make you a better teacher. If you know that a child between the ages of two and six learns best through concrete experiences or actual associations with his real world, you will know that the best way to teach him is to make sensory-motor experiences available to him: to make opportunities available for him to touch things, see things, smell things, taste things, and hear things. These experiences will help him build his repertoire and will thereby enhance his ability to deal with abstractions later.

But you can overstimulate your child if you do not understand his needs and read his degree of readiness. Remember that learning ability depends on maturation. The child must build a repertoire to be able to think. You must allow him to progress at his own rate.

148

Forcing him to read before he is mature enough can frustrate him, because those words don't mean much and because he wants to succeed but feels loathsome in your eyes because he is failing. Be wise in selecting activities for him. A child will give clues to his readiness through his actions and explanations. By knowing at what level he is working, you can add experiences that will help him and you can remove other experiences that will hinder him.

A parent can assist a child to work up to his maturity level but cannot push him beyond that level without distressing him. A good parent can challenge and help a child to reach his full capacity.

ACTIVITIES: DEVELOPING YOUR CHILD'S INTELLECT

1. Allow each member of the family to give an assignment to another person. For example, "Go to the coat closet, open the door three times, stand on one foot, and return to your seat." The instructions may be made more difficult as the child shows the ability to remember and follow through with each of the directions given.

2. Randomly select a volume of the encyclopedia and quickly thumb through to a relatively unfamiliar topic. A parent or older child (someone who knows how to read) should then quickly relate all the facts they can about the selected topic. The length of time spent and the depth of investigation should depend on the ages of the children involved and the interest shown. Questions should then be asked the group members about the information that was given.

3. Select a variety of items from around the house and place them one at a time in a paper bag. One member of the family should feel the item through the bag and try to guess what it is. Repeat this until all members of the group have had a chance to feel each item and to guess what it is.

One person should be blindfolded. Wearing gloves, he must feel the various objects and guess what each is.

While he is blindfolded, present one person various items, each having a distinct smell. The person tries to guess the name of each object after each has been sniffed.

Give a large, long-handled spoon to a blindfolded person. In the bowl of the spoon place various weighted objects. The blindfolded person must guess what each is.

149

CHAPTER 19
FOSTERING YOUR
CHILD'S PERCEPTION

One of a child's real needs is to gather information from the world around him and to assimilate it in his mind, in his central nervous system. Most children are born with the nervous system intact: in other words, they have the physical equipment to sense the world. Their eyes and ears operate, and they can gain information through their hands or their tongue. But having a nerve ending that can sense the world is not enough; a child has to pay attention to what is happening, and he must be aware of what is going on around him. He has to let an experience linger in his mind for a few seconds until it makes an impression and until it can be catalogued for future reference. This process of paying attention, or noticing the world around us, is called *perception*.

Differences in Perception

Children are born with differences in the ability to perceive. Some have a more acute sense of smell or taste or sight than do others. Children also differ in their ability to perceive because they have had different past experiences.

In a five-second learning experience you can demonstrate how it is possible to perceive the world differently because of having a different background. Write the words *tomato, banana,* and *avocado* on a sheet of paper and show the words to someone. Now, write on a piece of paper the letters r pe. Show your friend the word with the letter missing and have him fill in the blank with an appropriate letter. Next, write the words *knot, thread,* and *noose* on a sheet of paper and show the words to a second person. Then show the second friend the word with the missing letter (r pe) and have him fill in the blank.

When you showed your first friend the first set of words, he probably associated them with the word *ripe,* because *ripe* is a condition that describes fruits and vegetables. But when you showed your second friend the second group of words, he probably associated them with the word *rope* and wrote an *O* in the blank because *rope* is closely related to *knot, thread,* and *noose.* If your friends did write down an *i* and an *o* in the blank, this shows that they had a different mental set that was triggered by the different experience of the two sets of words.

The same principle is illustrated by what happened one day when two professors walked up a canyon. When they had reached the top, one said to the other, "Did you notice those lovely dandelions growing at the thousand-foot level?" "No," said the other. "I didn't, but did you notice the interesting rock formation down the trail about a half a mile?" The botanist, who noticed the dandelions, had missed the rock formation. The training of the geologist to notice interesting rocks and of the botanist to pay attention to plant life predisposed the men to see the world differently as they traveled side by side.

Everyone is constantly receiving stimulation from his environment, but it is impossible for him to learn anything from that stimulation unless he first perceives it. The following five principles will help a parent foster perception in a child.

Gaining Attention

First, before a person can perceive the world, he must be *paying attention.* You can show a child brilliant visual aids when he is sound asleep, but it's not going to do him any good. You need to alert him, to get his attention.

One day a farmer sold his neighbor a donkey which he claimed was very well trained. In a week the neighbor was back with the donkey, claiming that he had been cheated. The donkey wouldn't obey.

152

The farmer picked up a big piece of wood, hit the donkey on the head as hard as he could, and said, "Giddee up." The donkey got up and moved. "You see," said the farmer, "You just need to get his attention."

No one would advocate hitting children over the head to get their attention, but it is possible to browbeat people a little psychologically to get them to notice or pay attention to what's going on. One way to do this is to make an experience stand out. If you want a child to notice zebras as opposed to all other animals at the zoo, you need to do something to make the zebra cage stand out in his mind. Maybe when you got to the cage you could yell, scream, throw a temper tantrum, pass out on the ground, or put some candy into his mouth. Now, if the zebra cage is the only place where one of these unusual events happened in the whole zoo, he would clearly remember the zebra cage. When you're trying to teach a child a letter of the alphabet, making the letter stand out by making it a different color or size will focus his attention on that letter.

Redundancy

The second principle in fostering perception is *redundancy*. Practicing redundancy means giving someone repeated experiences with the same stimulus. It's not enough to show a child an item or an object once: in order to learn the nature of that object, he must have repeated experiences with it. Most adults don't like redundancy; they're always saying, "Get to the point. Cut out all the nonsense, and just give me the facts." The reason for this is that adults have had a lot of experiences in their lives and can therefore relate new experiences to past learning rapidly. They don't *need* redundancy. For example, a young couple who had grown up near one of the scenic canyons in the West saw the canyon about every way it could be seen. They went there on dates. They saw it in the morning and at night, in winter and in summer, and from the bottom and the top. Eventually they married and moved away. When their oldest child was sixteen, the family made their first visit back to the canyon. As the family reached the edge of the cliff and looked down into that gorgeous canyon, all the experiences that the mother and father had had as they were growing up were brought back to their memories, triggered by that one refresher look. The boy, who had not had any previous exposure to the canyon, said to his dad, "Gee, this is beautiful. Let's go down to the bottom and look at it." His father replied, "Now, if you've seen it once, you've seen it all." They got back in their car and drove on. This father made a mistake that a lot of fathers make: he assumed that his child's experiences in life were the same as his own. But of course that wasn't the case, and so while the father, with one glimpse, could call to mind many memories of the canyon, the boy couldn't. If the father had really wanted his son to get a notion of what the canyon was like, he should have let the boy have more than just that one fleeting experience.

Similarly, our written English language has become redundant for most of us. If you were to look at a word that had only the vertical lines of the letters printed, you probably could not read the word. But if some of the curved portions of the letters were added, you would slowly be able to recognize the word. You wouldn't need every letter in its entirety to be able to recognize the word. As an example, here is a word with the redundancy removed: ˡ ₁ ͻ ˡ Can you read it? Probably not. Now we add a little more redundancy: ˡ₁ ͻ ˡ ₎ . Now can you read it? Most of you will be able to see that the ⸢word says "help." All of these parts of the letters ⌐ ₑ₋₁ ∩ were redundant for you. You didn't need them. But you would be able to read it only because you have had many experiences with English written words in the past. If you were given a Hebrew or a Russian word from which half, or even a tiny bit, of each letter had been removed, you probably could not recognize the word. For instance, can you even tell what the letters here are: ᒡⱴ ʋ ⁊ˏ ⁊₍? These are the Greek letters for $\alpha\gamma\alpha\pi\eta$, and they spell *love* in Greek.

Children seek for redundancy on their own. They want all the experience they can get with new objects. Once a little thirteen-month-old girl who was used to eating mashed peas from a jar found herself eating real peas for the first time. She soon discovered that a pea would fit up her nostril, and before her parents noticed what she was doing she had pushed three or four peas up her nose. The parents rushed the girl next door to a nurse, who soon removed the peas with a cotton swab. The parents kept asking themselves, "Why would our daughter want to stick peas up her nose?" The answer might have been that she was building redundancy into her world; she was giving herself an experience with a pea besides just looking at it, and she was having something besides a visual experience. Maybe she had been trying to smell the peas. Young children are just like the wolf in the story about Little Red Riding Hood. A young child with a new object will handle it extensively, "the better to feel you with," explore it with his eyes, "the better to see you with," or put it in his mouth, "the better to taste you with." What such a child is doing is getting as much information as he can from the object. As an adult, you probably don't need this repetition, but if you're going to help children who have limited experience to perceive new objects and experiences accurately, it is essential that you give them more than one experience with those objects and experiences—that you build in redundancy.

Firsthand Experience

Third, if you want your child to learn about the world, try to give him *firsthand experiences*. In school having a firsthand experience means going on a field trip. Many parents are very good at providing firsthand experiences for their children by taking them to the grocery store, to the bank, or to the post office with them. They'll let their children work by their side, digging up the garden or gathering grass or making bread. Your children have probably had many firsthand experiences, but many children in the country haven't, and such children are intellectually deprived. One of the basic tenets of the Head Start Program—a federal program of compensatory education for young children—is to help them experience the real world, to give them varied firsthand experiences. When these children get to the first or second grade and are reading a book about an elevator or a grocery store, they will recall having seen such things and a mental image of the object described by the word will form.

Very little of what parents teach in the home is taught using firsthand experiences. Instead, the parents resort to representation, pictures, or verbal accounts. But the real world is the world of three dimensions; representations of things in the real world are usually only two-dimensional. There's an information loss that comes when you move from the world of three dimensions to the world of two dimensions. There is a loss when you go from the world of three dimensions, or the real world, to the world of representations of real things, or the world of two dimensions. There is no way to taste or smell a picture. All you can do with a picture is see it.

Whenever you have a chance to give a child a firsthand experience, you ought to do it. Sometimes, though, we can't give people firsthand experiences. For example, very few of us will ever make it to the moon to find out what that's really like, and so we're going to have to rely upon good secondhand experiences: the accounts of others, their pictures, and samples of the soil and rock. But even the best of that kind of information is inferior to being able to spend half an hour on the moon. If you want a little boy to find out

155

about dogs, you can show him pictures of twenty different dogs. Or you can let him hold a dog on his lap for half an hour. At the end of the half-hour that boy who held the live dog is going to know an awful lot more about dogs than the boy who learned from looking at pictures.

Frame of Reference

The fourth principle of fostering perception is that when you teach a child something new, you ought to tie it into his past learning. In other words, you ought to give this new thing a *frame of reference*. To keep the children from fighting and scrambling around on the floor of the bus during a nursery school field trip, the teacher pointed out the window and said, "Look! Look at all the goats." All the kids leaned toward that side of the bus and looked out. The teacher sat back with satisfaction because she had not only solved a discipline problem, but at the same time she thought she had taught the children what a goat was. But had she really taught them? Actually, she hadn't related the new object to any previously learned concepts; she hadn't used a frame reference. When the children looked out the window, they could see not only several goats in that field but also horses, cows, pigs, sheep, chickens, many kinds of buildings and farm implements, and several kinds of trees. Without a frame of reference, the first thing a child saw when looking into the field probably became a "goat" for him. If he had seen a tree when he was looking out of the window of the bus, then for him that would have become a "goat."

It would have been better for the teacher to put the concept of a *goat* into some kind of framework. For instance, she could have said, "Look at the goat out there. The goat is the animal that looks like a large white dog." That description requires a child to know four concepts—*animal, large, white,* and *dog*. Most four-year-olds have those words in their vocabulary, so that would have eliminated cattle, horses, pigs, chickens, trees, barns, and tractors. The only thing he could confuse the goat with at that point would be a sheep. And so the child might ask, "Are the goats the ones with the whiskers or without the whiskers?" Then it would be simple for the teacher to reply, "The goat has the whiskers." She could be sure at that point that the child knows what a goat is.

Sometimes we do this task about half right. We're committed to the idea of putting something in a frame of reference, but the frame that we use is inappropriate. Suppose the teacher had said, "The goat is the mammal that looks like a midget albino yak." *Mammal, midget, albino,* and *yak* are all good concepts—in fact, that's a good

156

description of a goat—but because most children don't have those words in their vocabulary, such a description would be meaningless and inappropriate.

Label

The final point is that to facilitate accurate perception you need to *label* objects. If you want somebody to remember what you're showing them, give it a name. In some South Sea cultures the people have only one word to describe all the colors of the rainbow in the range from blue through green. If you gave a child in that culture a pile of red, yellow, blue, and green chips and asked him to pile them according to color, he'd give you three piles: a red pile, a yellow pile, and a pile with the green and the blue together. He would not distinguish the green from the blue, because for him they have the same name.

The same thing happens in our own lives. When two objects have a similar or the same name, people tend to see those objects as the same even though they may have several different qualities. We don't worry very much about different kinds of snow. As a result we have few words to describe snow—powder or corn, heavy or fluffy white. But to people who live above the arctic circle, snow is an important element of everyday life; consequently their language describes a couple of dozen different kinds of snow, and because they have labels to describe them, they can recognize those many different types.

Perception is the foundation of all intellectual activity. To be able to notice the world accurately is a talent that can be taught to children. Children are born with differences in their abilities to perceive the world, and their experiences in life determine how they will perceive the world. Help your child by gaining his attention, giving him repeated experiences with the same object, giving him firsthand experiences with the object, and then placing it in a frame of reference and labeling it for him. Finally, children don't know which events or objects are the most important ones to perceive: they need guidance from parents in helping them store up concepts in their minds that will be useful to them in their later lives.

ACTIVITY: FOSTERING YOUR CHILD'S PERCEPTION

Materials:
   Pictures A–C in Appendix II and ten small objects from your home

A.

B.

c.

such as a spool of thread, a spoon, a pair of pliers, an old button, and so on.

Procedure:

1. Take nine of the small objects and arrange them about six inches apart in three rows of three. Now, pick out one of the objects that you want your child to notice more than the others and do something to make it stand out. Cover all nine objects with a towel. Bring your child into the room, uncover the objects for two seconds, then cover them up again. Ask your child what he notices.

2. Have your child handle the tenth object for about fifteen seconds. Then have him tell you all he knows about it. Have him look at any picture you find for fifteen seconds and tell you all he knows about it. List the responses.

3. Show your child Picture A for thirty seconds and Picture B for one second. Now show your child Picture C. Have him point out the figures that are like the two he saw in Picture A and Picture B.

4. Take your child on a field trip with you once a week to places in the neighborhood such as the grocery store, post office, and so on. Try to get to go behind the scenes where they cut meat and sort mail. Don't assume your child knows too much.

CHAPTER 20
CONCEPT DEVELOPMENT

What is a concept? Certainly it is not something we gain directly through only our senses. Instead, we are talking about the results that occur when we combine sensory *experiences.* For example, a young child with limited sensory experiences might think of a chair as an object with a straight back that he can sit on. As he modifies his concept of a chair through experiences with many different types of chairs, he will understand that *chair* can apply to many kinds of furniture—a wide, hard straight-backed chair; a long, tall, skinny chair; a large, soft stuffed armchair—any object designed for seating.

We classify objects according to our concepts, and those concepts are based upon the properties and functions of those objects. For instance, the fact that a footstool does not have a back and is not used at the table tends to disqualify it in our mind as a chair, even though it may be used for seating. The footstool's qualities, when compared with the characteristics of a chair, suggest that the footstool was designed principally for a purpose other than seating.

Once a concept is formed, there is understanding. If a child *understands,* then he recognizes the elements that make one thing differ from another. He can categorize and relate, and he begins to form a precise picture of his world. The more accurately he understands his world, the more easily he is able to change it and control it. If he sees a chair and a stool together, his understanding of *chair* and *stool* will help him to choose the one best suited to his purpose: he will understand that the steps on the stool can help him reach the cupboard, and he will understand that a chair is the best place to relax and read a book.

A child's adjustment to life will be greatly affected by his understanding of his environment, of people around him, and of himself. If an increasing understanding of concepts causes him to learn to recognize his strengths and limitations, he can begin to handle the changes in his world with a healthy attitude, realizing that further experience and concept development will afford him even more control.

Concepts are complex; they are continually changing, and they develop as a child gains experience and accumulates knowledge. They may be related to objects, people, qualities, relationships, and so on. To build concepts successfully, a child needs to assimilate information and to accommodate it.

First, the child receives information through observation, discussion, and sensory-motor experience. He needs many opportunities to observe objects with short time intervals between his observations. Second, he needs to discuss what he has seen so that he may find meaning for it. Once a woman riding on a train noticed some black and white spotted animals in a field. She asked the man sitting next to her, "What in the world are those things?" The man looked astonished, but he replied, "Oh, those are pigs." The woman replied, "That can't be! Pigs are pink with curly tails!" She had only seen pictures of pigs and had never seen the real thing.

A person exposed only to limited experiences or materials, or depending on only one source for his information, will have different concepts from those people whose experiences are many and diverse. If a person were to read all the time and if that were his only source of information, his concepts would differ from those who not only read but who also see pictures or objects relating to what they are reading about. For best development, a person should be exposed to learning materials and should experience frequent and diversified learning situations.

Because children are extremely curious, their concepts develop rapidly. Curiosity develops interest, and interest stimulates action. One very important means by which children develop their concepts

162

is language. As soon as a child is old enough to put words together, to ask questions, to understand the meaning of words spoken to him—usually at about age five or six—he begins to use language in concept development, asking questions almost incessantly. Even though he may sometimes annoy adults, answers to his many questions help him to hear things that build concepts and allow him to hear how words are put together to form thoughts and meanings. Sometimes he needs to ask his questions just for questioning's sake or simply to hear answers, to hear someone form words. Sometimes he asks questions to get information, and at other times he asks trying to find out what you'll do. He needs to know. Sometimes questioning is a way of getting attention: he may show little interest in your answer, but he is very concerned about asking the question because it's a way of getting you to spend time with him. All these types of questions are valuable aids to help young children develop concepts.

A child's concept formation is also assisted by pictures, comics, movies, television, and firsthand experiences. Many of you have seen *Sesame Street*. This production is primarily aimed at helping children develop concepts through observation. However, the program has more value if the child has an opportunity not only to observe, but to discuss the concepts with another person or to participate in the activities. For example, the television personality might show a picture and talk about the concept *under*, describing things that are happening *under* the table, *under* the light, *under* the ceiling, *under* the wastebasket. If so, the child who has an opportunity to experience the concept will learn its meaning faster than the child who merely observes the television personality.

Observation alone will not always establish concepts; although television programs attempt to be realistic, they sometimes contain elements that even a child may recognize as happening only on television. The result? Because the child may be unable to generalize or relate the concept to himself or his situation, his concept may be unclear or even misinterpreted. For example, movie, television, or cartoon parents are usually depicted as far more glamorous or exciting than anything the child has ever experienced firsthand. As a result, the child may develop critical and unrealistic attitudes toward his own parents. Thus, a child dependent solely upon the mass media for his information may form many misconceptions.

Children cultivate the values taught to them by their society, parents, teachers, and peers. For instance, in certain cultures a child learns to revere older persons; in some other cultures life is thought to be of little worth. Perhaps you have wondered why people have such strong feelings about being Democrats or Republicans or Independents. Usually such political concepts follow those expressed by their parents. Philosophies about treatment of the elderly or the value of life, as cited above, are products of a child's cultural background.

But even after information is received through observation, discussion, and sensory-motor experience, it is not really a part of a child's understanding—not until he utilizes certain skills to assimilate this information.

A child needs to be able to recognize differences and see relationships between objects and situations, particularly between old experiences and new ones. The greater the similarity between old and new, the more readily he will perceive the relationship. If, however, he cannot understand relationships between experiences, his understanding of unfamiliar situations will be limited; to the same extent, his ability to form concepts will be limited.

A child's ability to perceive differences and similarities is related to his ability to reason—to sift related information from unrelated information. The best way to help a child learn to recognize differences and similarities is to expose him to varied experiences, making sure that he feels secure. The best environment parents can provide is one in which there are enough differences to stimulate growth and enough security to provide rest. In those conditions a child may learn to deal adequately with differences and the stress that comes with them.

Parents who provide little opportunity for their children to experience minor difficulties will not prepare their children for more difficult situations, such as going to the hospital, being left with the babysitter, or spending the night with the scout troop. The child with limited experience will undoubtedly exhibit signs of stress and inefficiency in such situations, but the child who has been taught to react positively to unfamiliar situations will experience less anxiety. Children will be able to accept new situations if their prior experiences give them a basis of understanding; using such understanding they can trust the new situation and maintain confidence in their ability to handle the unfamiliar.

Another important aspect of concept formation is a child's need to comprehend underlying meanings. Children perceive surface needs and values but often fail to understand the not-so-obvious. Even older children find subtleties and abstractions difficult to understand. If we think back to some of the Mother Goose rhymes we were taught as children we can recognize political allusions that went over our heads at the time. Proverbs such as "Old dogs can't learn new tricks," "An apple a day keeps the doctor away," or "All that glitters is not gold" are similarly subtle. Sometimes when parents discuss things with a child they tend to use large or unfamiliar terms, jokes, and other things adults find interesting and clever but that are meaningless to the child. And because a child doesn't understand underlying meanings, sometimes a joke will make him feel confronted, if not threatened. We can best help a child to understand levels of meaning first by giving him information he can understand, and then by gradually helping him understand increasingly difficult material.

Abundant opportunities are essential for the child's concept formation, but parents should avoid rushing him through his learning experiences and should avoid unloading the whole cart when all the child wants is a small helping. It is wise to remember that a child learns by stimulation and rest. He can learn only when he has built a wide-range foundation to accommodate new materials or experiences.

ACTIVITIES:
CONCEPT DEVELOPMENT

1. Place a strip of masking tape down the center of the table, putting five cupcakes on one side of it and five juice glasses on the other side. Have the child count the number of cupcakes and juice glasses on each side of the line.

Move four of the juice glasses to one end of the table and one to the other end. Ask the child, "Are there still the same number of juice glasses as there are cupcakes?" Help him understand why they are the same.

Return the objects to their original position and move the cupcakes into a circle. Ask the child, "Are there the same number of cupcakes as there are juice glasses?" Have the child arrange the glasses in the same way as the cupcakes are arranged (in a circle) as you count them, pointing out that there are the same number of juice glasses as there are cupcakes.

Have a party. After eating a cupcake and drinking some juice ask your child, "Now are there the same number of juice glasses as there are cupcakes? Are there the same number of full juice glasses as there are cupcakes?"

2. For this activity you will need six pairs of shoes and stockings corresponding in size from small to large. Ask your child to put the shoes in order from the largest to the smallest, matching the stockings to the shoes.

Next, have him move the shoes in order from the smallest to the largest. Repeat the activity with the stockings.

Indicate to the child which shoes you want by referring to them by size relationships. For example, the second to the largest, the smallest, and so on.

Rearrange the shoes so that they are not in order and ask the child to bring the smallest to you, then the largest, and so on.

3. You will need the following materials for this activity:

Two bars of soap, one with its middle carved out, its middle filled with tissue paper, and returned to its wrapper.

Two cardboard tubes, one stuffed with tissue paper and the other filled with rocks.

Two jelly jars (or other glass jars or bottles) of the same size, one filled with water and the other empty.

One small, heavy box wrapped in foil and one large, light box wrapped in foil.

Two balls of identical weight wrapped in foil so that they look and weigh the same.

Put all of the above objects on a table and have the child identify which of each pair of objects is the heaviest.

4. Place two identical balls of clay in front of your child and ask, "Is there the same amount of clay in each ball?" Establish that the balls are equal.

Make a hot dog with one ball, leaving the other unchanged throughout the demonstration. Ask, "Is there the same amount of clay in the hot dog as in the ball of clay?"

Repeat the procedure, forming the clay into the shapes of a pancake, snake, and circle. Finally, reshape the clay into balls. Ask, "After we change the shape of the clay, is there still the same amount in the balls as there was before we changed them?"

Continue the discussion until the responses of the child indicate that he understands that the amount of clay stays stable throughout the various formations. Allow him to experiment by changing the shape of the one ball of clay by himself.

CHAPTER 21
LANGUAGE DEVELOPMENT

All animals have communication systems, but man's language is distinctly different from the forms of communication used by other animals. Most animals communicate in terms of survival behavior. Bees do dances that tell other bees where food can be found. Songbirds identify other members of their species by means of unique songs. Animals use odors to identify territorial boundaries. Little dogs concede to big dogs by exposing their necks, and in so doing, communicate to the stronger dogs that they know better than to fight. These types of communication are for specific purposes.

Animals are *born* with the ability to recognize certain inflexible patterns of behavior for survival, but children must *learn* man's language. Without such natural ability, he would never be able to distinguish words in the language from other meaningless sounds.

The culture into which a child is born has an established set of rules called a *grammar;* these rules regulate the way that words are combined to make sentences. As a child listens to the sounds, hearing and seeing the objects represented by those sounds, he begins to make up or *generate* rules that explain how those words and sounds work together. His speech is always based on the rules he has made for himself. This is a very natural, innate process.

Let's look at the critical issues involved in language acquisition. First, it is not exactly correct that what a child says is simply a repetition of what is spoken by those around him. If the sentences spoken by little children were nothing more than reproductions of things they had heard, the results would reflect an astonishing ability to memorize sounds and words. A two-year-old would make over 2,500 different combinations. But it is impossible for a child to echo the many different combinations of words they utter at age two. At some point a child must have begun to rely on some form of rules prescribing sentence structure.

Sometimes, however, it is obvious that a child *is* simply imitating. The first utterance of most children is only an imitation of what they have heard. The repetition of the first fourteen pairs of words is most likely to be rote performance. Such things as, "What dat?" "Drink water," "Night, night, Mama," "See shoe?" and "See wa-wa" can be rote performances. But consider these sentences: "All gone shoe," "All gone vitamins," "All gone lettuce." These utterances cannot be imitations, because they are all inversions of the corresponding adult models, "The shoe is all gone," "The vitamins are all gone," and "The lettuce is all gone." And because the child has never heard the adult invert the normal sentence structure, we conclude that the youngster has created a rule of his own telling him how to combine two words. Measured by adult standards, the rule is incomplete, but it fits somewhere in the changing structure of the child's grammar.

Children all over the world do the same thing to make sentences, passing through the same baby-talk stages at about the same time and making about the same kinds of combinations. (Of course, the rules that each child generates are determined by the language of his community.) This cross-cultural similarity supports the idea that each of us has an *innate* mechanism for acquiring language.

Now let's see if we can determine how this mental equipment works. What are the basic requirements for normal language acquisition? First, the child must be able to *hear;* he cannot learn a language unless he hears it. And we fulfill our part simply by talking—the more the better. Beyond that there is little we can do besides offering moral support and lots of encouragement, having lots of patience and a good deal of love, because, as we have seen, biology takes over.

Assuming that a child can hear, what does he do with what he hears? He classifies each sound according to a set of discriminative, inborn mental categories: how loud it is, how fast it is, how long it lasts, from which direction it comes, and so on. Every utterance, every single word, has certain tonal qualities. Sounds have certain stresses or accents, they have a distinct pitch, and the pauses between sounds also carry meaning. And a normal infant hears all these things. In his early years he begins to distinguish sounds that he recognizes as language from sounds that mean nothing to him. This is the beginning of his rule making. He begins to isolate sounds and to classify each according to its association with different situations and things. The frequency and the quality of these sounds is extremely important at this age. And this is where parents can make a real contribution. Overstimulation—that is, providing so much "noise" that a child cannot distinguish consistent kinds of sounds—may be harmful to him. Consequently, repeating patterns that are familiar to him is very important. It is important to infants that their parents respond using the same words when referring to similar kinds of objects.

After a child has listened to sounds, organized them, and generated rules about them, he then attempts to reproduce or "match" them. Very few such attempts are made during the first few months of life. There is evidence, though, that infants can have several different meaningful cries; in fact, most mothers will testify that a cry of pain is distinctly different from a cry of hunger. This differentiation of cries is an early indication that a child is generating rules based on the response to each type of cry.

By the time a child is six months old, certain vowels and consonants emerge and are combined. Such sounds as "ma ma" and "ga ga" are usually some of the earliest. Acquiring all the rules of adult speech is a long and difficult process: children are still trying at ages ten, eleven, and twelve. However, by age four a child will have learned most of the rules of grammar—through hearing others speak.

What can we do to help children use language meaningfully and to grow to maturity in speech? First, parents should remember not to simplify their vocabulary when talking with their children. Children very often adopt new words and use them correctly if the meaning is clear and inherent in the context.

Many oral language experiences center around real-life situations involving real-life problems and interests. A young child's growth in language is directly related to the experiences and practice he gets.

From month to month, children develop steadily in their choice of words, their ability to use longer and more complex sentences, and their adequacy and clarity of expression.

Second, parents should never explain anything without first giving their child the opportunity to explain. If you're showing slides in your home, let your children be the first to explain what's going on in the picture. You may add other things later. Give them the opportunity—don't beat them to it. Many times parents will interrupt a child and complete his sentences for him. This only discourages him. When your child wants to tell you about an exciting experience, let him. Be interested, listen, and he will develop his language. He needs language to express his feelings, and if you're willing to listen, he'll keep trying to explain his feelings to you meaningfully.

When you're reading books to a child, ask him to explain the pictures: "Could you tell me about this picture? Who do you see in the picture? What's happening? Where do you think the children are going? What do you think will happen when they get there? What's the boy thinking? What would you do if you were the little boy?" You can stimulate a lot of conversations by encouraging a child to compare himself and his own experiences with the children and activities in pictures and stories. When a child shows you his indoor or outdoor playthings, ask him questions like, "What can you tell me about this kind of truck? Who would use this kind of hat at work? What would happen if I dropped a rock to the floor? What if I dropped a feather? How many balls would fit into this basket? Why do you think so? How does your airplane differ fromm a jet or a rocket?"

In summary, a child's language ability is directly related to his experiences; consequently, language power grows in a stimulating environment, one that offers opportunities for firsthand experiences. In other words, to speak fluently the child must have interesting things to talk about. Of course, he also needs a vocabulary that allows him to express his thoughts clearly. Interested parents, who model situations for their child and provide him with experiences for speaking are affording him the best opportunity for such a vocabulary. At the same time they are teaching him to use a pleasant voice, to interest listeners, to listen politely to others, to pronounce words correctly, to enunciate words correctly, to use words correctly, to speak in complete sentences, to develop and use a well-chosen vocabulary, to speak so others can hear, to think while he speaks, and to reduce infantile speech patterns.

Hearing and speaking are the basic steps that a youngster goes through, but they don't make up the whole picture. The child must perform some very important thought processes before he can understand or reproduce language.

Language formation includes the notion of *acceptance*. Every set of sounds that comes in from the environment, from his parents and the children he plays with, is processed, and he has to decide whether he is going to accept it as meaningful or reject it as irrelevant; in other words, he is constantly generating rules about things that he hears people say. These rules help him determine (1) whether or not to accept a particular sound as having meaning, and if he does accept it, (2) the function of the sound. For example, you might say to a youngster, "Get me some juts for the carolee." The fact that these unfamiliar words come associated with certain familiar sounds gives the child a clue as to their function. *Carolee* is preceded by an article, which makes it a noun (a rule automatically understood by the child who has constructed a grammar). *Juts,* with the *s* on the end of it, is plural. Very young children become familiar with almost all new words this way.

Before age six, children will accept almost any word that they hear and—using their grammatical rules and other nonverbal clues in the environment—will try to get meaning out of it. After six or seven, however, their ability to accept unusual sounds begins to diminish, and by twelve years of age, they accept very few strange sounds. For example, if we hear somebody say "¿Cómo está usted?" we do not seriously consider the functions of those unusual sounds; we simply reject them because they are not our own.

Besides determining the functions of new words, the child must also determine their meaning. But how does he go about gaining meaning from words? Compare, for example, these sentences: "Colorless green ideas sleep furiously" and "Healthy young babies sleep soundly." Although both sentences have the same construction, the second is less difficult to remember, because each word is in a context that helps explain its meaning. Similarly, a child interprets each word by the company it keeps.

We also get meaning from the spacing between words. For example, if you say, "37, 32, 69, 6," the spaces between those numbers suggest false meanings. But if you say, "373 2696," it is immediately identifiable as a phone number. Consequently, how we say things is significant in speech development and interpretation.

The next thing a child does with language is to determine the meaning of a statement from the circumstances or the context in which it is uttered. This step is formally called *understanding*. Think about this: an older brother comes in and says, "Mom, Theresa dropped a glass." That kind of statement—all too familiar around the house—implies that somebody—probably Mom—must clean up the broken glass. There are some very serious implications in this for parents. Frequently, we, too, say things that have double meanings. If too much of what we say is characterized by double meanings, our children will have a difficult time understanding which meaning they are to attend to or which meaning would be best to respond to. For example, when a mother says to her child, who just dropped the glass and broke it, "Boy, you're no good," she may say it with a loving, humorous intonation that implies the opposite of what was said, but the child may infer from it, "My mother doesn't like me. I really am no good because I broke a glass." Many emotional problems develop because of double meanings, particularly when the child is unable to decide which meaning he should respond to; because of this, it is important to send clear messages to children.

The final stage of processing something that we hear is *belief*. When somebody comes rushing in and says, "I saw five lions in the garden!" you may hear it, you may match it, you may accept it, you may interpret it, and you may understand it, but at this point you don't believe it. This is a particularly significant issue for very young children. Preschool-age children are very imaginative and are filled with fantasy, and they generate all kinds of verbal concepts that are fantastic. They are playing a very healthy kind of play with words and with facts. Encourage your children to use language as a tool for imaginative and creative expression; this kind of play does not imply distorted perception. Everyone has the tendency at some stage in life to verbalize something we want or recognize. Sometimes the results are quite humorous. Children will come home and tell you that they sang the song, "A Pup in the Sky," or might repeat the Pledge of Allegiance with this interesting twist: "I pledge allegiance to the flag ... one naked individual. ..." Sometimes a child will sing a song in church and then will come home with some of the craziest interpretations you can imagine. Typically these youngsters are believing, but they are simply repeating—not understanding—what has been said.

Language is complex, but children are born with the ability to handle it. Parents can help by speaking clearly and distinctly, by being unambiguous, and by offering plenty of opportunities for their children to verbalize and to express their feelings. Most of all, parents should never be terribly concerned when what their child says isn't quite right; he'll get it eventually as long as he has effective, loving models.

ACTIVITIES: LANGUAGE DEVELOPMENT

Sound Discrimination

1. Collect a box of objects including such things as a fork, a pan, an eraser, a piece of paper, a pencil, and so on. Drop two objects on the table or floor one at a time and ask your child to identify which was loudest. Then ask him which was softest. Continue this process with each of the objects. For variation of this activity, ask the child to guess which object will make the loudest sound before the objects are dropped.

Listening

2. Send the child out of the room while someone else places a small toy in an unexpected place. It should be in full view. Have the child return to the room and try to find the toy as the other family members give clues to its whereabouts. Everyone in the room should clap louder and louder when the child approaches the object and softer and softer as he moves away. Continue the game as desired.

Sound Identification

3. Instruct your child to close his eyes and to listen to what you are doing. It is his responsibility to identify every sound he hears. Suggestions for you include closing a door, skipping, crumpling paper, dropping a book, and so on.

Sentence Completion

4. Begin several sentences such as these for your child to complete:
   "When it is cold, I wear . . ."
   "I feel happy when . . ."
   "I sleep in a . . ."

If he enjoys particular nursery rhymes, recite portions of their phrases and allow him to complete them.

Interpreting Tone of Voice

5. Ask your child how he would say "Oh" if he were afraid, happy, or sad. Then, have him repeat the following sentence: "Bobby's puppy ate my spaghetti." Now ask him to say the sentence again to ask a question. Continue this exercise, having him express surprise, anger, sorrow, or joy.

Repeat the activity by allowing your child to guess the feeling you are expressing as you quote a sentence. Guide his vocabulary if he indicates difficulty.

6. Clap your hands in an irregular sequence of three to five taps and have the child imitate the series. The number of taps used can be increased as the child shows the ability to repeat the pattern accurately.

Other suggestions for stimulating language development:
1. Encourage your child to tell you what he is doing or to express how he feels about a situation.
2. Allow your child to interpret pictures in a book.
3. Assist your child in learning and reciting poetry.
4. Read to your child often.
5. Talk to your child while you work, identifying to your child what you are doing.
6. Identify for your child foods and objects in a grocery store, on a walk, on a ride, or in the house.

UNIT V
CREATIVITY IN CHILDREN

At times we hear the comment, "Doesn't that art work show the author's great creativity!" or, as parents and teachers of young children, we are frequently admonished to exercise caution so as *not* to "stifle" their creativity.

The question arises, "What is creativity?"

Creativity is defined as the ability to create, to produce, to invent, or to use imagination. As we observe those around us, we recognize that there are many creative people—the mother who bakes and decorates a child's birthday cake, the engineer who designs and builds a bridge, the carpenter who builds cabinets with skill and care, the child who draws a picture. Each of these is doing something requiring some degree of creativity.

How then are we to insure that whatever amount of creativity a child has or may develop can better be realized? This section presents various chapters devoted to helping young children develop and beneficially use their creative abilities. Through studying such topics as art, literature, science, writing, and play and play materials, parents and teachers of young children will find some helpful and practical suggestions and activities they may use to enhance a child's development of creativity or will find ways to further his abilities to create.

CHAPTER 22
CREATIVE WRITING
FOR CHILDREN

Some of the skills your child learns in school, such as the multiplication tables or basic word attack skills in reading, will be mastered in a measurable period of time. Other skills must develop over long periods of time—some as long as a lifetime. Writing is one of those processes that human beings master slowly over a period of years. We may never *completely* learn to write. It is not surprising that many adults find writing a difficult and sometimes frustrating task, since everyone is still in some stage of development of writing skill.

A young child is in the critical first developmental stage of his ability to communicate in writing. The attitudes he develops at this time and the degree to which he masters basic writing processes will have a major influence on how successfully he writes throughout the rest of his life. Your most important goal in helping him with writing skill at this time is to make his writing experiences satisfying and successful. Few of the efforts you make to help your child academically will pay greater dividends than the time and energy you spend helping him to enjoy writing.

What is writing, anyway? Why is writing skill so important for human beings? Man is set apart from animals by his capacity to translate his experiences in the world around him into words, which can then be communicated to other human beings. At the simplest level, a man interprets his environment and feelings by attaching to them labels, which we call words, and which he organizes as thoughts in his mind. He shares his thoughts by speaking, and he receives the thoughts of others through listening. In sophisticated cultures such as ours he also has a system for recording his thoughts—writing—and a system for receiving the recorded thoughts of others—reading.

Writing, then, is basically the process of recording thought for communication to others. Skill in writing depends first of all upon skill in thinking. In learning to write well, techniques of correct expression, though important, are secondary to the thought process.

Finding Something to Write About

The first way you can help your child to write is to help him find something to write about. Many parents underestimate the potential contribution of the child's everyday life to his writing. When you talk with your child, when you listen to him interpret his environment, you are helping him to gather the raw material for writing. Most of us recognize the importance of providing varied experiences such as family outings and vacations to broaden the child's horizons and introduce him to new ideas. However, these occasional, spectacular events are less important in the long run than is the way you help your child to look at his *everyday* surroundings, his *daily* tasks, the changing seasons, his relationships with others. Encouraging the child to talk about his experiences, reinforcing his ideas by your reactions and encouragement, and helping him find new words to describe his thoughts can be done every day in the course of ordinary living. Help your child to write by helping him to think, and particularly by helping him to think about what happens to him.

It has been observed that a child's success in school is influenced by whether or not his family has their meals together, and particularly whether breakfast is a family meal. Perhaps there are nutritional reasons why this is a helpful procedure, but certainly the nourishment of thought that occurs through conversation and interaction between adults and children at mealtime is also important. Regular reading and discussion of information found in newspapers and magazines, discussion of television shows, and sharing information about father's or mother's work, as well as discussion of family plans and decisions, helps a child to grow mentally.

178

Finding a Purpose for Writing

A second way to help your child communicate is to guide him in finding a purpose for writing. It is logical for him to ask why things need to be written down. Actually, there are only three good reasons for writing anything: (1) the person for whom you are writing the information is not in the same place you are, so you can't simply tell him your message; (2) the information needs to be preserved for a later time, either for yourself or for someone else; or (3) the writing is imaginative and is meant to be entertaining.

You must decide whether you really believe writing is important. Ask yourself these questions: "Does my child ever see me write at home? Have I written a letter or anything else lately? If I did, did my child see me do it? Have I written anything to my child lately? How does my child know that writing is a useful skill for me?" As you plan family writing activities, include yourself as a participant. There is no better way to create purpose for your child.

Opportunities for writing at home are countless once you begin looking for them. Begin with the child before he goes to school. Give him paper and crayons, and when he has produced a drawing—even if it is only a scribble or a few lines—ask him to tell you about it. Help him by writing a caption, title, or story about the picture as he dictates the words to you. Show him that you are writing his own words as he says them. Let him know that words on paper represent ideas people have thought about.

When your child goes to school and learns to write himself, look at the papers he brings home and praise his early efforts. Make paper and writing implements available to him at home. Take advantage of the pride a child feels in his new skill by suggesting that he show you how well he is learning to write.

Ways to Stimulate Writing

As the child grows in writing independence, new and different ways to stimulate writing become important. Perhaps the most natural and purposeful writing activity done in the home is writing letters. The whole family can participate in writing and mailing letters. The occasions are numerous—thank-you notes, birthday greetings, get-well messages, hello notes, or business letters such as requests for information or orders for purchases. Less formal notes and messages may even be exchanged between family members.

A family bulletin board is another good writing stimulator. Written work from school may be displayed, and messages, reminders, lists, and creative writing done especially for family sharing can be posted.

Some children enjoy keeping diaries, but most can't maintain interest in a long-term detailed journal. Try a short-term diary covering a special time or experience. For example, give your child a notebook on the first of December and encourage him to write something in it every day describing his activities and feelings as your family prepares for Christmas. A vacation journal is a good way to keep track of special experiences on a trip, and also provides something for a child to do when he becomes bored with a long journey. Remember to pack crayons that can be used for liberal illustrating.

Another good way to stimulate purpose for writing is to dignify the child's product in some way. Bind it into a book or mount it on a chart or in a frame for wall display. Creative stories or poems carefully written and illustrated make special gifts for friends and family members.

Try a family bulletin or newspaper. Everyone can contribute. Include news stories about your family and friends, an editorial suggesting possible solutions to family problems, jokes, riddles, poems, advertisements, and illustrations. Newspaper projects are self-motivating and provide real reasons for writing for children at all stages of development.

Don't forget the everyday reasons for writing. Let your child keep minutes or notes of family meetings and of sessions to plan for family projects. Ask him to keep a perpetual shopping list for you to which items are added as needed. Teach him to write clear telephone messages and messages from people who call at your home when you are away. Let him help you inventory family food or clothing supplies, keep lists of family chores, and write daily or weekly menus.

Creative writing in the form of stories, poems, essays, or dramatic plays may be produced at home. Creative writing is closely related to one's feelings: you will find that your child's favorite writing subjects are likely to be nature, seasons, holidays, and his family—all topics that are emotionally involving.

School Writing Assignment

Sometimes you will be asked to help your child with a writing assignment from school. Get him to identify his purpose for writing; once he has clearly established his purpose for writing, it will be easier for him to gather information and to organize his thoughts for writing. Talk through his ideas with him before he begins the actual writing.

How to Help Children Write Well

Once you have stimulated your child to write by helping him to think through his ideas and by establishing a purpose for writing, your third consideration is how to help your child write well.

Two major characteristics determine the quality of a piece of written work: (1) the content, or how well the ideas are stated and organized; and (2) the mechanics, or how well the writer has followed correct forms of spelling, punctuation, word usage, and sentence structure. Both are necessary for clear written communication.

In order to help your child with the content and mechanics of his written work, you should be familiar with the developmental patterns children follow in learning to write.

Before the child actually writes for himself, his teacher or his parent writes sentences for him as he dictates his ideas. He also copies sentences that were written by others. Help him at this stage by writing his ideas for him and writing simple sentences for him to copy. Be sure you use the same manuscript letter forms he is or will be using in school.

Independent writing—written work that the child creates himself rather than copying from some other source—usually begins sometime during the first grade. Some children write independently before the first grade, and some do not write on their own until later. A child needs to have some reading skill, handwriting skill, and a beginning sense of spelling before he is able to write by himself.

A child's first independent sentences are often incomplete and may even be written backwards. Sentences usually improve with experience, but a child who has difficulty writing his own sentences may need more practice in dictating sentences to an adult and in copying correct sentences.

The content of first writing experiences usually consists of a record of personal experience; the child usually writes about something that has happened to him or something he has seen. At first his sentences are short, factual description: "I saw a dog." Soon he recognizes sequence, and he writes a series of sentences that tell what occurred in time or space: "I saw a dog. He was digging in the dirt. He buried his bone." Later the child begins to interpret with some sort of value judgment: "He was a good (or bad, or funny) dog." He learns to distinguish between fact and fiction and begins to write simple "pretend" stories. Some children write free verse and simple rhyming poetry in the beginning writing stage.

181

Children at this stage of development benefit from games or exercises that help them see events and ideas in sequence. Reading the comics in the newspaper with your child gives him excellent practice in noting sequence. Cutting out a series of pictures, scrambling their order, and asking your child to place the pictures in the order of "what happened next" is also helpful. Some children may be interested in drawing a series of events in pictures (similar to a comic strip).

During this early period, punctuation and spelling are not emphasized. The child is encouraged to write his ideas freely without worrying about mechanics. Original spelling is accepted, even encouraged, since the child needs to experiment without restriction with new language skills. When your first- or second-grade child writes at home, he may be concerned about how to spell words and he might ask for your help. Tell him how to spell words as he asks, but do not correct the spelling in his written work nor attempt to teach him words you think he should know. There is no surer way to discourage the development of writing skill than to emphasize mechanical considerations too soon. Most children begin formal spelling instruction sometime during the second grade. Help your child learn the words on his spelling list if he brings it home, but do not place great emphasis upon spelling at this stage.

During the latter part of the second grade and in the third grade, most children do much of their writing independently. Organization of ideas is still chiefly related to sequence in terms of time or space, but critical thinking gradually becomes more evident and the child begins to interpret his experience as well as to describe it: "I wish the dog had buried his bone somewhere else because he dug up my mother's flowers. Mother was really mad. I don't blame her."

At this stage creative stories begin to have plot characteristics including climax, conflict, and resolution of problems. It is important to relate what the child is writing to materials he reads, pointing out how authors organize their work.

Some children like to retell familiar stories or fairy tales in their writing. Occasionally this worries a parent who is concerned about plagiarism and the child's apparent lack of creativity. At this stage of development, though, some children need the security of a proven formula, and the process of thinking through a story and writing it on paper, even if the plot is not their own, is worthwhile. Often this kind of writing opens the door for original writing later.

Some mechanical aspects become important at this stage. Those aspects include spelling, punctuation, and content and mechanics.

Spelling

Increased attention is given to spelling at this stage, but instruction should be limited to helping the child spell the words he asks about as he writes and to build skill through formal spelling study. You still should not correct spelling errors in the child's written work.

You can help your child study assigned spelling words at home during this period. First, give him a pretest·on the words in his list. When you give a spelling test it is important that your child correct his own paper as you spell the words aloud to him. The process of his taking a test and correcting it himself is a valuable learning experience in itself. You may find that he already knows how to spell many of the words on his list and does not need to study them.

Once the words he needs to study have been identified through a pretest, help him follow a systematic study method. The method of copying the word over and over again is not efficient because the child is not required to use all the clues—sight, sound, and feeling— that help him to learn to spell. Another problem is that often he has not copied the word correctly in the first place, and he ends up practicing his errors instead of learning the word. A better study method is found in the following eight study steps. Instruct your child to:

First, pronounce the word. Sometimes a child does not spell a word correctly because he does not hear or say it right.

Second, look with your child at the parts of the word. Notice any unusual letters. Find word parts that occur in other familiar words.

Third, say the letters out loud in proper sequence with your child while you are both looking at the word.

Fourth, have your child shut his eyes and try to see the word. Have him say the letters in sequence with his eyes shut.

Fifth, ask the child to look at the word again. Have him check to see if he spelled it correctly with his eyes shut.

Sixth, have your child write the word without looking at it.

Seventh, have your child look at the word again. Ask him to check to see if he wrote the word correctly.

Eighth, if he did not write the word correctly, begin over again with the first step and repeat the procedure until your child has learned how to spell the word.

When the child has studied all the words on the list that he could not spell on the pretest, give him another test on the entire list. You will find that the study system described here can be followed with only a few minutes of study each day.

183

Punctuation

Punctuation is also given attention during this stage of development. By the end of the third grade most children use periods, question marks, and exclamation points correctly. They are also able to correctly use commas after the salutation and after the closing of a letter, to set off items in a series, between the day of the month and the year, and between the name of the city and the name of the state. They use apostrophes in common contractions such as *isn't* and *aren't*. By the end of the primary grades a student can also use capital letters appropriately in most situations.

Content and Mechanics

In the intermediate grades, writing skills in both content and mechanics increase rapidly as the child gains experience. Children of this age are often helped by giving them a four-step sequence to be followed in completing any kind of written work. These four steps include (1) notetaking, (2) writing a first draft, (3) revising and proofreading, and (4) writing the final draft.

During the notetaking step the child makes a list of the ideas he wants to include in his written product. These notes may be in the form of single words, phrases, or short sentences. Some fourth-graders and most children in fifth and sixth grades are able to follow a simple outline in arranging their notes.

The child then uses his notes to write a first draft of his report, story, letter, essay, or other written work. At this point the important part is to concentrate on content and to get ideas on paper without worrying too much about the mechanics. The child's first concern should be what he is trying to say.

When the ideas are safely on paper, the child can then go back and look for incorrect spelling, punctuation, word choice, and sentence sense. Usually it is better to wait until the next day or even later before revising and proofreading a written piece.

This revision stage is the time when the parent or teacher can be of most help, but the child should be encouraged to make his own evaluation and corrections before asking for adult criticism. Children can help each other with the revision and proofreading step; it is helpful to have a friend read a paper aloud to see if it makes sense both to him and to the writer as he listens to his own work. As you help your child revise his work, resist the temptation to change his wording or to add your own ideas. Your function should be to help him talk through his ideas and to find his own errors, not to edit his writing.

Once the child is satisfied with his work, he writes a final draft in the form which has the most use for him. Written work may be done in a variety of forms, including charts, books, newspapers, or notebook sheets. When the final draft is completed, consider it done. Accept your child's efforts wholeheartedly without further criticism.

The intermediate-grade child continues formal spelling study and will benefit from the eight-step spelling study procedure described earlier for younger children. In addition, he is ready to benefit from having spelling errors in his written work called to his attention. Misspelled words found in his writing should be added to his formal spelling list he brings home from school to be studied by the eight-step process until they are mastered. He is also ready to use commas to clarify meaning in sentences, semicolons and colons to add variety, apostrophes to show possession, and quotation marks. He frequently gives attention to even margins, centered titles, and other matters of general form and appearance.

In summary, parents help children to become good writers by providing enriching experience and stimulating thinking to give the child something to write about, helping the child find purpose for writing through suggesting meaningful activities, and guiding the development of quality in writing in terms of content as well as language mechanics.

ACTIVITIES: CREATIVE WRITING

1. Take twenty minutes to sit with your child to watch, discuss, and praise his efforts as he illustrates a series of pictures having to do with things he is grateful for. (This activity could be preceded by a discussion of things that make him happy.) After he has completed each of his pictures, tell him you are going to write what he says about them on each page as he tells you what to write. Record his statements. Fasten the papers together and enclose them in a cover made from either construction paper or some other appropriate material. Label the book "My Thankful Book," and put your child's name on the cover. Read the book to the child often and show pride in his accomplishment.

Other books could be created using such topics as "My Family," "My Friends," "My Trip," "The Sleepy Penguin," and so on.

2. Show your own interest in creative writing by writing a journal of family activities for a period of one week. Emphasize in the journal the activities of each child. At the end of the week, read your journal to the family.

3. Allow your child to dictate a note of remembrance or thank you to someone special. Write it for him as he dictates to you. Let him illustrate the note and let him prepare it (with your help) for mailing.

4. Each time your child draws a picture, ask him to tell you about it. Record under the picture exactly what he tells you. Point out to him that you are writing down exactly what he says.

5. Cut a comic strip out of the newspaper and divide it into sections. Scramble these sections up and ask your child to put them back in the correct order. Let him tell you the story as he sees it in the pictures.

CHAPTER 23
CREATIVITY THROUGH
PLAY AND PLAY MATERIALS

What is play? Many early childhood education writers have suggested that play is the child's work; others think that play is the child's world. Play might also be defined as an activity engaged in for the enjoyment it gives, with or without consideration of the end result.

Games, manipulative toys, and play equipment for children do provide an opportunity for learning many things, but when we start approaching play seriously and solemnly with the goal of aiding specific school learning, it is in danger of no longer being play. Play could lose its spontaneity and become the conscious tool of adults who want to manipulate children toward an academic goal.

Even with these conditions in mind, playtime probably is the best time for learning. Perhaps learning isn't obtained only in structured, cognitive concepts (as, for example, in math or symbolic abstracts); from babyhood through adulthood, learning through play is part of our everyday living. We see groups and individuals playing at home, at school, and outdoors; in almost any suburban backyard we see families participating together in organized activities, or children just playing on their own.

187

Play provides an opportunity to learn to work alone or to enjoy oneself in a group, to experiment with a medium, or to use imagination and to enjoy oneself fully. Some adults may need to set the stage for play by planning a specific activity, by opening possible avenues, or by saving the right materials to promote more constructive play, but every child at any age will probably find spontaneous ways to play.

Categories of Play

There are different categories of play. *Sense-pleasure play* begins in infancy and continues throughout life. As the name suggests, sense-pleasure play is play in which the participant receives pleasure from touching, tasting, and other sensory experiences. In organized nursery schools or other organized groups for young children, many of the creative experiences come under this domain.

Dramatic play. A touch of imagination and resourcefulness plus a child who is ready to explore and experiment are the chief ingredients for rich play experiences. Dramatic play (or *domestic play,* as it sometimes has been labeled) is the reconstruction, or dramatization, of life as it is seen through the eyes of a young child.

Dramatic play is especially common among three-, four-, and five-year-old children. As they dress their dolls and become part of their family in a group of children, they identify various roles: "You be the mommy, and I'll be the daddy; you be the baby, and you be the dog. You go out to work and be Uncle Harry, and you be Aunt Sally. You stay and make all those cookies." As other children enter the group they acquire a role in the dramatic scene.

Children most often imitate the home setting, because that is what is important to them; they center their dramatic play around episodes and experiences such as a trip to the zoo, a visit to the farm or to a friend, or a trip to a serious place such as a hospital or the dentist.

Observing a child involved in dramatic play helps adults learn about a child's concept of the real world. It especially reveals how he sees his parents and their role in the family. Dramatic play can also open avenues that help the child clarify his concepts and thereby help him to better understand the real world. A teacher or a parent observing a group of children "going to the store to buy a baby" might ask them, "Do you know where babies come from?" When they express interest, he might explain, "They aren't made like a doll or like a package of macaroni that you buy at the store; instead they grow inside a mother." This would probably suffice for a group of three- or four-year-olds, and would help them to clarify a concept.

Dramatic play is an essential part of a child's learning about the world. One day in a nursery school a fireman came in his fire truck to visit the school. The head teacher noticed that everyone was present but one girl. When the teacher went inside, she found the little girl hiding in a closet. She thought firemen started fires instead of putting them out. Her past experiences had somehow helped her form a misconception or false concept about the role of a fireman. Such misconcepts can be corrected through dramatic play.

Skill play. While some children at the preschool age become involved in play such as learning to ride tricycles, such play that demands or develops skills is usually participated in by school-age children. Some of these activities that we call "play" involve the actual application of a child's skills. Young girls who make clothes for their dolls must acquire the ability or skill to manipulate a mechanical tool—the sewing machine or a needle and thread—in order to accomplish their play. They must also develop the skills of fitting patterns and cutting. Young boys who want to "play" in a basketball game need to learn to dribble the ball, make baskets, and shoot free throws.

Forms of Play

In addition to three different categories of play, there are three different forms of play: solitary play, parallel play, and cooperative play.

The child involved in *solitary play* is, as the label indicates, playing by himself. Much of a young child's play is of this type. He may become completely lost in his play, totally oblivious to what is going on around him. While infants, toddlers, and often preschool children may engage in solitary play, the activity is most characteristic of the very young.

Parallel play involves two children playing side by side. Whether or not they are playing the same game or using the same equipment is unimportant; the definitive characteristic is that while playing they are not totally dependent upon each other.

But while they *can* carry on their play independently without getting involved with each other, they might interact. One might say, "Mine wiggles when it walks," or, "Yellow, yellow, yellow, yellow." The other might respond, "When it walks it sometimes falls down," or, "I'm painting yellow, orange, yellow." What one says may not at all apply to what the other is saying; however, they will take turns,

189

waiting for each other to say something as though they were carrying on a conversation with each other.

The departure of one child may disturb the other's play. Parallel play is demonstrated most often by two-year-olds and three-year-olds and sometimes by four- and five-year-olds (although these older children are usually ready for experiences with other children and are therefore ready for cooperative play).

Cooperative play is characterized by the interaction of two or more participants. It emerges as the predominant type of play among four- and five-year-old play activities.

All three forms of play will be found in the home setting. The baby usually plays alone. The three-year-old digs a hole in the garden alongside his father or plays beside his mother in the kitchen, or he may sit down with a book, looking at the pictures or trying to read while his older brothers and sisters are doing their homework. (You see, they're working with books, and it's important for him to be able to do the same.) Your organized family activities frequently depend on the participation of several or all family members in cooperative play.

Toys: The Equipment for Play

The child at play does not need a lot of props. In fact, it is better that he have too few than too many: too many can stifle his imagination and his initiative. Any toys he does have should be suited to his abilities, should be designed to stimulate and challenge him, but should not be so difficult that they discourage him—children are easily discouraged by demands that go beyond their ability to achieve.

Toys can be divided into three chief categories according to the stimulation they provide: (1) those that stimulate the imagination and invite initiative, effort, and fun, such as building blocks and art activities; (2) those that help the child attain adult skills, such as brushes and brooms, scissors, and hammers and nails; and (3) those that help develop physical and mental abilities, such as construction toys and climbing equipment.

In recent years we have seen numerous "educational" toys appear on the market. Some are helpful to the child and suit his interests and needs, but many are of little value. But parents should consider whether or not the child is going to enjoy the toy, and whether he will have pure and simple fun with it. A professional child-developmentalist went to a large department store at Christmas to purchase gifts for some young children. The saleslady brought out many attractively boxed "educational" games and, in trying to sell them, explained how very valuable each would be for a young child because of its educational value. These would help develop basic concepts in arithmetic; those, eye-hand coordination and perceptual development. But not once did she mention that a game was for enjoyment, or fun. It is not good if all of a child's games, equipment, and activities are designed solely to aid specific school learning.

Criteria for Selecting Play Equipment

Certain guidelines will help in establishing some criteria for the selection of play equipment. First, the plaything should be as free of detail as possible. A child needs freedom to express himself by creating his own childlike world, and too much detail hampers him. Those who respect the child's world will not choose equipment that reflects adult interests in structure and realistic details; rather, they will look at the child's playthings from the standpoint of what will be best for the child. Unit blocks are an outstanding example of prime play equipment that is free from detail and can therefore be used in many creative ways.

Second, check the durability of the plaything. It's frustrating to have an exciting new toy that breaks almost the first time it is used. You should also consider whether the plaything is sturdy enough to be used by more than one child.

Third, the construction of a toy should be so simple that any child could determine how to use it. Many times even adults have been frustrated by trying to figure out how even a young child's plaything works.

Fourth, the plaything should actively involve the child; playing with it should require some effort. Physical activity such as the large-muscle manipulation necessary to ride a bicycle or the mental exercises required by some kinds of games involve the child and add value or commitment to the plaything.

Some basic guidelines will help parents select the best play equipment for their children. The following questions should be considered:

1. Is the material safe? Is it free from dangerous corners, splinters, and nail points? You can write to Toy List, Federal Drug Administration, Washington, D.C. 20016, for free information concerning toys that have been banned and why this action was taken.

2. Is the toy repairable and durable (this especially applies to outdoor equipment)?

191

3. Does the plaything challenge the child's imagination and stimulate his thinking?

4. Does the plaything deal with the child's real world?

5. Can several children be involved simultaneously in the use of the toy?

6. Does the toy stimulate the child's muscular and physical activity?

7. Does the plaything require manipulation, experimentation, and construction, and if so, how much and how detailed?

8. Is the plaything suitable for the age and interest of the child using it?

9. Is there adequate space for the use of the material or equipment and adequate storage when it is not in use?

10. Does the toy or material have more than one use?

Summary and Conclusion

From the information provided we see that children use play to learn about and understand the world around them. They advance through various categories of play: *sense-pleasure* play beginning in infancy and continuing throughout a lifetime; *dramatic play* involving imagination and resourcefulness of a child as he imitates and explores various adult roles and behaviors; and *skill play* involving actual application of learned and practiced skills.

The forms of children's play are: solitary play, where the child plays alone; parallel play, where two children play side by side, but not particularly with each other; and cooperative play, characterized by the interaction of two or more children.

Play and toys are sometimes considered synonymous, but toys are categorized according to the stimulation they provide: (1) toys that stimulate the imagination and invite initiative; (2) toys that help children attain adult skills; and (3) toys that help develop physical and mental abilities.

Guidelines are necessary when selecting toys for children. Toys should be selected according to the purpose they are to serve (academic, physical growth, pleasure, relaxation, diversion, and so on). They should be examined for durability, safety, complexity, adaptability, and appropriate age-level usefulness for the child. In selecting a toy for a child to play with, an adult should invest time, thought, and an effort to meet the child's needs.

Most important for children's play are patient, understanding, and benevolent adults, parents, and teachers who are aware of the child's needs for and interest in play and who recognize how truly essential play is for the child in his unceasing search for orientation and for self-awareness. Children *do* learn those things through play: they learn what they can do and what their limitations are, and they learn what can be accomplished through their play and their interaction with the significant people in their world.

ACTIVITIES: ASSISTING YOUR CHILD'S CREATIVITY THROUGH PLAY AND PLAY MATERIALS

1. Have a field-day with boxes.
   A. With your child, select durable boxes of fairly large sizes. Find a smooth, grassy slope and take turns sitting in the boxes and sliding down the slope.
   B. Build a playhouse out of boxes that vary in size. Cut, tie, glue, and paint the masterpiece in whatever way, shape, and color you and your child desire.
   C. Select several boxes varying in size. Cut them, paint them, stack them, and shape them to represent animals, cars, machines, and other familiar objects.

2. Make a zoo with rocks.
   Plan an outing through the neighborhood, mountains, or backyard; collect as many different kinds of rocks as possible. Glue these rocks into various shapes to represent animals found in a zoo. Paint the creations with tempera or acrylic paints. If tempera is used, spray it lightly when it is dry with a fixative or varnish. The finished animals can be used in pretend games or can serve as bookends, paperweights, knickknacks, or gifts.

3. Make a creative treasure.
   Put some props that can be used in dramatic play in a large box. These props might include kitchen utensils, old shoes, hats, adult clothing, dolls, books, empty food packages, and other similar items. Instruct your child that he may use this "treasure box" to play with and perhaps even to create his own play.

4. Teach your child about high, low, in, and out through play.
   Stretch a broomstick between two chairs. Encourage your child to go over, as well as under, the stick in as many different ways as

he can without touching it—forward, backward, skipping, crawling, and so on. The height of the stick can be adjusted to provide a greater challenge.

5. Play "Giant steps, baby steps."

The object of this game is to count the number of steps each person takes in moving from one side of the room to the other. Each person should take turns telling the other how many as well as what kind of steps to take. For example, instruct your child, "Take three baby steps." Be sure the child counts each step aloud as it is taken. The game can be adapted to see who can get across the room first.

6. Have a bean toss.

Give the child a small container of beans. Place an open show box on the floor a few feet from a marker or line. Standing behind that marker or line, the child should throw one bean at a time toward the box, attempting to get as many beans into the box as possible. When all of the beans have been thrown, help the child count the number of beans he got into the box. Show him how to keep a written record so that as he continues to play the game he will know if he does better or worse each time through. For an added challenge, move the box further away from the throwing line.

7. Play "Clap loud, clap soft."

There must be at least two people to play this game. One person is chosen as "It"; he leaves the room, while someone remaining partially hides an object. "It" comes back to the room to look for the object. He is given clues to its whereabouts by the clapping hands of observers. As "It" gets close to the hidden object the clapping should become loud. As he moves away from the object the clapping should get soft. When the object is found, "It" chooses someone to take his place while he hides the object.

8. Practice sorting.

Put four or five each of twelve different objects in a wide-mouthed jar, can, or box. These objects could include buttons, nails, coins, safety pins, beans, paper clips, or other tiny objects found around the home. Using an egg carton, demonstrate to your child how to sort like objects into each of the compartments of the egg carton. After the child has learned to sort the objects by himself, and if he desires, let him race against the clock to complete the task. A kitchen timer that rings at the end of the time period is ideal for this activity. Set the clock for five minutes the first time. As your child becomes more proficient at sorting, the time can be lessened.

CHAPTER 24
YOUR CHILD'S CREATIVITY
IN SCIENCE AND THE WORLD

A young child's world is a magical place that he is constantly exploring to satisfy a basic drive to know and interpret, to understand and then control. Nothing is too basic or simple, because a child is a person of limited experience. This energetic approach to life, this desire to explore everything, is rudimentary to scientific activity.

An adult can aid a child's scientific learning in two major ways: by sharing in the excitement of scientific discovery and by providing opportunities for this learning to take place.

Scientific Discovery

A child should be encouraged to *discover* the world rather than to merely memorize facts about it. Urge your child to develop his own routes of exploration, to make intelligent guesses, and to speculate. If his idea is not feasible, he should be encouraged to try again; dwell on his successes, and diminish his failures. If he persists in developing his own ideas, he will approach understanding in wide zig-zags, adding bits and pieces each day. The adult who knows where the child is in his thinking can help him clarify and summarize, thus aiding the child's learning for the rest of his life.

To share in the excitement and joy of discovery presents a great challenge: such discovery does not occur quickly. As the child watches, wonders, studies, and questions—experiencing science as a part of everyday living—he gains an appreciation of the world around him and keeps alive the sense of wonder. Steadily, as he comes to understand the orderliness of the universe, he develops a method of thinking and of finding answers to questions.

The following list, adapted from "Young Children and Science," a pamphlet published by the Association for Childhood Education, International, offers a meaningful description of scientific discovery. Science for the child is: (1) pausing to wonder, reflect, and speculate; (2) questioning conditions and events, (3) seeking explanations from reliable sources; (4) doubting generalities and looking for deviations; (5) sharing ideas; (6) recording findings mentally before recording them materially; (7) organizing, interpreting, summarizing, generalizing, and applying information; (8) gaining knowledge; (9) bringing order to scientific learning; and (10) having experiences involving change, variation, adaptation, space, interrelationships, and energy.

Aids to Scientific Learning

Parents can promote a child's scientific discovery by daily providing rich, exciting, scientific experiences for young children rather than leaving such scientific experiences to chance. For example, if teachers and parents wait until the child is asking about only a specific scientific phenomenon or is studying only the thing he seems interested in, his learning may become restricted to that one area.

It is important that you encourage a child to explore all areas. You must be flexible and prepared, and you need to be acquainted with the areas of elementary scientific discovery. In the event that your child asks a question that you can't answer, you can say, "I don't know. Where can we find out?" or, "I'll help you find out."

Success in helping a child learn depends largely on the skillful use of questions. For example, such questions as, "What do you mean?" or, "How would that work?" help the child to clarify his own thinking. Questions such as, "Have you noticed that?" or, "This is puzzling. How do you suppose it happened?" help to focus his attention on a subject, "Have you ever wondered about ...?" or, "Have you thought of it in this way?" may seem rather sophisticated questions for a young child, but he can learn what you mean by the question and can later utilize the same type of question in his pursuit of new ideas.

A parent or teacher who wishes to help a child develop an idea should have an objective in mind. These methods will help a child develop his thoughts: (1) introduce a concept with a demonstration; (2) follow such a demonstration with pertinent questions; (3) lead the child into a discussion; (4) listen to the child and elicit his ideas; (5) encourage the child to draw conclusions, to make discrete, accurate observations of *exactly* what he saw (not what he *thinks* he saw); (6) plan experiments and repeat experiments, supplementing such experiments with pictures on a bulletin board or a flannel board; and (7) read to the child.

Teaching Scientific Concepts

There are a number of ways to teach scientific concepts. The first way is to help the child to observe specific things within the home, such as the evaporation when water dries or the conversion of water into steam that disappears in the house when mother is cooking. Let the child go outside and observe what happens after a storm; let him watch the water on a sidewalk until it dries and disappears. Take a walk with your child and try to see things as he sees them by walking slowly and by observing and questioning as you go. Such questions help clarify, help direct the child's attention, stimulate the child's thought, and cause the child to speculate.

A second way to teach scientific concepts is to visit or to invite into your home a person who knows a lot about something the child may be interested in, and who is capable of presenting it in a way that the child can understand.

A family with young children who were interested in pretty rocks returned from their vacation with quite a rock collection. They didn't know how to classify these rocks, but because their neighbor was a geologist, they invited him to their home for an evening. He told the children some basic differences in rocks and helped them label each rock with a scientific name. The experience was an extremely beneficial one. Although the scientific names were more difficult than the parents could remember—and certainly more difficult than a child could be expected to remember—the children nevertheless accepted the challenge, remembering and using the scientific names when referring to the rocks. They were also able to find some distinctive characteristics in each class of rocks.

A third suggestion is to provide meaningful excursions. A young mother in California made a list of all the places in her community that might interest her children: museums, zoos, farms, businesses, and organizations. The list also included the address of each and its items of particular interest. If the place required an entrance fee, this was indicated on the mother's list. After each listing was her evaluation of her children's reactions to the excursion. Then she gave the list to friends as a way to help them provide meaningful experiences for their children. To be meaningful, such an excursion must be planned ahead of time and some directions and objectives need to be outlined.

Fourth, capitalize on special occasions, seasons, changes in the weather, holidays, or special events. For a number of weeks David and his sister and brother had watched a caterpillar spin a cocoon and then hibernate in the cocoon. The family wondered if the caterpillar would come out of the cocoon at about the time of David's birthday, and, sure enough, on the day of his birthday the cocoon broke open and the butterfly emerged. David's mother captured the butterfly without harming it. On the next day, the day of the birthday party, David's mother took the children out onto the back lawn and celebrated the birthday by setting the butterfly free. The children clapped with glee as the butterfly flew away. They followed it from tree to bush, around the yard and down the street, over into the next lot, until they finally lost sight of it. Those children had not only developed a better understanding of this magic event, but had remembered it better because it was part of a special occasion.

Many such experiences can be associated with special occasions. Certain manufacturers have capitalized on the fact that some holidays are associated with specific smells and tastes: they have published books with textural content and such holiday smells as pine, peppermint, and pumpkin pie.

It is important, then, for adults to use observation, resource individuals, excursions, and special occasions and events to encourage children to formulate ideas about the scientific world around them. A child who learns about the world around him will subsequently enjoy it more.

ACTIVITIES: ASSISTING YOUR CHILD'S CREATIVITY THROUGH SCIENCE AND THE WORLD

The four approaches used in teaching scientific concepts include:
1. Accurate observation.
2. Discussion with a resource person.
3. Meaningful excursions.

4. Studies of special occasions, seasons, changes in weather, holidays, or special events.

A child's learning can be facilitated by the skillful use of questions. They can be used for:
1. Clarification—"What do you mean?"
2. Directing attention—"Have you noticed . . .?"
3. Stimulating thought through speculation—"Have you ever wondered about . . .?"

Water

1. Provide your child with a small tub or bottle of water and some food coloring. Allow him to mix them together to form different color combinations. Guide his discovery of colors by asking him to verbalize his findings and to guess their results: "If you add yellow to red you get (color)."

2. Give your child two jars. Ask him to fill one with water. Next, have him put a few drops of detergent in both jars. Ask him to tell you what happens. Have him hold the jar without water in it under the faucet, and turn the water on. Again, ask your child to tell you what happens and to guess its reason.

Light

3. Turn on a small light in a dark room. Standing between the light and the wall, have the child make shadows with his hands or body. Discuss with your child why shadows are made by blocking out the light.

4. Do plants need light to grow? Let the child put a can upside down on the lawn in a place where it won't be knocked over. Leave the can there for three days before lifting it off. What happened? Discuss the results with your child.

Air

5. Make a balloon jet by blowing up a balloon. (The child may need help in blowing up the balloon.) When the balloon is full of air, release the open end and let it fly.

6. Let your child stuff a piece of tissue into the bottom of a small glass so that it is secure and doesn't fall out when the glass is turned upside down. Now, have the child push the upside-down glass straight into a large bowl of water and pull it straight out. Did the tissue get wet? Did the air in the glass keep the water from going inside the glass, too?

Collections

7. Assist your child in collecting, properly categorizing, and displaying pebbles, shells, leaves, insects, and seeds.

Excursions

8. Go exploring with your child. He may find a bird's nest, a bee gathering pollen, or a butterfly coming out of its cocoon. Discuss with your child the things he finds. This is a marvelous way to stimulate discovery.

Reflection

9. Give your child a mirror and a piece of paper with his name on it. Let him look at himself in the mirror as he puts his name in front of the mirror as well. What does the mirror do to his name?

10. Using a silvery-bright spoon, ask your child to look into its bowl. What does he see? Now have him look at himself on the back of the spoon. Does he look the same?

Seeds

11. Soak a few seeds in a glass of water overnight. (Seeds for peas, corn, and beans are very appropriate for this experiment.) In the morning, cut the seeds open and have your child look at them under a magnifying glass. Is he able to see a baby plant inside each of the seeds?

12. In the summer, look for a ripe dandelion. What happens if your child blows on it? What will happen to the seeds? Milkweed pods split open in the autumn and are also appropriate for this experiment.

Other suggestions for basic science experiences can be found in books from the library.

CHAPTER 25
YOUR CHILD'S
CREATIVITY IN ART

When a child is only beginning—and often with very limited success—to express himself in words, introducing him to art in its various forms serves him in more than one way. Not only can he thrill to the creation of something beautiful, but he has been given a way other than words to express his feelings.

The bright and dark colors of paint; the delightful pliancy of clay and the thrill of seeing it take on a recognizable shape; the development of coordination through cutting, pasting, coloring, and arranging (and the satisfaction derived from mastery of those skills); and the joy of making and giving a gift—all of these are important to a preschooler's development. An alert parent observing a child as he paints or as he vigorously twists and thumps a ball of clay can learn a great deal about the child and his needs.

Helping Your Child with Art

The teacher is frequently asked, "What should I do to help my child with his painting, drawing, or clay modeling at home? I know absolutely nothing about art!"

Answering such a parent is easy: you don't need to know *anything* about art to give your child all the help he needs.

It is hard to say what creative art *is*, but it is easy to say what creative art *isn't*: it's *not* something obscure, mysterious, and "highbrow"; it's *not* found only in museums with frames around it or pedestals under it. Art is and always has been a part of everyday living.

When your child paints a picture in poster colors or draws a scene in crayon or models an animal in clay, he doesn't think of himself as "making art"; he is setting down his reactions to the amazing world around him. If this is true, evidently you need to know just two things to help your child with his art activities: (1) you need to know your child, and (2) you need to know the amazing world around you. If time has dulled your own amazement with the world, you may really have to work to regain the viewpoint you had at age seven, five, four, or three when you joyfully discovered that the tall sticks you had drawn for the legs of a standing-up man would, if bent in half, make a sitting-down man.

To do this, to become a child again, you will have to sweep a lot of useless rubble from your mind. Sweep out first your notion that you know what things look like. You don't. All you know is the way they look to you. Young children do not draw things the way they look to an adult. They draw and paint their own world the way they see it. The very young child is not concerned with using color as it appears in nature: to him, a cat may be green or a house purple. This element of fantasy is consistent with the exciting impossibilities of fairy tales. Your child sees the world intensely: to him things aren't just things—they are pleasing, mean, swift, heavy, happy, dark, comforting, rhythmic.

Your Response Makes a Difference

Once you have accepted the fact that things look different to different people, you are ready for your role as an enthusiastic audience. The hardest part of that role is holding in check your urge to bring your visual experience to your child. He does not want or need your secondhand experience; he is having his own firsthand visual experience right now as he sits at the table working away at a big sheet of paper, covered with what to you are assorted scratches and scrunches. Do you smile and say, "That's nice, Son. What is it?" If you do, your score as an audience is zero. You may get an "Oh, Daddy!" as an answer, but you probably won't be shown many more pictures by this squelched child.

Instead, really work at understanding your child's artwork. Study it. Then maybe you'll discover that the little group of squiggles in the center, with four violently active lines sweeping down from each one, represents horses. You note the greatly exaggerated bridle on each one, and suddenly you recall that last Sunday at his grandfather's farm, Danny had at last worked up enough nerve to mount a horse. The bridle must have seemed pretty important to him then. It certainly is in this picture.

Finally you see the reckless riders on the horses' backs, and you comment, "Boy, those cowboys sure are built into their saddles!" Danny's face lights up. He waits as you keep on looking. You ponder the meaning of those big lines at the top of the picture. Now you see. They are mountains—forty-thousand-foot-high ones. And those marks that you thought were where he sharpened his pencil are cactuses. The black smudges over the mountains are clouds. And at last the whole story breaks. In the middle of a vast landscape, under a threatening sky, gallops a brave, if tiny, group of men. You look at Danny in complete understanding. "They've got guts," you say. Danny's expression is pure bliss.

You have done for him as much as any parent can possibly do. In fact, your performance was perfect. In just three words you summed up the essential mood of the picture. The mountains weren't important. The cowboys weren't important. What was important was that these frail human beings were not merely coping with but dominating that fearsome country. Maybe that horse at grandfather's farm really had seemed pretty terrifying!

Through our actions and attitudes, we convince young children that we have complete faith in their ability to express their own ideas. Danny wasn't picturing a mood; he was in a mood. Nor was he trying to produce a work of art; the art was a byproduct. He worked rapidly; technical problems were solved instinctively as they came up. You noticed that the horses' legs were four violently active lines—violently active because Danny was trying to show you the speed of the horses, not the anatomy of their hooves or their fetlocks. He was setting down an idea that was clamoring for expression.

Art Changes Occur as the Child Develops

As the child changes, so does his art. At around two, three, and four years of age your child will scribble purely for the muscular pleasure of it. As a stage, scribbling before drawing is just as important as is crawling before walking.

203

Next your child will give names to his scribbles ("Look at the big jet plane!"), and finally—a big jump—he will name his scrawls in advance. But by then he's in the four-, five-, and six-year-old group. "This is going to be Daddy," he says, and you'll see a huge circle with dots for eyes, maybe a nose and a mouth, and a pair of lines hanging from it for legs. Well, why not? For most of his early life "Daddy" meant just a head looming over the crib. But Daddy does go away; hence, the legs. If you want to, you can ask, "But where are Daddy's arms? What could he pick you up with?" Then, if he is ready, Danny will add two lines for arms, probably branching out from where the ears should be.

This readiness must be respected. Just as you possess a reading vocabulary far larger than the one you use in speaking, so a child always has a store of knowledge that he is not yet using. The able teacher (and the wise parent) watches for the right moment to bring out these new concepts. Boredom, by the way, is one signal that the "right moment" has arrived.

Have you ever heard someone humming a piece of music to himself—thinly, annoyingly? Yet in his inner ear he hears the whole orchestra. It's the same thing, often, when the young child paints or draws. The painting of "The Bride" may look to you like a rectangle, a triangle, and a collection of circles, but its maker saw flowing, bright satin and fragrant flowers. In the same way, you use symbols constantly: "Turn left when you come to a white picket fence"; "Mr. Jones is the one with the bushy eyebrows." They are shortcuts. Similarly, if you are tempted to draw for Danny what a man "really" looks like--stop! Maybe you'd just be showing him *your* symbol.

If you follow the development of Danny's art, by the time he reaches age nine, you will have become quite attached to his fearless self-expression, and you will regret its passing. You will have learned a lot about Danny and Danny's world. And you definitely will have removed yourself from the group of those who "know nothing about art."

At age nine, Danny will start off on a new task, a more complicated one. But the basic part of your job is done. By entering, as a quiet but appreciative guest, into Danny's own amazing world you have helped him develop his creative powers and kept them apace with his physical and mental growth. All you will now need to do is simply continue counseling him to be himself.

Essentials of a Creative Experience

Consider the essentials of a creative experience:

1. There must be an understanding adult. As the child finds that

his mother feels he has good ideas and can express them, he relaxes and his expression becomes more free, flowing, and meaningful.

2. A child needs ready access to a number of varied creative media—clay, fingerpaints, large sheets of paper to allow free expression, crayons and chalk that are rich-colored and soft enough to mark easily, and tempera paints (used with large brushes to assure ease of handling).

Children who are given a ditto sheet to color are not being given an opportunity to grow very much creatively, intellectually, or emotionally. The child who only colors another person's outline misses the opportunity of trying to visualize and draw the object himself. He becomes a technician and not an artist. It is difficult for a child who has learned to "color pictures" to get emotionally involved in his work. His "art" does not become an emotional release for him. About the only good that comes from such an experience is that a child learns good eye-hand coordination. He really learns how to "stay in the lines." But then you recognize that "staying in the lines" is not a principle of art.

3. Time is a third essential factor affecting creativity. A child needs enough time to express himself adequately when he wants to. A family's busy schedule must allot each family member the privacy and time to develop his own abilities.

4. The fourth aspect of creativity is space—space to move in, space to build in, space to create in. Adults would hate to be limited to the top of a school desk when they were making a dress or building a cabinet. Just the same, a child shouldn't be confined to this small area of space. A large enough area should be provided so that dramatics, dancing, building, or painting won't be cramped or inhibited. The creativity of children can easily be stifled by adults who don't take the time and effort to create an appropriate atmosphere in their homes.

Whenever a child works—whether with clay, pencil, or paint—enthusiastically, rapidly, and unfalteringly, and is himself satisfied with the result, that result is a work of art—a perfect welding, that is, of idea, emotion, and design. It is an approach your child shares with all great creators. The master artist is one who succeeds in recapturing the fresh, uninfluenced viewpoint he had as a child and in welding to it all he has learned of the world through experience. As you can see, the child needs freedom and opportunities to express himself. And he needs your confidence that he can succeed. With that he can feel comfortable in being creative.

Conclusion

In conclusion, to recognize creativity in art requires an understanding of children and a willingness to examine children's art in light of their level of ability and experience. As the child changes through the passing years and increases in experiences, his art undergoes changes in form and complexity. A child's early symbols are not those expressed by adults. He sees things differently and expresses what he sees in his own way. However, the adult's responses and actions express to the child the worth of the child's work and have a marked influence for good or ill.

The essentials outlined to produce a creative experience for a child are: (1) an understanding adult; (2) access to various creative media such as crayons, chalk, paper, scissors, and paste; (3) time to express himself within the family environment; and (4) space necessary for him to create.

Creativity in art is a valuable form of expression for young children who have a desire or a need to communicate their feelings and experiences, because children create from what they live.

ACTIVITIES: ASSISTING YOUR CHILD'S CREATIVITY IN ART

Easel Painting
1. Fasten a large sheet of paper to an easel. Provide separate one-half- to one-inch-wide brushes for each container of paint, and allow the child to paint freely.

Finger Painting
2. Painting may be done on the table top or on a piece of paper. If paper is used, the table should be wiped with a wet sponge before placing the paper on it. When the painting is completed, hang the paper to dry.
    Suggested painting media include:
    1. Pudding, such as Danish pudding, or soft jello
    2. Ivory soap flakes beaten with dry tempera paint and water
    3. Liquid starch mixed with dry tempera paint

Sponge Painting
3. Dip sponges into thick paint and make printed designs on a piece of paper.

Ink Blots
4. Fold a piece of paper in half and reopen it. Place a few drops of paint on one side of the paper and refold it. Press the paper firmly closed. Reopen the paper and let it dry.

Murals
5. Provide your child with a long sheet of butcher paper, paint, and encouragement. He will do the rest.

Vegetable Printing
6. Cut a potato, carrot, or other vegetable in half and cut designs into its flat surface. Dip the design into paint and press it on a piece of paper.

Straw Painting
7. Put paint on a piece of paper with a spoon. Blow through a soda straw, spreading the paint on the paper.

Spool Painting
8. Nick the edges of a spool as desired. Loop a coat hanger through the spool for a handle. After dipping the spool in paint, roll it over a piece of paper.

String Painting
9. Dip a piece of string into paint and place it on half of a sheet of paper. Fold the other half of the paper over the string. Place one hand on top of the paper to hold it in place while you pull the string out of the paper.

Salt Painting
10. Color a shaker full of salt by mixing it with dry tempera paint. After putting paste or glue on a piece of paper, shake the colored salt over it.

Watercolor and Rubber Cement Resist
11. Paint a picture on a piece of paper with rubber cement. Allow the rubber cement to dry before painting over it with watercolor. After the paint has dried, clean away the rubber cement by rubbing it with your finger or a pencil eraser. A white outline of the picture will remain.

Clay
12. Add food coloring to one cup of water. Mix the liquid with two cups of flour and one cup of salt.

Collage

13. Provide a number of different materials that the child may use as his imagination dictates for cutting, arranging, and pasting on large sheets of paper. Such things as ribbons, string, buttons, beans, macaroni, cereals, fabric scraps, colored pieces of paper, and so on are ideal for this type of activity.

CHAPTER 26
CREATIVITY
THROUGH LITERATURE

Almost every child enjoys looking at books and listening to stories. At the same time, the experience helps him learn important language skills and fulfills certain of his needs. In addition, parents can enhance the experience by learning criteria for selecting books, and especially books of poetry, for three-, four-, and five-year-olds, and by becoming acquainted with sources available to aid parents in selecting appropriate books.

Exposure to Books and Stories Enhances Language

Story and poetry books for children afford a child experiences in listening and also in speaking. As the words in the books are read aloud to him, he hears the verbal representation of the objects he sees. He hears new words (a process that helps increase his vocabulary). He hears about his world, and he also hears ideas that support his firsthand experiences or lay a foundation for future experiences.

He makes such comments as, "I have a dog, too," and asks questions such as, "Where are they going?" He relates ideas: "If I do this, then that will happen. Right?" In other words, he interacts with the reader and the story. Reading books together in this way can be satisfying to both the child and the adult, and can provide a time to sit down and enjoy being together. The physical contact, the undivided attention, and the sharing of an experience can all add to a personal relationship.

Stories or poetry can be read at a special time during the day—just before supper or prior to nap or bedtime—or they can be used spontaneously. While the enjoyment a child gets out of a book should be reason enough to spend time reading to him, the quietness of the activity will also soothe him. So, if your child tends to be restless, overactive, or bored, try sitting down with him and enjoying a good book.

Children's Needs Met through Literature

The needs of children can be fulfilled through the use of stories and poetry. One need of considerable importance to the child is *security.* It is critical that he knows he is wanted and loved; he needs to have a high self-image. He especially needs exposure to stories about things he can do. You as a parent want him to develop confidence in his abilities; this feeling of one's own worth and ability can be enhanced through appropriate stories.

A young child can identify with a story of a boy or girl who is about his age and who is engaged in activities familiar to him. He can understand when the story child takes the dog for a walk, empties the garbage by himself, or picks up his toys when he has finished his playtime. He likes to hear about other children doing things he also does.

Another need is evidenced by the fact that a child likes to feel that he *belongs.* He wants to belong to a family, he wants to belong to a peer group, and he wants to belong to society. A child may be accepted by family members mainly because he, too, is a member of the family. But when he moves outside the immediate family unit, he needs to know that there are other people in the world who are friendly who will accept and like him. As a child first attends an organized group away from home (such as nursery school or Sunday School), or has a new babysitter or an unknown visitor to his home, hearing the adult who is not a family member tell a story or read a book gives him comfort. The enjoyable experience of hearing a story and the warm personal contact with the stranger adds to the child's acceptance of new situations and unfamiliar surroundings.

The need for *achievement* is also strong in the young child. He needs to feel that when he attempts a task, he can succeed at it. If he constantly meets with failure, he ceases to try. Why attempt something when you know you will fail? On the other hand, if he experiences success in most of his attempts, he will continue to try because he knows that a good feeling comes from accomplishing and achieving and that such success is within reach.

The need for *intellectual* security, or the desire to "know," can be at least partially fulfilled through the use of books. A child's world can be widened through the variety or kinds of books available to him. When selecting books to meet this need, it is important to select those that are on the developmental level of the child, that contain words he can understand. Picture books will encourage him to ask questions.

A child derives pleasure in hearing stories and seeing pictures of new things and places. His endless question, "What's that?" is a measure of his quest for new experiences. He is also eager to hear stories about and see pictures of familiar objects and things. He seems to never tire of rehearing his "favorite" dog-eared book or story whose details he knows by heart. Books and stories provide him with experiences both new and familiar to him.

The interest span of a child is much more limited than that of an adult. The need for *change* appears often in the child's life. While it may be difficult to visit the park, explore the seashore, see the circus, or do other exciting things *all* the time, such visits can be recalled through the use of books. Similarly, the child can have a variety of experiences with the part of the world in which he lives, but books will help him to explore beyond this close-knit world.

Criteria to Use in Selecting Books for Preschoolers

How does one select books for three- and four-year-olds? Are there any guidelines to make the task easier? It is most important to remember that each child is an individual, having a unique combination of abilities and inabilities, likes and dislikes, securities and insecurities, and needs, opportunities, interests, moods, and environmental influences. Each child should be treated as the individual he is. Therefore, books need to be selected to fit his own personal and individual needs and desires.

But there are also some general factors that should be considered in selecting books for very young children.

First, books for preschool children should present things as they really are. It has been established that most preschool children cannot distinguish reality from fantasy. For them, anything is possible. Just listen to these suggestions: "Let's flush John down the toilet because he doesn't play nice," or, "You be the dog and I will be the garbage man." And because their acquaintance with the real world is in the here and now, they need a solid foundation with their immediate realistic world before they branch out to the unknown. Their stories should be about things with which they are familiar, or about experiences they could also share.

Second, the book should have one central character, preferably one of the approximate age of the child. When too many characters are introduced, the child is so busy trying to keep track of the characters that he loses track of the plot.

Third, the story should be a happy one. The character who does something that delights the child or makes him laugh is very welcome; that character can be a good influence. The child may be inclined to imitate such a character. Humor is very important to a young child, even though he may laugh at things that are not at all amusing to adults, and vice versa. Books that stir the emotions are disturbing to the child who has not yet gained control over his own emotions.

Fourth, stories that have a slight element of surprise or suspense hold the interest of a young child. He likes to guess at what will happen next or what is on the other side of the page. Even if he has heard the story before, he will still express excitement at the suspense.

Fifth, because language is fairly new to the young child, he enjoys the sounds that the spoken words bring into his life. He likes the rhythmic sound of repeated sayings or catch phrases ("It swam around, and around, and around, and around, and around, and around, and around."), and he likes the rhyming of words ("Molly took her dolly to see Polly."). Ideal books for young children are those that are full of repeated sayings, catch phrases, and fun-sounding words without being too lengthy or containing adult humor and concepts.

Sixth, the length of the story must be determined by the intensity of the child's interest at the time the story is read. Most young children can sit still for at least ten minutes when a story is read to them, but their interest will differ from time to time and from story to story. If a child is very interested in the story, you could stop and talk about the pictures or ask the child questions to lengthen the story. If the story seems to be too long for him, you could talk in general terms about the pictures as you skip through the text. The length of time spent in story reading should be determined by the child. He'll stay if he is interested, and he'll want to leave if he is bored. Make the storytime a relaxed, enjoyable time rather than a forced one. If you insist that the child sit quietly until you have completely read the story when he isn't interested, he will shy away from books and reading. Do everything you can to make reading enjoyable.

Seventh, the story should be of interest to the individual child. Most children enjoy similar topics but *all* children do not enjoy *all* topics. Select the story for the particular child. Reading about things beyond his understanding or remote from his interests detracts from the enjoyment of the occasion. Be aware of his needs, interests, attention span, and maturity level so that you can select his books wisely.

Eighth, illustrations should be clear, simple, and closely representative of the written text. Children enjoy colorful pictures, but some of their favorites are black and white, with or without the addition of one or two colors. More important than color is the authenticity of the reproductions. Modernistic drawings are confusing to young children, who want to see a picture of the object as it really is. Similarly, many unnecessary details detract from the picture. There could be some subtle or interesting things portrayed in the picture (a ladybug on a blade of grass or a rainbow in the background when the book is about horses, for example), but when the entire page is so cluttered that it lacks a focal point and the child doesn't know what to look at, he becomes confused and actually loses interest in the picture and the story.

The visual representation and the written text should coincide exactly. If there is a picture of a brown cow and the story talks about a black cow, for example, the child becomes confused, wondering whether the color he sees is brown or black. Or if the story is about three ducks but only two are pictured, the child wonders if his counting is wrong or what happened to the other duck. When the visual and written representations support each other, they strengthen concepts for the child. Misconceptions are often very difficult to correct. Photographs instead of illustrations can be very useful, especially when accompanying factual materials. Photographs can show comparative sizes of different objects, can picture things realistically, and therefore can help children clarify concepts.

Ninth, the amount of written text per page is also important. Young children like to move rather rapidly through the book. Remember, they are looking at the pictures and don't like to wait long periods of time looking at the same picture while the adult finishes reading the written text. Several sentences per double spread of pages take about as long to read as most young children are willing to wait.

Tenth, although some authors are noted for writing books for preschool children and can be relied upon for that age group while other authors write for different age levels, select the book for its own merits and not simply on the basis of the author's name. Select the book because of the values it can offer the child.

Eleventh, have plenty of time when you sit down to enjoy a book with a child. Let him know that reading is fun, that it's a way of sharing with each other, and that it deserves undivided attention. You will improve your child's later reading habits if you stress these aspects.

Criteria to Use
in Selecting Poetry for Children

The criteria for selecting poetry are the same as those listed for stories. Too often at the mention of poetry there are groans, shrugs of shoulders, and indications that poetry brings unpleasant memories. But that need not be. There are many delightful poems written for young children, and if they learn to love poetry at a young age, they will enjoy it forever.

Poetry can help children listen carefully. It is a tremendous vocabulary builder and allows children a different way of expressing their own feelings. Because poems are generally short and direct, they can be used when appropriate situations arise in a child's life—not when he is forced to learn it, but when he learns it because of his interest in the situation the poetry treats.

Poetry can be used for a number of reasons: its rhythm is pleasing to the ear, it is a concise way to convey a message, it helps the child increase his auditory awareness, and it gives him an opportunity to try new ideas and words. If you enjoy it, the child is sure to enjoy it. And if you will just try it, you will probably like it.

It seems that weighing the relative merits of these eleven points in selecting books for young children would cause you a great deal of time and concern. Actually, though, many books meet two, three, or more of the criteria. The important thing is that you select the book best suited to your child's unique needs. And how do you determine that? Read it!

Take your child to the library. Let him see where the children's books are. Show him several appropriate books, and let him select some from among them. He'll be using books for the rest of his life, and he needs a positive attitude toward them.

Sources Available to Help Parents in Selecting Children's Books

There are some sources that can help you select books, whether you are purchasing them or checking them out from the local library. The next time you go to the library, ask the librarian to direct you to the picture books or books for preschool children. She can assist you. *The Horn Book Magazine,* which should be available at the public library, gives information on books for young children. The Association for Childhood Education, International, in Washington, D.C., publishes two helpful pamphlets (which are revised every two years): *A Bibliography of Books for Children* and *Children's Books for $1.25 or Less.*

Other sources on children's literature include the following:

Children and Books, by May H. Arbuthnot, published by Scott, Foresman & Company.

Books Before Five, by Dorothy White, published by Oxford University Press.

The Years Before School, by Todd and Heffernan, published by Macmillan Company.

A Child Goes Forth, by Barbara J. Taylor, published by Brigham Young University Press.

Articles and book reviews in publications like *Childhood Education, Young Children, The Early Years,* and *Parents' Magazine* could also be used as aids in selecting books. Each year the Newberry Award is given for the best contribution to children's literature. The local librarian could refer you to the list of Newberry Award winners. The Caldecott Award is also granted yearly for the best illustrations in a child's book; books receiving this award are also listed at the library. But while these awards cover the general area of children's literature, they are not necessarily limited to books for preschool children. So, even if the book has received one of these awards, you should read it to determine its appropriateness for your preschool child.

Now, what happens if you do all these things (select the books carefully, sit down in a nice relaxed atmosphere, and so on) and the child doesn't want to listen to the stories? Should you give up? By no means. Instead, take his indifference as an extra challenge: watch for things that really interest the child—whether it be airplanes, cars, bugs, or whatever—and then find an interesting book on that topic.

You might begin by simply looking at the pictures with your child. You might just leave the book where he is bound to see it. Don't force him to look at it or read it with you. Talk about some of the things in the book in a very relaxed way. "Yes, ladybugs are red with black spots on their backs. I wonder what they like to eat. Maybe we could find out in this book." Suggest that he look through the book. Glance through it yourself, letting him know that there are some interesting things about ladybugs that you didn't know either. Find a ladybug and compare it with a picture. Tell him that he can find out more about it by reading the book.

If your child still isn't interested in books, don't get upset. If you make them enjoyable and desirable, he'll be attracted to them, even if it takes a while.

Many possible factors could make a child seem uninterested in books. Perhaps his visual perception is impaired. If he doesn't hear clearly, the words may sound like one long string of meaningless sounds. Maybe he has been forced too often to sit and hear a story when he would rather build with blocks or play with someone. Maybe the books haven't met his needs. Could it have been that they were too advanced for him in concept or language?

Unnecessary details, morals, unrealistic ideas, or other elements that a child can't relate to will confuse him. Perhaps he resents books because Mother or Daddy has been buried in a book or newspaper whenever he wanted their attention, advice, or action. If any of these, or other, reasons apply to your child, don't dwell on the past; set a new goal to help him enjoy books.

Many children who have not had the opportunity to hear stories at home will have a difficult time sitting still long enough to hear stories, information, or instructions at school. The interest span of such a child is so short that he won't know how to respond to such demands. No matter how limited a time schedule parents have, no matter how many children are in the family, no matter how much parents may prefer other activities, the child still suffers if he doesn't have a pleasant introduction to books, stories, and poetry. Can you afford to let him suffer when there is such a wealth of good literature at our fingertips?

Summary and Conclusion

Books, stories, and poetry are valuable aids to the child's development of proper language. Hearing correct sentence structure, though simple in form, helps children to learn vocabulary and correct verb usage, and to gain confidence in their own speaking abilities.

Some basic needs of a child can be filled through being with an adult as he listens and shares stories and ideas. The child's sense of security, self-image, intellectual stability, and acceptance by others outside and inside the home is greatly increased through such times of closeness, quiet, and sharing of good literature.

ACTIVITIES: ASSISTING YOUR CHILD'S CREATIVITY THROUGH LITERATURE

1. Take your child to the library and show him where he can find books appropriate to his age and interest. Allow your child to select books for reading at home. If he does not already have his own library card, now would be an ideal time for him to get one.

2. Make a commitment to take the time each day to read to each of your children. Note the time you spend reading to them each day for one week, the results of each experience, and any suggestions for improving future reading experiences.

Day	Time Spent	Results	Suggestions for Improvement
Monday			
Tuesday			
Wednesday			

Thursday			
Friday			
Saturday			
Sunday			

What is your goal regarding reading with your children for the weeks to come?

Criteria for the selection of children's literature
  Realistic
  One central character
  Happy mood
  An element of surprise or suspense
  Repeated sayings and fun-sounding words
  Length appropriate to the interest span of the child
  Subject should be of interest to the child
  Illustrations which are clear, simple, and representative of the text

Available sources to aid in the selection of children's books
  The Horn Book Magazine
  A Bibliography of Books for Children, from the Association for Childhood Education, International, Washington, D.C.
  Children's Books for $1.25 or Less, from the Association for Childhood Education, International, Washington, D.C.
  Children and Books, May H. Arbuthnot, Scott, Foresman and Company.

Books Before Five, Dorothy White, Oxford University Press.

The Years Before School, Todd and Hefferman, Macmillan Company.

A Child Goes Forth, Barbara J. Taylor, Brigham Young University Press.

Also valuable are articles and book reviews in publications such as *Childhood Education, Young Children, The Early Years,* and *Parents' Magazine.*

UNIT VI
ACADEMIC AND
PHYSICAL SKILLS

One distinguishing characteristic that separates man from the lesser creatures in his world is his ability to think and reason and be concerned about his world and be actively involved in it. In order for man to exist, he must use his abilities to develop certain skills and tools. Most skills are learned; those related to man's physical growth require repeated attempts at mastery (or refinement), along with exercise, physical exertion, and abundant activity.

Academic skills, too, are learned, used, refined, or extinguished, depending upon the amount of exposure to new experiences and new situations and the relevance of past experiences. Learning new skills provides man with various avenues of response. He receives strength and power from some physical and academic tools and skills, he gains added experience and new-found abilities from others, and he receives sheer enjoyment or entertainment from still others.

This unit presents ways for parents to understand their children's progress in acquiring certain skills and tools and instructs parents about how to help children develop or increase their proficiency in other skills and tools.

CHAPTER 27
DEVELOPING THE HANDWRITING
OF CHILDREN

One writer recently estimated that businessmen in the United States lose over one million dollars a week due to mistakes, delays, and problems resulting directly from illegible handwriting. The Post Office reports that millions of letters end up in the dead letter office each year because the addresses are so poorly written that postal employees are unable to decipher them.

Even in this day of typewriters and computer printing, good handwriting is an important skill. As parents, you are concerned about how well your children write. You recognize that it is important that good writing habits be established early in a child's school career. But many parents are confused about how to help their children with handwriting skills. Some hesitate to comment at all about the child's work, while others set impossibly high standards for their children, not knowing what is reasonable for the child's age and maturity. Yet parents are in an excellent position to help their children with writing skills, because handwriting is one school subject the child uses often at home. Letters, notes, telephone messages, family schedules, shopping lists, and reminders all require a child to use handwriting skills at home.

How to Help Children Develop
Good Handwriting Skills

How can you help your child with his handwriting? You can show by your attitude and performance that you believe legible handwriting to be important and possible. Parental attitudes expressed in comments such as, "Of course Bill doesn't write well. Look at his father's writing. What else can you expect!" or, "You never could read Uncle George's writing and he's done very well professionally," or, "I wish he could do better but maybe someday he'll learn to type anyway," are bound to influence the child's feelings negatively about the importance of good writing.

The best way to show your child that you believe good handwriting to be important is to write clearly yourself. This may require conscious improvement on your part and the changing of long-established habits, but as your child sees your efforts he will realize that good writing is a worthwhile goal. Create situations where you need to communicate with your child in writing, such as dropping a note in his lunchbox, sending surprise letters or postcards to him in the mail, writing him instructions for household chores, posting lists and reminders for the family on the bulletin board, and writing down telephone messages. Show him by the care you take with these communications that you take pride in your writing.

Modern Handwriting Instruction

Another way to help your child is to become aware of the goals of modern handwriting instruction and to learn what you can reasonably expect from your child at different stages of development.

Not too long ago, children were taught to write by a series of tedious exercises that were designed to perfect various writing strokes or letters but did not have any relationship to meaningful communication. Perhaps you remember the old "push-pull" exercises from your childhood. Today, it is recognized that the first purpose for writing is to communicate ideas in written form, that instruction must be related to meaning, and that exercises and practice should grow out of real communication needs. Every child, as well as every adult, delights in receiving his "own" note expressing a personalized message or individualized instruction from someone interested in him. These messages convey direct concern and are a good example of how ideas can be communicated.

The first criterion for deciding what is adequate or inadequate writing performance is whether the written message can be read. This does not mean, however, that as long as writing can be deciphered it doesn't matter whether it is neat and attractive, but major emphasis is always placed upon meaning. Usually legible handwriting has a pleasing appearance. As you work with your child, your goal should be to help him communicate his ideas clearly in writing. His desire to please you or his teacher or his desire to earn a good mark on his paper should never be as important to him—or to you—as his desire to make himself understood.

Expectations of
Handwriting Skill Development

How does handwriting skill develop and what can you expect from your child as he progresses through school? Before entering school, most children have a desire to write, and many actually begin forming a few letters. The first words a child writes are usually his own name and the names of others in his family. It is useful at this point if the parent has a copy of the manuscript alphabet the child will use in school; the child should be shown correct forms as he begins to write. One common problem with kindergarten children is that some have already formed incorrect writing habits that may be difficult to correct. For instance, many children begin to write by using all capital letters. They can learn to write small letters just as easily if parents help them begin that way. A child's first writing attempts should be with large paper and crayons or on a chalkboard with chalk, since his fine muscle coordination is probably not yet fully developed.

The first alphabet the child uses is *manuscript writing*. These letter forms are commonly called "printing," since they resemble the forms found in books and other printed materials. Manuscript letters are formed using straight lines, slanted lines, circles, and parts of circles. The writing is straight up and down, not slanted, and each letter is formed separately. Words are separated by leaving extra space between one word and the next. Manuscript writing is preferred for young children because it requires less muscle control and has fewer different strokes than cursive writing, which is learned later.

Children vary widely in their readiness for beginning writing. The kindergarten or first grade teacher watches closely for motor coordination, desire, and other signs of readiness. The child's first writing attempts in school are carefully guided, with the teacher avoiding undue pressure and accepting the child's efforts enthusiastically. *Reversals* (letters written backwards) are common in the beginning writing stage, and the child usually corrects these errors himself as he gains experience.

If your child is in kindergarten or first grade and is beginning to write in school, help him by praising his work and by giving him opportunities to show you his skill at home. Provide lined paper, if possible. If you do not have regular lined school paper, you can draw the lines yourself, about one inch apart, alternating light and heavy lines. The capital letters fill the space between two dark lines, while small letters occupy the space between a light line and a dark line (with the exception of t, d, f, h, k, l, and b, which have strokes beginning above the line, and q, y, p, g, and j, which have strokes ending below the line). As the child matures, his writing becomes smaller and the lines should be reduced in width.

At first your child will not know the letters from memory, and you will need to supply a copy of the material he wants to write. Be certain the letter forms you give him to copy are the same as those he has learned in school and that they are about the same size as you expect him to write. Avoid having the child trace your work. He will learn more quickly if he forms his own letters with your copy as a reference only.

Most children learn manuscript writing quickly and are able to use it as an effective tool throughout the first and second grade years. Sometime during the third grade, and occasionally earlier or later, the child is ready to make the transition to cursive writing. Cursive writing differs from manuscript in that the writing slants, letters within words are joined, and letter forms are different from those found in printed material. Most children are anxious to learn cursive writing since it represents "grown-up" writing to them.

You can help your child become ready for cursive writing by helping him read cursive forms. It is important to obtain a copy of the cursive alphabet your child's school uses, since there are a variety of systems and it is possible that some of the letter forms you normally use in your writing will differ from those your child will learn in school. It is not necessary for you to change your customary handwriting, however, as long as you point out to your child the differences in letter forms so that he will not become confused.

As the child increases his skill in using cursive writing, emphasis in writing instruction is placed more and more upon helping the child evaluate his own written work and upon maintaining quality in his writing. A child in the intermediate grades is ready to learn the characteristics of good handwriting and to be helped to judge his own written products.

Special Problems Affect Handwriting Skills

Thus far we have been talking about normal development for most children in writing. However, some children have special learning problems—motor, neurological, or visual handicaps—and will need special consideration and may require more time to develop handwriting skill. Often such children have difficulties with cursive writing, but can master manuscript writing readily.

In many instances it is better for a child with a problem to continue using manuscript writing throughout his school career. However, the decision as to whether he should make the effort to learn cursive writing should be left to the child, since there is a high social premium attached to "grown-up" writing by his classmates. Many children who do not have learning handicaps prefer manuscript writing and continue to use it even after they learn cursive.

Another individual difference important in learning to write is the child's hand preference. The left-handed child needs special instruction as he learns to write, but he should not be considered nor labeled a "problem child." With one or two minor adjustments, the left-handed student can learn as readily and easily as his right-handed classmates. When writing manuscript letters on paper or at the chalkboard, the left-handed child should hold his pencil or chalk further from the point than the right-handed child so that his hand will not cover his work as he writes.

With cursive writing, the left-handed child slants his paper to the right instead of the left and holds his pencil a little further back than usual. In the past teachers were concerned when the left-handed child slanted his letters to the left rather than to the right or when his letters were vertical rather than slanted. If the slant to the left is uniform and not so extreme that it interferes with legibility, or if the vertical letters are legible, there is no reason why the left-handed child should be expected to change the slant to the right.

An Approach toward Handwriting Legibility

Now that you understand the objectives of handwriting instruction and are familiar with the developmental steps a child takes in learning to write, you can learn to analyze your own and your child's handwriting to discover why it is legible or illegible and you can discover what specific changes need to be made to improve legibility. It is not enough to label a handwriting sample as "good" or "poor" or to constantly remind your child to "write better." Unless he knows what to do to change his writing, he cannot do any better.

227

Whether or not a detailed analysis of handwriting problems is useful depends, of course, upon the stage of development the child is in. Children in the beginning stages of either manuscript or cursive writing are not helped too much by having their errors pointed out to them. Continued practice with a correct copy of the alphabet readily available helps more at this point than a detailed analysis of problems. However, you may wish to use the analysis techniques without discussing the information with your child so that you can encourage him to practice the letters or characteristics that he needs. When the child has become proficient in either manuscript or cursive writing, an understanding of the characteristics of legible handwriting and practice in evaluating his own work against some criteria are helpful.

Evaluation of Handwriting Characteristics

The characteristics of handwriting that may be evaluated include: (1) letter forms (are the letters made correctly?); (2) letter size (are the letters consistent in size and in relationship to each other?); (3) spacing (is the space between letters and between words consistent and not too close or too far apart?); (4) slant (is manuscript writing consistently vertical; is cursive writing evenly slanted or consistently vertical?); (5) alignment (is the writing even on the bottom?); and (6) line quality (are the letters too light or dark and are they consistent in darkness or lightness?)

How are these characteristics evaluated? Begin by looking at a sample of your own handwriting. Find something you have written recently—a letter, a note, or a telephone message. If you can't find anything, write a few lines as a sample, using your normal handwriting. Now consider the sample against each of the six characteristics separately.

Letter Form

To evaluate letter form, take a small card and punch a hole in it with a paper punch or cut a small hole in it with manicure scissors. Place the card over your handwriting sample and look at each letter, one at a time, through the hole. Do you recognize the letter easily when it is isolated from the rest of your writing? Sometimes illegible letters are not detected because the word can be deciphered in context from the rest of the letters, but the same letter formed incorrectly in another word may make the word unreadable. Keep a record of any letters you do not form correctly. Some common cursive letter form problems include failure to fully close a's,

228

o's, and d's, making them look like u's; a's mistaken for o's; i's either not dotted or dotted too far away from the rest of the letter; failure to make an open loop in the e; making b's, d's, t's, and l's too short; failure to make a sharp point at the top of r and s; making the loop below the line too small in y, g, and p.

Letter Size

Size of letters may also be evaluated with the punched card. By looking at several letters, one after the other, it may be determined if some letters are definitely too small or too large in relationship to the rest of the writing.

Spacing and Slant

These may be evaluated together. Place the edge of a card or the edge of a piece of paper under your line of writing. Draw a line through the center of each letter, following the degree of slant, and extend the line onto the card. Move the card away from your writing and look at the lines you have drawn. Is the slant consistent, or are some letters slanted more or in a different direction than the others? Look at the space between letters. Is it uniform and consistent? Look at the space between words. Is it adequate and consistent, or would your writing be better with a little more or less space between words?

Alignment

Now place the edge of the card underneath the writing again. Look for alignment. Do all the letters touch the edge of the card, or do some rest above or below the card?

Line Quality

Now look at the writing sample as a whole. Are the letters evenly dark or light? Some problems with line quality are a result of the writing instrument, but uneven quality—inconsistency in lightness or darkness—may result from holding the pencil or pen too tightly or not tightly enough.

Once you have identified your own problems, you can improve your handwriting through practice. If you have difficulties with letter forms or letter size, practice your specific problem letters by finding words in which the letters occur and by writing those words several times. Problems in slant and alignment are often due to writing in a cramped position, writing too quickly or too slowly, or not slanting your paper when writing. Experiment with writing position and speed until you see improvement in these areas.

229

After you have analyzed your own handwriting, take a look at your child's work, keeping in mind the basic goal of legibility and remembering also his stage of development. Don't forget, too, that analysis means finding strong as well as weak points. It is probably more important to praise your child's good writing features than to criticize his mistakes. If your child is writing fluently without having to refer to copy, he is probably ready to assume some responsibility for his own improvement and can benefit from doing his own handwriting evaluation.

In summary, it is important to remember that handwriting is definitely a skill and is improved with guided practice just as skiing, dancing, or any other skill is improved. The most important steps a parent can take in guiding development of handwriting skill are: (1) to believe it is important to write well and to show your child that you care by your own handwriting; (2) to recognize your child's stage of development and accept his efforts, giving deserved praise freely; and (3) to be specific with recommendations for improvement. Consider the outlined handwriting characteristics given here as a guide for evaluating your child's progress and for defining areas that need attention or improvement.

ACTIVITIES: HANDWRITING

1. During the period of one week show the value of good handwriting by using it daily to take and give messages, to make family schedules and shopping lists, and to remind your children of daily responsibilities. Other suggestions might include dropping affectionate notes in their school lunches or sending surprise letters or postcards in the mail. Remember the value of good handwriting as an example to your children.

2. Make an appointment with the teachers of your children to discover how you can best help your children with their handwriting. Perhaps you could get a copy of the handwriting guide used in the classrooms to further inform you and to guide you in assisting your children's practice at home. The teachers will also be helpful in making you aware of the recommended performance level for each child.

3. Evaluate your handwriting. Punch a small hole in a 3" x 5" card. Place the card over a sample of your handwriting, looking at each letter individually through the hole. Do you recognize the letter eas-

ily when it is isolated from the rest of your writing? Check for the following:

1. Letter form (are the letters made correctly?)
2. Letter size (are the letters consistent in size and in relationship to each other?)
3. Spacing (is the space between letters and words consistent, being neither too close nor too far apart?)
4. Slant (is manuscript writing consistently vertical; is cursive writing evenly slanted or consistently vertical?)
5. Alignment (to check, hold the card underneath your writing. Is the writing even on the bottom?)
6. Line quality (are the letters too light or too dark? Are they consistent in darkness or lightness?)

List the areas in which your handwriting can be improved.

Practice your handwriting.

4. After you have analyzed your own handwriting, take a look at each of your children's work, keeping in mind the basic goal of legibility as well as each child's stage of development. Don't forget that analysis means finding strong points as well as weak. Praise their good writing features often. If they are writing fluently without referring to copy they are probably ready to assume some responsibility for improvement and may benefit from doing their own handwriting evaluation. Be specific when giving suggestions.

CHAPTER 28
PHYSICAL MOVEMENT
AND RHYTHM

If you have ever tried to hold a young child on your lap during a church service or struggled to keep a preschool boy or girl quietly confined to a small area, you know that children have to move and to be active. What we often overlook is the fact that movement is essential to physical growth. Physical activity stimulates bone growth, develops lung capacity, and aids in blood circulation. Only through movement can the muscular strength and coordination necessary to sit, stand, and walk be adequately developed.

Movement Results in Learning

In addition to promoting the physical growth that comes as a result of being active, children also move in order to learn about themselves and the world around them. Through random, thrashing movements, the infant gradually learns to control his arms enough to reach for and grasp a bright object that is dangled in front of him. He discovers, after frequent attempts, that he can bring his hand to his mouth whenever he desires. These early learnings about himself and what he can do with his body are a result of movement.

As a child's muscular strength and coordination increases, he learns to creep, to stand, and to walk. These skills not only help him become independent, but they expand his world and the things he can explore. As the young twelve- to fifteen-month-old learns to coordinate his legs and his arms, he is also learning about the world surrounding him. This is the age when children discover, often to the dismay of parents, how to open drawers and cupboards, how to climb onto tables and benches, and how to get out of cribs. Although this stage of development is often difficult for parents, it is an important time for young children to develop the motor coordination necessary for learning other more complex skills later in life.

Once children can walk and run with ease, they can begin to learn about themselves and space through a variety of physical activities. The child discovers that the world looks different when he is hanging upside down from a horizontal bar or while he is standing on the top of a slide. Things look and feel different to a child if he is spinning around, crawling under something, walking backwards or sideways, or riding in a wagon. As the child explores the world around him in these many ways, he also learns to coordinate his movements accordingly. If he is going to jump from a bench, he must assess the distance, judge where he will land, and finally coordinate his movements.

Through motor activities of this kind, a child can begin to develop confidence and self-control. He learns what he can do as he takes risks and tests himself in situations that require power, strength, and skill. Who can doubt a child's feelings about himself when he shouts, "Hey, look at me!" after he has climbed to the top of the slide all by himself?

Within recent years some educators (Coghill, Piaget, Strauss, Kephart, Doman, and Delacato) have been looking at physical activity and its importance in the lives of young children in still another way: movement can be important in the development of learning, because the very first things a child learns are those things that involve moving. These scholars maintain that all later learning is based on these early motor learnings. In fact, Dr. Newell Kephart believes that if a child has difficulty moving in a coordinated way, he might experience difficulty with future learnings as he begins school.

A number of studies have supported this idea. One study using fourth-, fifth-, and sixth-grade children showed that there was a high relationship between achievement in school and the ability to balance and coordinate movements (Ismail, Cowell, Kephart). Another study done with children who were experiencing academic difficulty in school showed that those same children improved scholastically after they participated in a physical education program that emphasized mastery of basic movements such as running, jumping, throwing, and climbing.

Although these studies relate to children of school age, preschool children should master many foundational skills involving movement and the physical body. These skills help provide the necessary background experiences that will enable children to perform tasks expected of them as they enter school. These learnings involve basic body awareness, directionality, eye-hand coordination, and balance. Each of these skills will be more fully discussed later, and suggested activities will be described.

To move is not only fun for the young child: it is essential. By participating in the activities of play, children aid their body's physical growth, learn about themselves and their world, gain self-confidence, and prepare themselves for more complex learnings.

Helping Children Develop Physical Skills

Because physical activity is so important to the growth and development of the preschool child, it should not be left to chance. The following principles and activities provide guidelines for parents who desire to help their children enjoy a physically active and healthy childhood.

Principle 1: Vigorous activity is essential to promote physical growth.

Physical exercise stimulates growth of the body's tissues, organs, and bones. If you have ever broken an arm or a leg and had it immobilized by a cast, you know how quickly muscles decrease in size when they are not used. Lack of exercise also affects the lateral growth of bones. Likewise, normal growth of the heart and lungs can only be stimulated by vigorous exercise.

In our urbanized society modern conveniences—such as automation and television—deprive children of the essential motor exploration and activity that is necessary for physical development. In the busy routine of everyday living, even adults often don't take time for adequate physical activity; this is frequently reflected in the lives of their children. On a winter day it is often easier to encourage a young child to watch television than to take the time to help him put on boots, mittens, a coat, and a hat so that he can go outside for vigorous play. In addition, increased urbanization has resulted in fewer places where children *can* play. In some instances, the nurturing and growing of grass that can be a showpiece seems more important than providing a space for children to play and engage in physical activity.

It is estimated that preschool and school-age children need four to five hours of physical activity each day (Lawrence, Rarick). Recognizing this, it is essential that parents provide places and time for their children to engage in vigorous play activities. Consider the following:

1. Plan *specific* times each day when your child can participate in vigorous play activities. Don't schedule other things—like practicing the piano or accompanying you on a shopping trip—that will take the child away during his play time.

2. Participate with your child. (Adults need activity, too!) Plan enough time so you can walk to the neighbor's house or to the store. Encourage your child to run ahead and then run back to you. Challenge him to run to the last tree before you count to ten, to return back to you before you count to five, and so on.

3. Designate a specific area in your yard that can be used for play activities. Keep in mind that children need a fairly large space so that they can run and climb. Ropes tied securely to a tree or pipes sunk in cement provide inexpensive but practical play equipment. (Note: Climbing activities help to develop upper arm strength, but little is gained in terms of coordination or strength from simply swinging in a swing. You might consider replacing swings with climbing ropes on home playground equipment.)

Principle 2: Some basic motor skills are necessary for future academic learning. These skills include body awareness, directionality, eye-hand coordination, and balance.

1. *Body awareness* means that a child knows the names, movements, functions, and locations of his body parts. Without this knowledge, a child cannot develop an adequate image of his body and what it can do.
   To develop this awareness, a child should experience a variety of movements that require using the whole body as well as a variety of movements that involve specific body parts. The following activities help the young child develop body awareness:

   A. Point to some part of the child's body, and ask him to name the part.

236

B. Name a body part, and have your child touch it. "Simon Says" can be used for this activity: the child touches a body part only if the adult says, "Simon says touch . . . ." If the instruction is not preceded by "Simon Says," the child is not to touch a body part. (Note: Use *all* body parts, not just the common ones. Consider asking the child to touch his head, eyes, eyelashes, eyebrows, ears, nose, cheeks, chin, mouth, forehead, neck, shoulders, chest, back, abdomen, waist, hips, buttocks, arms, elbows, wrists, hands, palms, fingers, legs, knees, ankles, feet, toes, soles, and heels.)

C. Have the child lie down on a large piece of paper while you draw a line around the child's body. Ask the child to point to various body parts. A puzzle can be made by cutting the paper body into pieces and having the child assemble it.

D. Using magazine pictures of people, ask the child to cut out designated body parts such as feet, hands, head, ears, and so on.

E. Ask the child to touch one body part to another body part (for instance, "Touch your elbow to your knee"). "Simon Says" can be played with this game.

F. If you need a game for a small group, have each child choose a partner. An adult or older child calls out the name of a body part, and the partners touch this part together (for instance, "knees to knees" or "hands to hands"). On the command "change" the children find new partners.

G. Have the child sit inside a hula hoop or circle made of yarn or rope. Call out body parts, and have the child respond by placing the designated body part outside the hoop. More than one body part can be called. A variation is to call a number, and the child must put that number of body part outside the hoop. You can then ask him to identify which body part he has used. To make this game more difficult, you might say, "Put three body parts outside the hoop, but you cannot use your hands or feet."

2. *Directionality* is the ability to move the body in a controlled way into space in all directions. It is important to develop directionality in order to be able to move in space, to make judgments about space, and to solve problems in space. The following activities aid in the development of directionality:

A. Ask the child to identify the top, bottom, and sides of himself and of various objects around him. Have him identify the top, bottom, and sides of the room.

237

B. Instruct the child to move to certain places in the room. ("Stand near the refrigerator." "Stand with your back to the couch.") This can be modified by asking the child to point. ("Point to the wall nearest you." "Which chair is farthest from the table?")

C. Set up an obstacle course that requires the child to go over, under, and around various pieces of furniture or household objects. Have the child verbalize what he is doing. Chairs, wastepaper baskets, bottles, boxes, ropes, and yarn are good objects for making obstacle courses. Let children make their own obstacle courses and then tell you about what they do.

D. Direct the child to move in specific patterns within a given space. ("Run forward ten steps and walk backward five steps." "Put your feet together and jump to one side.") If children are under five years of age, give only one direction at a time.

3. *Eye-hand coordination* is the ability to work the eyes and hands together as intended. Control and accuracy are needed in this skill, which is essential for success in school. Eye-hand coordination is needed in order to button a coat, catch a ball, cut with scissors, color, print, or write. The following activities can aid in the development of good eye-hand coordination:

A. Give the child a balloon. He can do the following: hit the balloon with his hand as high and as many times as possible without letting it touch the floor; hit the balloon in the air with a wooden paddle or a paper plate; hit the balloon to a partner; rebound the balloon off a wall; or hit the balloon with different parts of his body.

B. Have the child pound wooden pegs into holes, using as few swings as possible. After accuracy and strength develop, use real nails and allow the child to pound them at random or in a definite formation.

C. Soap bubbles provide an excellent activity for developing eye-hand coordination. Have children pop the bubbles by poking them with different fingers, clapping them between hands, or hitting them with different body parts (head, elbow, and so on).

D. Have the child stack wooden blocks or paper cups as high as possible.

E. Children can develop eye-hand coordination by using clip clothespins. Clothespin activities include: the child holds a clothespin in each hand and grasps cards or pictures being held in the hands of an adult; child quickly puts clothespins on the edge of a cardboard box; child attaches colored clothespins to matching colors on a color wheel.

F. All ball throwing and catching activities are good for developing eye-hand coordination. Use a ball at least eight inches in circumference for young children.

4. *Balance* is the ability to maintain equilibrium. Lack of balance makes it difficult for children to move in a coordinated manner. A child who lacks balance falls frequently and bumps into objects. Help a child develop balance by helping him with the following:

A. While standing on both feet, have the child move his arms in various positions and instruct him to place his feet apart, close together, heel to toe, right foot in front; and heel to toe, left foot in front.

B. Put a ladder on the floor and have the child walk inside the sections. Then have him balance while walking on the rungs and edges of the ladder.

C. With a small group, play "statue"—have the children move around freely until you say "Freeze." The children must then balance in the position they were stopped in until you give the command to move again.

D. Roll a ball toward the child and instruct him to kick it back with his right or left foot.

E. Have the child jump or hop in place and maintain his balance while doing so.

F. Attach looped ropes to shortening cans or regular number ten cans through holes punched near the top. Have the child hold onto the ropes and walk with his feet on the cans.

G. Jumping (two feet together) is good for learning balance. The child can jump several times in succession, jump in various directions, jump over objects, jump a rope while it is being held stationary, and jump in and out of tires.

Principle 3: Physical activity is fun and can be enjoyed by the entire family.

As you make plans to encourage and promote your family's participation in physical activities, keep in mind that such activities are best enjoyed with others. Consider:

1. When planning family outings try to select activities that will allow children to get physical exercise. Having a picnic in a park meets this objective better than going to a movie.

2. When you are going to purchase a game for a child or for the family, look for games that involve physical activity or the skills of balance, body awareness, or eye-hand coordination.
3. Remember—example is the best teacher. Play *with* your child. Show him that *you* enjoy physical activity, too!

In conclusion, movement is important in the lives of young children; we have discussed three principles that stress this importance. These principles and the activities suggested to implement them are just a beginning. Hopefully, they have helped you understand and appreciate the importance of physical activity in your child's life. Are you ready to accept the challenge? Begin *today* to plan for and participate in physical activity. Remember—it's as vital for you as for your child.

ACTIVITIES: PHYSICAL MOVEMENT AND RHYTHM

1. Plan specific times each day when your child can participate in vigorous play activities. Provide a large space in the yard for the explicit purpose of play, to include both running and climbing.

2. Participate in physical activities with your child. Plan enough time to walk to the neighbor's house or to the store. Encourage your child to run ahead of you and then to run back. Challenge him to run to the farthest tree before you count to ten, to return to you before you count to five, and so on.

3. Have your child lie down on a large piece of paper while you trace the outline of his body. After you have completed this, have him point to the various body parts on the drawing while he names them. A puzzle can be made by cutting the paper body into pieces.

4. Participate in this game for a small group: Each child needs a partner. An adult or older child calls out the name of a body part. The partners are to touch this part together; for example, "knees to knees" or "hands to hands"). On the command "change," each child is to find a new partner.

5. Play "Simon Says." The child is to do everything that is preceded by those words. For example, upon hearing "Simon says to wiggle your nose," the child should wiggle his nose. "Touch your eyes"

should not be followed, because it was not preceded by "Simon Says."

6. Have your child touch one body part to another. For example, say to him, "Touch your elbow to your knee." "Simon Says" can be played with this game.

7. Have your child sit inside a circle made of yarn or rope. As you call out the names of body parts, the child should respond by placing that part of his body outside the circle. More than one body part can be called at the same time.

8. Ask your child to identify the top, bottom, and side of himself and of various objects around the room.

9. Instruct your child to move to certain places in the room ("Stand near the refrigerator" or "Stand with your back to the couch"). This game can be modified by having the child point or by his giving the instructions.

10. Set up an obstacle course that requires the child to go over, under, around, and on top of objects placed in his way. Have him verbalize what he does. Chairs, wastepaper baskets, bottles, boxes, ropes, and yarn are good objects to use in making the obstacle course.

11. Direct your child to move in specific patterns within a given space. Such instructions as "Put your feet together and jump to one side" or "Run forward ten steps" can be used.

12. Give your child practice at hitting nails into a piece of wood with a hammer.

13. Fill a balloon with air and allow your child to do the following activities:
   A. Hit the balloon with his hand as high and as many times as possible without letting it touch the floor.
   B. Hit the balloon in the air with a wooden paddle or a paper plate.
   C. Hit the balloon to a partner.
   D. Rebound the balloon off a wall.
   E. Hit the balloon with different parts of the body.

14. Allow your child to play with a large ball. All ball throwing and catching activities are very beneficial. The ball should be at least eight inches in circumference if a child under the age of five is involved.

15. Ask your child to swing his arms while he moves his feet apart, close together, heel to toe, and so on.

16. Put a ladder on the floor and ask your child to walk inside the sections. Then have him balance while walking on the rungs and the edges of the ladder.

17. Roll a ball toward the child and instruct him to kick it back with his right or left foot.

18. Attach ropes securely through the tops of two large cans. The child should be able to hold on to the ropes while he stands on the cans, using the cans as stilts.

19. Jumping of any kind is good for learning balance. The child can jump several times in succession, jump in various directions, jump over objects, jump a rope while it is being held stationary, and jump in and out of tires.

20. Plan a family outing. Try to select an activity that will allow your child to get physical exercise. A picnic in a park meets this objective much better than going to a movie. Join in and have fun.

21. Together, take up a family sport: choose an active sport such as cycling, tennis, bowling, and so on.

CHAPTER 29
READING AND
THE YOUNG CHILD

Because a child's success in school depends largely upon his reading skill, nothing he does in school is more likely to concern his parents than how well he reads. Perhaps you remember your own experience in learning to read; if you do, you probably recall that the process brought you either great satisfaction or great frustration. There are a number of reasons why reading is so important and why so much attention has been—and should be—given to reading in the school curriculum.

Reading Expectations for the Child

First, a child's reading skill is inseparably connected with his feeling about himself. A good reader usually has high self-esteem, while a child with reading problems nearly always has a low concept of himself. Cause-effect is not clear here: whether a poor self-concept prevents a child from learning to read or whether reading failure causes a poor self-image cannot easily be answered. It *is* clear, however, that improvement in reading strengthens confidence and self-esteem. We also know that experiences that build confidence will

243

help a child learn to read. Thus, in our culture, learning to read is necessary not only for academic achievement, but also for good mental health.

Second, reading is a basic tool for acquiring information and for broadening experience vicariously. Until the advent of radio, television, and similar instant forms of communication, reading was the only link most people had with the rest of the world. But even today, with all the electronic aids for learning, the written word remains our most constant, dependable source of information.

Third, written records are the basic means for passing on our culture from one generation to the next. Man is separated from animals by his ability to learn from the experience of others through oral and written communication. Reading enables man to accurately interpret such communication.

Fourth, reading is an important form of recreation. Enjoying the creative efforts of others, escaping into worlds of fantasy, and living with people who are separated from us by time and space adds depth and color to our lives. No movie, play, or television show offers the satisfaction obtained from stretching one's imagination with a good book.

What Is Reading?

What should a child do if he wants to read well? First, he should take part in activities that encourage good speaking, listening, or writing. These three skills, together with reading, constitute what we call *language*, the process by which humans communicate ideas. Speaking and writing are the means of expressing ideas; listening and reading are the means of receiving those ideas. All four skills are related because they require an understanding of words and other symbols that represent ideas. It is critical to all four that both the sender and the receiver of information share common experiences. Thus, activities promoting good speaking, listening, and writing will also help reading.

Recognizing and Understanding Symbols

Second, we must remember that writing, like speech, is composed of symbols *arbitrarily* adopted to represent ideas. Our alphabet, grammar system, spelling, and vocabulary have cultural rather than natural roots, so reading skill can be acquired not by natural, biological maturation, but by systematic teaching and conscious learning.

For many years it was thought that parents lacked the training required to teach children, and that children could not absorb—and therefore should not be exposed to—formal reading instruction until the magic age of six. Thus, it was believed, the teaching of reading should be left to the school and, preferably, to the first-grade teacher.

Recently, however, numerous studies have shown that many children are ready to read and do learn to read long before the age of six. And, as a result, the popular press and other media are now giving wide publicity to various reading programs for the preschooler. In fact, some writers have suggested that parents who do not begin a child's formal reading instruction before he goes to school are derelict in their responsibility. These same writers feel that children who are not instructed at home will be intellectually handicapped for the rest of their lives.

On the other hand, many educators and psychologists view with alarm the trend toward early reading. They warn that such programs place young children under a stress that may be harmful.

Parents are caught in the middle.

Much disagreement about early reading has arisen from the misinterpretation of data concerning the intellectual development of young children. The fact that *some* children *can* learn to read at a very early age does not mean that *all* children *should* learn to read before going to school. Even though quantities of data have been collected, our knowledge about early mental development is still sketchy. While it is clear that parents must stimulate the intellectual growth of young children and that the home environment has serious and long-lasting effects upon mental development, it is *not* clear that such stimulation must include formal academic instruction. On the other hand, there is no evidence that structured learning activities at home are always harmful.

How to Recognize Reading Readiness

How is a parent to decide? A common-sense approach might include several guidelines. First, the most valuable help a parent can give his child is to broaden the child's experience. Give him something to think and talk and listen and write and read about. Second, remember that language skill is built through interaction; talk to your child about his experiences, define the meaning of new words you use, and listen to his reactions. Third, answer your child's questions about whatever he is reading. Most children are curious about words, and they learn a great deal when you identify familiar letters and sounds on food cartons, in books, on highway billboards and other signs, and in newspapers. Fourth, use games with words and sounds to stimulate your child's interest in reading.

The key to deciding whether an activity is appropriate and worthwhile is to determine how much your child enjoys it. If the activity seems to be drudgery for him, if his attention wanders, or if he exhibits negative behavior, chances are that he is not ready for, and therefore will not profit from, the activity. If he is eager to participate and asks for more, the activity is probably good for him.

Learning games should also be fun for parents. Many parents, mothers especially, become so concerned about doing the "right" things that they forget to relax and enjoy their children's development.

Occasionally ask yourself, "Does my child ask questions about words, or do I ask all the questions? Is he really interested in sounds and letters, or am I the one who wants him to read?" This doesn't mean that you have to wait passively for his interest to develop. Plan games and activities that lead to reading interest, but be extremely cautious about insisting that your child participate. Learn to recognize the difference between a stimulating environment and a stuffy one. Work toward achieving relaxed, easy guidance rather than forced instruction.

Stimulating Language Development

What are some specific activities for stimulating language development and reading interest in the preschooler? While playing, most small children like to be near their mother or father, so develop the habit of talking to your child as you work. Describe what you are doing. Attach word labels to objects and experiences. Encourage your child to tell you about his play, to describe what he is doing. Help him find new words as he needs them.

Take your child shopping with you. Talk to him as you push the grocery cart down the aisle; tell him the names of objects on the shelves, and listen to what he says about the things he sees. Talk about what he can see out of the car window: "Is that a bus or a truck? What color is that car? How many houses can you count?"

It is especially important that *both* parents read to their children. Establish a regular time each day for reading together, and don't forget to talk about the pictures as well as the story.

Write stories with your child. Ask him to describe the weather and other simple bits of his experience. Write his comments exactly as he says them, making sure that he knows that the words on the paper are really his own speech, written down so it can be read by others. Then let him illustrate the story with crayons or paints. At another time you might begin by letting him draw the picture; then write a caption, label, or several sentences about the picture as he dictates to you. Let him watch you write, noting that you are writing from left to right on the page. Be sure to read his story to him when it is finished. You may even wish to keep a collection of your child's stories in a notebook or file folder to be read again and again.

Watch television with your child. Help him interpret what he sees, and guide his selection of programs. Television's value or its vice depends on how it is used.

Talk about word sounds with your child. What objects or names can he think of that begin with the same sound as his first name? Call attention to rhyming words and words with similar beginnings and endings.

Write the names of family members on their belongings. Usually, the first words a child learns to read are his own name and the names of those close to him. Stimulate his interest in reading by having these familiar words readily available for practice. If he shows a great deal of interest in word recognition, you might try labeling other objects around the house with small signs. Use your best handwritten lettering, and write with lower-case letters; the child whose first experience with reading consists of words written in capital letters is often confused later when he tries to read words written in lower-case letters.

Again, remember that the child will learn best if he thinks well of himself and if he believes he can learn. If he finds that your expectations are reasonable and interesting, he will feel successful. Don't forget how important your example is. Make sure that your child sees you read, and let him know that reading is important for you. Even babies will be interested in books if they have parents who read.

When your child begins to read in school, the best way to help him is to reinforce the school reading program. There are numerous approaches to beginning reading, but most start by helping a child recognize words quickly and easily. Differences between programs arise from the materials used and the emphasis placed upon the various techniques for decoding words.

Common Approaches Used for Teaching Reading

The most common approach to teaching reading is the basal-reader program. You were probably taught to read with a basal-reader: remember Dick and Jane or Alice and Jerry? A dozen or so different publishers produce basal-reader series, which consist of a set of graded books with controlled vocabularies. Word recognition and other reading skills are introduced gradually and reinforced by repetition. Using these readers, the teacher presents a sequence of lessons to children who are generally grouped according to skill levels.

Most basal-reader programs begin by teaching the child to recognize a number of whole words called *sight words*. These are then used to introduce sound/symbol relationships (commonly called *phonics*). Other programs begin with phonics, teaching children to recognize sounds and put them together into words before attempting to remember whole sight words.

Another method, the language-experience approach, utilizes the student's own writing as his reading material. This approach concentrates on whole sentences before it attempts mastery of single-word analysis.

Another new approach, using a set of sequential workbooks that consist of programmed exercises, gradually introduces the child to phonics and other reading skills.

Find out which approach your child's teacher uses. Become familiar with the materials and procedures of the program, how you can help. Many times the best assistance you can give is your constant interest and encouragement. Few children need reading lessons at home, but all children need reading practice and recognition for their efforts.

Continue the word and sound games your child enjoyed as a preschooler. Expand his experience through taking family excursions, walking around the block, looking at nature together, and sharing home responsibilities. Continue reading to him and helping him write his own stories. Build a family library of easy-to-read books. Several publishers are now producing books especially suitable for children; most schools will help you order these books at a discount. You may also purchase many titles in commercial bookstores.

At this stage it is important that you listen to your child read regularly. Reading for a few minutes every day is better than spending long periods of time infrequently. A few guidelines will help make this time profitable and fun for you and your child:

1. The material your child reads to you should be familiar to him. Sometimes he will bring home books that he has already read and

knows well. If he wants to read something new, allow him to practice by himself first.

2. Tell your child the words he doesn't immediately recognize. Your reading time is intended to help you enjoy the story together and to build your child's confidence; it is not the time for teaching your child to analyze words. Nothing will discourage him more rapidly than your turning a shared story into a phonics drill. Usually he will learn the word faster if you simply tell him what it is in a kind tone of voice before it has seriously interrupted his reading.

3. Talk about the story together; mention funny, sad, exciting, and interesting parts. Let him know that you are interested in the story, not just the words.

4. If your child seems to be losing interest during reading time, change the pace. Try reading with him, each of you taking alternate pages or sentences. Or read the story or page to him first.

5. Keep a mental record of words your child misses as he reads, and look for a consistent pattern of errors. Does he use substitute words that make sense in the sentence but that are very different in form from the printed words—such as glad for happy? If so, he is probably reading for meaning and is not concerned with accuracy of words. This problem usually clears up with practice and experience. If, however, he substitutes a word that looks something like the correct word but has no relationship to the meaning of the printed word, such as there instead of three, he may be reading individual words rather than reading for meaning. Contextual clues can be helpful for such children. You can teach him to watch for such clues by writing short, easy sentences with a critical word left out, such as "John hit the _____ with the bat," or "the mother _____ has three kittens." Let your child supply the missing word. Have him practice distinguishing between pairs of similar words written on small cards.

Does your child have trouble with words that have regular phonic spelling? If so, he may not know all the letter sounds, or he may have difficulty putting sounds together. Play games with sounds, and call attention to similar sounds in his reading.

Many children who have little difficulty with words that follow regular phonics pattern do have trouble with words that do not follow word-analysis rules, such as said, many, or friend. Such words can be learned only by remembering their visual form. For the child troubled by such words, write them and use them often for recognition games.

The Poor or Slow Reader

Suppose your child does not seem interested in learning to read or appears to have unusual difficulties. Remember that there is a wide variation in the ages at which children are ready for reading: don't be too quick to label your child a problem reader. Give him time before you become too concerned.

Of course, some children *do* have problems that make reading very difficult. Many suffer from perceptual or motor difficulties that affect reading and other language skills. Emotional difficulties and problems with vision and hearing frequently have similar effects. If you suspect that your child has unusual learning problems, seek professional help. Begin with the family physician, who has probably followed the child's development since infancy. If you have not had a regular family doctor, consult a pediatrician, who can make a thorough examination and, if necessary, refer you to another source of help. Work closely with your child's teacher to plan special help.

Recognize Possible Reading Problems

What else can you do to help your child learn to read? As important as your home reading activities may be, the most valuable contributions you can make may not be directly related to reading instruction at all. Some children don't do well in school because they arrive in the morning either tired or hungry. While it is commonly believed that children from deprived families are the only victims of inadequate rest and nutrition, study has shown that the number of children who come to school without breakfast simply because their parents didn't get up in time to feed them exceeds the number of those who miss breakfast because they didn't have food to eat. Late television shows and irregular family schedules are usually the reasons for inadequate rest.

Good Physical Health

Two other factors affecting a child's school success are his attitude toward work and his ability to accept responsibility. Performing regularly assigned jobs and taking responsibility for helping in the home are essential preparations for learning in school. Even the child who is eager to learn must exercise self-discipline to complete all the tasks required in school. But some children never participate in meaningful work until they come to school, and such children may be handicapped learners.

Another reason for expecting a child to assume regular home responsibilities is that there is no better way to build his feelings of self-worth than to let him contribute his share to the family. Such feelings are necessary for achievement in reading or in any other academic skill.

Finally, your total relationship with your child has a major effect upon whether or not he will be successful in reading. Think for a moment. What have you done lately to let your child know that you value him, that you know he can succeed, that you are proud of him? Is home an oasis where he finds total acceptance regardless of what has happened to him elsewhere? Is he happy at home? If so, chances are good that he will also be a successful reader.

ACTIVITIES: PRESCHOOL AND BEGINNING READING

1. While you are on a ride or at home, have your child look for objects that start with a certain sound. For example, "I am thinking of something that starts with the letter c."

2. Play letter bingo. A set of playing cards can be made by randomly writing a letter in each of the nine squares on a six-inch square card. A smaller packet of cards should also be made, each containing one letter of the alphabet. Each letter of the alphabet should be represented. As one person draws a small card from the stack, a marker should be placed on the corresponding bingo square if that letter is represented on it. Macaroni, buttons, or colored squares of paper can be used for markers. The first person with three markers in a row wins. The game can be repeated as desired.

3. Cut a comic strip from the paper into sections. Allow your child to put the sections in their proper sequence as he tells you the story represented in its pictures.

4. Ask your child to tell you a story. Record his words exactly as he says them. Then, let him illustrate his story. Another time, after he has drawn a picture, ask him to tell you something about it. Let him watch as you write what he says, noting that you write from left to right on the page. Be sure to read his story to him when it is finished. You may wish to keep a collection of stories in a notebook or folder to be read again and again.

5. Watch television with your child. Help him interpret what he sees, and guide his selection of programs.

6. Write the names of family members on their belongings. If your child shows a great deal of interest in word recognition, label other objects around the home with their names. The labels should be printed with lower-case letters.

7. Make two sets of simple words, each set containing the same words. Give the sets to your child and assist him as he matches those words that are alike.

8. Ask your child to listen as you say a sentence that he must complete. Listening to the content of the sentence should aid him in finding a correct word. Examples include the following:

John hit the _____ with the bat.
The mother _____ has three kittens.
I ate _____ for breakfast.

CHAPTER 30
YOUR CHILD'S MORAL
AND VALUE DEVELOPMENT

When a child is born into a society, he doesn't know its rules. Whether the society is as big as a country or as small as a family, he has to be taught which behavior is acceptable—which means that he could be reared equally readily as a pickpocket or a priest. Whichever preparation his teachers provide, it is important for them to know a sequence of moral development that seems to typify children of all cultures.

At first, children seem to follow rules out of fear of punishment. Just as we train animals by hitting them, so we can train a child not to touch books in a bookcase by punishing him when he does play with the books.

At a slightly older age, children conform to rules not to avoid punishment but to gain something good. If a child at this age follows a rule but gets nothing good in return, he will feel cheated. To him, it's as though the moral system has broken down, and he may have a temper tantrum.

At the next stage of development, the child conforms to rules just because they exist. He has no notion of whether a rule is good or bad: if he has read or been taught that rule, then it is automatically good to him. To his way of thinking, people ought to keep the rules just so they can help the society maintain itself.

But all of the above stages are characterized by low levels of moral development. The child is doing the right thing for the wrong reason: he is following rules to avoid punishment, to obtain a reward, to please the authority, or to maintain the social system. But although people often start out doing the right thing for the wrong reason, right behavior for any reason is better than wrong behavior.

After having passed through these initial stages of moral development, a child should learn to abide by the rules of society because they promote the welfare of everyone. Such behavior implies an increasing concern for the rights of others.

Some have suggested that the highest level of moral development is based on a set of individually discovered ethical principles: one person discovers a set of principles that seem to work best for him, and another person might discover a different set that works best for him. These principles have to do with maintaining the dignity of the individual, helping people maximize their potential, and so on. When internalized, these principles act as a moral gyroscope: if we get blown off course a little bit, they pull us right back on course again.

Most preschool children will be operating at one of the earlier levels, striving to avoid punishment or to get something in turn for conforming to rules. Such children are oftentimes very egocentric, seeing what is right from their own viewpoint only. As a result they have difficulty weighing extenuating circumstances. By their standard a person who steals a loaf of bread just on a lark is no more guilty than a person who steals a loaf of bread to feed a starving child. There are no shades of gray; things are either right or wrong. Sometimes, however, the consequences of an action determine for a child whether that action is right or wrong. For instance, if a person gets caught and punished, then what he did was obviously wrong; if he does not get caught or punished, his action must not have been wrong.

In teaching high-level moral development to children, you cannot afford to say, "When my child is old enough to decide for himself, he can pick out the value system that he wants to live by." Taking that approach is courting disaster: instead of helping a child to understand the systematic value system that you believe in, you are leaving a vacuum in his life.

Every parent ought to feel that his value system is the best approach to life. The first thing you must do is learn to feel that the way you live and the way you believe is a good way, the best way. When you have that conviction, you won't have qualms about trying to teach your value system to your child. Furthermore, it is best to reach that conviction and to begin teaching it to your child very early in his life. Some specific methods will help you to teach your child your value system.

First, teach each value in a way that your child can understand. You can't use fuzzy language; you can't speak in euphemisms. The clearer you can make a value system, the more you can expect a child to live it.

Suppose that you were trying to teach your teenager acceptable dating behavior. Saying, "You're not fiddling around with the girls, are you?" won't help. What does "fiddling around" mean? That is about as fuzzy a concept as you could possibly convey. Instead, try saying, "You should always keep your hands off this part of the body and this part of the body. And you should never do this activity for over five minutes." Spelling things out very clearly removes all the leeway, the slippage in what you are trying to communicate to your child. By communicating in this way, you can rest assured that your child has understood you.

Second, you can teach children general rules. For example, suppose you are trying to teach honest behavior. You *can* teach a child not to take mail out of another person's mailbox, not to take candy out of a corner drugstore, not to take apples from another person's tree, not to take a chicken from another person's yard, and not to take toys off another person's porch. But you can also see that, using this technique, you may have to teach one thousand separate behaviors. Of course it is much better to determine the general principle and to then teach that general principle. For honest behavior the general principle might be that when an object does not belong to you, you don't take it. If you've taught your child that, then all your child must do when he sees an object is to make a simple discrimination: "Does that belong to me, or not?" If the answer is "It doesn't," then he will automatically know not to take it.

He's learned a general principle. It's apparent that this method is much more efficient than trying to teach each specific example.

Third, you must make your value system meaningful to your child. People want to know *why* they should behave in a certain way. You must be able to tell your child, "I believe in this value system for this reason." If you can't think of a good reason why your child should behave in a certain way, perhaps that behavior shouldn't be part of your value system. Of course your reason can always be, "Because I said so." But that just doesn't satisfy most people. In fact, most will rebel against that approach. The more satisfying the reason you give, the more you can expect your child to live the rule.

As long as there are flaws in your reasoning, people will use those "loopholes" to justify violating the rules. Suppose, for example, that the reason you give your child for refraining from premarital sexual intercourse is that by doing so he won't get any girls pregnant and will avoid venereal disease. When he reaches high school, he is going to know several ways besides abstinence to prevent pregnancy and avoid venereal disease. If your whole rationale for abstinence was based on those two consequences, your child, who knows how to avoid those consequences, feels free to go ahead with premarital sexual intercourse.

You have to give a reason for your values that can't be circumvented. But while it's not always easy to think of the right reasons why people should live a value system, the job of parents is to think of the right reason and then to point it out to their children.

The fourth way that we convince people to live a value system is to be a model, to be an example in our own lives. We have to show people that this value system is working for us, that it pays off, that it has some benefit in our lives. Especially with teenagers, we have to avoid evil and even the very appearance of evil. We can't even look as though we *might* break the value or bend the rule.

A final suggestion for fostering moral development in children is to be a warm, nurturant parent. There is a lot of evidence that the development of conscience in children is facilitated best by warm, loving parents of the same sex. Little boys who have warm, nurturant fathers develop conscience faster than boys who do not have such a relationship. The same holds true with girls whose mothers have those qualities. No matter how good a job you've done, your children will sometimes walk right up to the line marking the limits of proper behavior, and may even cross it. They are going to experiment, they are going to dally a little with what you've taught. But if you've given them a ball park that they can operate in, if you've established the rules and the boundaries, they know how far they must go to get back. They know when they can get back safely before all is lost, so to speak. If you have made your moral standards clear and meaningful, most children will adopt them—even those who have temporarily violated them.

ACTIVITIES: YOUR CHILD'S MORAL AND VALUE DEVELOPMENT

1. Write down five values that are meaningful to you that you want your child to adopt.

2. Take any value from the above list that both you and your spouse agree is important. Without letting your partner see what you are writing, express that value in the clearest, most general terms you can.

3. Together, write down the reason why a four-year-old should want to adopt and live the above value. Ask yourself if the language is something a four-year-old child could understand.

4. Look at the rating sheet below.

	Poor 1	Average 2	Good 3
Clarity: how clear the value is to your child			
Reason: the reason you have given your child to keep the value			
How well *you* keep the value			
The quality of your relationship with your child			

Rate each other's values for clarity and reason. Next, rate yourself on how well you live it and your relationship with your child. You could also have an independent source, such as a friend, an older child in the family, or someone who knows you well rate both of you. If you get a score of seven or eight (and the points fall within the shaded area) you could expect a child to adopt and live the value. If you got a score of six you should be able to see the areas that you could strengthen. A score of less than five probably means your child will not adopt the value.

5. Formally teach the above value to your child.

257

CHAPTER 31
SEX EDUCATION
IN THE HOME

Many of today's parents were raised in an era when information regarding either reproduction or maturation was not discussed in the home. This silence can be ascribed to at least two things. First, parents may not have known what to tell their children; that is, they may have lacked specific information. Second, they may have been so emotional about the topic that they couldn't approach their children about it: embarrassment, fear, shame, or guilt would inhibit communication. In an attempt to prevent a repetition of that silence among today's parents, this chapter describes seven principles that will help parents teach their own children about sex and reproduction.

Principles of Sex and Reproduction

1. *Teach children about sex and reproduction in the home.*
   The first principle to remember is that while every child should receive an education in sex and reproduction, he should receive it in the home. Reproduction and sex are subjects clearly related to a person's values. And because schools aren't equipped to teach each

individual person's particular value system, no person should rely on the school to teach his children about sex. The only reliable place to teach about reproduction is the home, and parents ought to do the teaching.

To be able to teach effectively, parents must prepare themselves in two ways. First, they need to know what they're talking about. (This chapter will not attempt to specify what should be taught.) Nearly any bookstore or library has books on the topic. Familiarize yourself with what you want your children to learn and take the time to study things you are unclear about. Second, because even the best information is useless to a child who can't understand it, and because the best way to deliver this information is through one-to-one communication, you must first establish a suitable relationship with your child. You can't wait until he is ten or fifteen years old before sitting him down to tell him about reproduction. If you haven't built a meaningful relationship from the time he was very little, if you haven't learned to talk to each other freely, you're not going to be able to give him all of that good information you have.

2. *Never violate your own integrity.*

The second principle is that a parent should never violate his own integrity. In other words, you should never teach or do anything that would make you feel awkward or embarrassed. When parents have these feelings, a child will often pick them up. Right now you may think, "I don't think I could tell my child *anything* about sex without feeling embarrassed." If this is true of you, your course of action is clear: prepare yourself so that you *can* handle the topic comfortably. You might have to practice telling the story of where babies come from by yourself locked in the bathroom. Then tell it to your partner. After a couple of rehearsals out loud, you'll be able to tell it to your child.

3. *Never violate your child's integrity.*

The third principle is that you should never violate your child's integrity. Help him learn only as he desires knowledge. This is especially applicable when he is a preschooler. Telling him about reproduction before he is interested or before he is ready to handle the information can lead to confusion or anxiety for him. Rather, you should let him take the lead and ask you the questions.

However, there are a couple of exceptions to this rule. If you have a child in the first or second grade who has not asked you where babies come from, then you ought to approach him with the subject in a very casual, matter-of-fact way, letting him know that

260

you are willing to talk about it. For instance, upon seeing a friend that's pregnant you could say something like, "Gee, look how big Mrs. Jones's stomach is getting. It looks as though she's just about ready to have her baby, doesn't it?" This opens the door for your child to say, "Uh, yeh, well, but ah ... where did the baby come from to start with?" He can then ask questions that may have been bothering him if he knows you're willing to talk. The slowness of some children to ask questions about reproduction isn't because they're stupid or uninterested. All children are interested in where they came from. And your child is smart and alert. But suppose he's been next door playing with a friend who tells him, "I asked Mother where babies came from, and she slapped me and made me stay in my room all day." Your child, because he's smart, will think to himself, "Okay. I'd better not ask my mother where babies came from because I don't want the same thing to happen to me." And so his curiosity is never satisfied.

Another exception to the policy of letting children take the lead is that you should teach your children about the changes their bodies will undergo at puberty before they happen. Don't decide to "wait until the nurse comes over in the fifth grade and shows her little film to my daughter" or "until my son goes down to his eighth-grade gym class." You, the parents, should explain the processes and changes that your child can expect in his body before those changes happen. The child isn't going to say, "Listen, I think I'm getting ready to menstruate. What is this process?" Here you're going to *have* to take the lead.

The third exception to letting the child set the pace is in the area of teaching values. Even before your children are old enough to know what is going on, you are teaching them the values and attitudes you want them to have. Through your example, the things you say and do around the home, you will be teaching your child your values in both a subtle and a direct way. If you are not pleased with your value system, then you had better change. Your children will learn what you believe.

4. Teach your child about sex in a positive way.

Fourth, you should always teach sexual values and factual information with a positive attitude. It's easy to make sex sound dirty and worthless, and you can even frighten your child in an attempt to keep him from experimenting with sex. Those obviously are not good teaching techniques—and they probably won't work anyway. A child ought to feel that the sexual part of his life isn't something to be ashamed of or frightened of; instead, he should learn that it can be a wholesome, powerful, unifying force in his marriage.

5. *Teach on the child's level.*

The fifth principle is that a parent should teach on the child's level. It would be quite appropriate, for example, to tell a four-year-old, "Babies grow in a special place in the mother's stomach. They get started when a seed from the father gets together with a seed from the mother." But you don't talk that way to a sixteen-year-old. You use such terms as *uterus, ova,* and *sperm.* And you would probably explain much more of the process than you would to a preschooler.

a. *Teach correct terminology.*

It was fashionable for many years for parents, in their anxiety about the subject of reproduction, to make up cute little toilet words for their children to use such as "wee wee" and "tinkle." These words serve no useful purpose. In fact, when parents use them, children soon realize that their parents are anxious about the whole process.

You will do better to teach your children correct terms from a very early age. Boys have a penis, girls have a vagina, and we all urinate. You may know other words for parts of our reproductive anatomy, but most of those other words are inappropriate. Use the correct terms. There is some risk involved, because no matter how many times you tell your child to talk about reproduction only at home, he will forget. His using the correct terms in public may cause you some embarrassment. But you should be able to live with whatever embarrassment may come to you because of having taught your children correctly.

There is an added benefit that comes from teaching correct terminology to begin with. When you are asked to explain where babies come from, you have the vocabulary. Imagine trying to explain reproduction with terms like "Daddy's widdeler" and "Mommy's number one." You couldn't keep a straight face.

When answering your child's questions about sex, you will do well to remember that most children who ask questions about sex and reproduction already know the answers. But because the process seems pretty far-fetched and difficult to believe, they want to hear it from someone they can trust: you! Think about the story of how a baby gets started. Perhaps a child has heard something about it from a friend or has seen something on television. He thinks he understands the process, but now he's coming to you, a reliable source of information, for verification. If you say something like

"Babies come down a magic slippery-slide from God" or "They're found under cabbage leaves," he may go away thinking, "Thank heavens! I thought maybe the father and mother together had something to do with getting the baby started."

b. Understand the question.

Make sure you understand the question that your child has asked. Everyone has probably heard the old story about the boy who came in breathlessly to his mother and asked, "Mother, Mother, where did I come from?" His mother thought, "This is it," and sat down for a half-hour and told him the story of reproduction. His eyes got as big as saucers while he was taking all this in. When she had finished, she took a deep breath, let out a sigh, and, being very pleased with herself, asked, "What made you ask that question?" Her son replied, "While I was outside playing, Bill said he was from Chicago and Jerry said he was from New York. I wondered where I came from."

It is always a good practice to ask, "What do you mean?" when a child asks a question. That technique will do two things: first, it will give you a few seconds while you clear your mind and refresh your brain about the information you're going to use; second, you will be certain that you understand the question. Once you understand the question, you should give the child a little less information than he asked for. That will act as a safeguard against your violating his integrity. If he asks a very large question, answer part of it. If you haven't answered it all, and if you have good communication with him, he'll ask, "Why?" or "How?" or "What's next?" Then you can answer that part—and so on, until he says, "Oh," indicating that you've finally answered what he wanted to know.

Another thing to remember about answering questions is that you should answer them when they're asked. That's when the child wants to know the information. Don't put off a child by saying, "Wait until you are in the sixth grade," or "You don't need to know that, you nasty boy," or "Wait until you're married. On your honeymoon you'll discover all of that." If a question is asked, answer it.

The person who is asked the question should be the one to answer it. It isn't necessary that fathers talk to boys and mothers talk to girls. If a daughter approaches her father, he ought to answer her. There's probably a good reason why she selected him. At that particular time she may feel closer to him than to her mother. Of course, her mother should not become defensive, thinking, "She likes you better than me." Instead, both parents should be grateful that the child would come to one of them to discuss this important area in her life.

c. Human sex and reproduction is not like animal reproduction.

It is not a good idea to base all of your teaching examples on what animals do. Parents will sometimes teach children that a human birth is essentially the same as what the child has observed when a pet cat has delivered babies. The mother cat is alone all the time. Perhaps she had her kittens outside in the middle of the night (in the dark!), or out by the furnace. Nobody was there—certainly not the father of the kittens. That isn't anything like what happens with most human births. In most human births the father feels responsible and is close by, sometimes in the very room, at delivery. He loves and supports his wife. Many other people also help and support the mother during the process. It's a joyous occasion in the family. Friends drop by and bring gifts. Thus, the analogy of reproduction and childbearing between animals and humans isn't very good.

The sexual behavior of animals and humans differs also. Animals mate only to have young. In fact, if a male approaches a female in times other than when she could conceive, she will become very hostile and may even attack the male. Certainly she will not be receptive. But that doesn't have to be true of humans. Sexual experience within marriage can serve many functions besides that of producing children; it's a way for parents to express tenderness towards one another, a way of feeling close and of relieving tension. If you believe this, you ought to communicate it to your children. You have to be very careful that the child doesn't get the idea that what he sees animals doing is a direct copy of what human beings do. It isn't.

6. Be natural about sex.

Sixth, sex isn't something that you isolate, bringing it out for discussion only on special occasions and then for only twenty minutes at a time. The best teaching takes place in the context of total family living. Parental attitudes, expressions, and experiences will rub off on children. Every child should know that his mother and father care for each other and have a sexual life together.

Part of the naturalness and wholesomeness that a child develops toward his own body comes from being able to take baths with other brothers and sisters. In that way he learns that his body is not something to be ashamed of that should be hidden. In fact, if he wants to occasionally bathe with his parents he ought to be able to do that. Familiarity with his own body and with the differences between male and female bodies will not encourage immorality or preoccupation with sexual thoughts. In fact, just the opposite seems to be true. Because you have handled the matter naturally and matter-of-factly, your child will probably be *less* interested in all kinds of exploratory behavior. Among children who have been raised in a loving home where they've seen brothers and sisters, and even parents, without their clothes on, the incidence of "doctor-nurse games" drops off. (And later in life those same children seem to have less of a need to neck and pet.) Furthermore, such familiarity in the home affords parents a good opportunity to teach values. They can say, "These things are all right at home, but we don't do them with our friends or neighbors or out in the street."

We're not advocating that people run around nude at home. We are simply advocating a common-sense approach to the situation and suggesting some easy ways to teach children within the home. Remember, though, that you must never violate either your integrity or your child's. Never force anyone to take a bath with someone else if both parties aren't completely comfortable.

7. *Develop and defend your own personal value systems.*

Principle number seven is that each parent ought to feel that his value system is the very best one there is. If you don't feel this way, then your responsibility is to find a value system that expresses what you really believe. It's going to be difficult to teach a value that you don't believe in. Parents who tell their child not to take drugs but who are themselves taking many kinds of pills for various reasons are defeating their own purpose. Nor can you teach him that sex will be a good thing in his marriage if he sees you using sex as a tool in marriage to control your partner. He won't learn to be morally clean if you read pornographic books or magazines or flirt with men or women other than your spouse. So make sure that you avoid the very appearance of evil in situations that involve value teaching.

Home truly is the proper and most effective environment for children to learn the value systems of their parents concerning sex education, because it is a very personal issue to be handled between parent and child.

ACTIVITIES: SEX EDUCATION IN THE HOME

1. Value clarification and application.
   A. Describe in detail your values pertaining to sex.
   B. Describe those values and understandings you desire your children to have by the time they are eighteen years old.
   C. Consider things as they are and the goals you have established regarding values. How can you better teach those values to your children?

2. Obtain a book about human reproduction or physical maturation and study the sections on maturation and reproduction. Review the questions below and record appropriate answers, keeping in mind the truthfulness of the answer and the age level of the child indicated.
   A. A four-year-old child asks, "Where do babies come from?" and "How does the baby get out?"
   B. A six-year-old child asks, "How does the seed from the daddy get together with the seed from the mother?"
   C. A fourteen-year-old boy wants to know what "making out" is.

3. Practice using the correct words for the parts of the body involved in reproduction.

4. Tell your spouse the story of reproduction.

Remember the basic principles of sex education:
   1. Sex education should occur in the home.
   2. A parent should never violate his own integrity.
   3. The child's integrity should not be violated.
   4. Values and information should be taught with a positive attitude.
   5. A parent should teach on the child's level.
   6. The teaching of sex should take place in the context of total family living.

CHAPTER 32
FEEDING YOUR CHILDREN

Pediatricians say that fifty percent of all children brought to them are there because parents feel that the children are not eating properly. One noted doctor said, "With all our rules and regulations as to when, where, what, and how much to feed children, we have succeeded in doing one thing: we have taken away their appetites."

Height and weight charts often alarm parents: they fret if their child doesn't conform to the specified standards. But what is really important is not that your child reaches or exceeds an average, but that he grows.

Of course proper development depends upon eating the right foods in sufficient quantities, and for that reason families worry that they don't know enough about foods. In fact, families frequently worry more about foods than they do about children. But we are beginning to realize that we need to know more about *children*. In recent years, a number of studies have added to the understanding of the development of human personality; although we still have much to learn, using what we know now will help us feed our children more successfully.

Feeding Made Easier

Feeding children can be easier if you know three things: (1) what to expect from them, (2) what foods they should have, and (3) how to bring children and food together happily.

First, let's consider what to expect from children. The preschool child does not eat as much in proportion to his size as he did when he was an infant because he's not growing as rapidly. But beyond that it's more difficult to generalize, because no two children are exactly alike. Children differ in body build; whether your child will be a short stocky type, a tall string bean, or somewhere in between depends mostly on his inheritance of genetic characteristics. Lack of proper food could prevent him from gaining his full stature, but stuffing him with food won't change him from one height to another (and will probably make him overweight).

Children grow at different rates. Jack gains weight more rapidly than his cousin Mary, who is the same age. He wants and needs considerably more food than she does. Every child may go through periods when his growth rate spurts ahead and then slows down; in a spurt he eats more food because he needs it, and when growth slows down he eats less.

Just as children grow in height and weight, so they also grow in their abilities. Patsy wants to try using her cup and spoon by herself before she is a year old. Mike, on the other hand, may be several weeks older than Patsy before he tries to feed himself. Any child will find it difficult to feed himself at first, and those whose muscle control is not yet developed will find it even more difficult than others who have been able to develop muscle control. Some children feed themselves before they are two; others don't try this until after they turn three. Don't hurry your child—let him take over when he shows he is ready. All children at this stage need patient parents.

A child between the ages of one and five will be very active. He changes from a helpless baby to a busy little person who is trying to do things for himself. His muscles must be used before he can learn to direct them. Give him safe opportunities to run, climb, and explore; then he may be able to sit still and eat a meal. If he would rather stand than sit, you may as well feed him standing up. This is usually a phase, and will pass with time. Soon he will eat sitting down, because he sees you eat that way.

Second, your child may show some contrariness. Irritating though his repeated "no" may be, it represents his growth and development. He is discovering himself and is trying to express likes and dislikes of his own. At this early stage, his vocabulary is limited, so that he responds to things he dislikes: he can say "no" or act "no" more easily than he can tell you what he wants or what he would like to do. When he closes his mouth against food you are feeding him, he is not trying to be annoying; it is his way of saying that he doesn't like it or that he has had enough.

Third, you can expect your child to do a lot of imitating. His choice of foods likely reflects the choices and attitudes of someone dear to him. Consider the experience of a father who had three sons under the age of six. As he came in the front door just before the evening meal, the smell of scorched milk hit his nostrils. Seeing the distraught look on his wife's face, he said in an honest but pleasant way, "What's that smell? It must be something new for dinner." When he sat down at the table with his boys around him, he smiled and said, "Mom has really fixed up some special soup tonight." The boys watched their daddy eat the soup without any complaints; so did they. He turned what could have been a very unpleasant situation into a pleasant one.

Fourth, a young child needs routines. The preschool child has his own regular body demands: an orderly pattern of mealtimes, playtime, bathtime, and bedtime seems essential to his emotional and physical well-being. Such routines give him security.

Fifth, a child can be expected to dawdle or play with his food. When the first keen edge is taken off his hunger, he will be in no hurry to eat. He has no adult sense of time to push him. Trying to make him hurry will only spoil his pleasure in eating. If there is a reason to hurry, you'd better help the younger child eat and explain the reason for the rush to the older one.

Sixth, he can be expected to go on food binges. He may want peaches and oatmeal for supper every night for a week, and then suddenly refuse to eat either for a spell. If his menu choices are not too impractical and you can be casual about it, be accommodating; that way he is not liable to stick with the binge for long.

Seventh, your child needs limits—but keep them few. Too many rules confuse him. For instance, instead of insisting upon a clean plate before dessert, simply give him small portions. He'll get used to the idea of completely finishing one dish or course before starting another. If he plays with his food, remove it without threats. He'll learn to eat without fuss and play. Every child needs to do for himself whatever he is able to do. His first efforts will be awkward, but they should be encouraged, because they are steps toward healthy and happy growth.

If parents place too much stress on eating, there may be trouble. From infancy on, your child is smart enough to recognize your anxiety, and he will learn that his "not eating" will gain him attention. A relaxed, happy atmosphere at mealtime—and at other times—without undue emphasis on the clean-plate routine will probably eliminate most mealtime difficulties.

On the other hand, don't ignore a child with a problem. If your child persists in not eating, then it is your responsibility to try and find out why. Is the child sick, vomiting, or having diarrhea? If illness and emotional problems are both ruled out, then ask yourself the following questions: What am I feeding him? Am I feeding him too much? Am I offering him enough freedom of choice? Answers to these three questions may solve your child's feeding problems.

Foods Children Should Have

Young children use a large amount of energy—both for developing and replacing body tissues and for physical, mental, and emotional activity. It goes without saying that no one food or group of foods meets all those needs. Everyone needs a properly balanced diet. Milk products, meat products, vegetables and fruits, and bread and cereal products are foods known to supply the essentials.

Milk and Milk Products

No other food will do as much for children as does milk: it furnishes protein that builds muscles and body tissues, supplies calcium and phosphorus that build bones and teeth, contains vitamins A and B that promote growth and health, and provides easily digested fat and sugar as fuels that convert into energy.

The recommended amount of milk for children is three to four cups daily, but many preschool children who are in slow periods of growth simply cannot hold that much. In fact, some children under three may not be able to drink even two cups a day. However little your child drinks, don't try forcing him to drink more. Force will only make him balky, and you can't afford to let him get set against milk at this age. Recognize that each person, no matter what his age, can consume just so much milk—and no more. One way to assure that a child will drink as much milk as he should is to protect its flavor: children have sensitive taste buds and can detect a taint much quicker than adults can. Keep milk cold and tightly covered, and be sure that it is pasteurized.

To include more milk in a child's diet, cook with it and make dishes he likes, such as milk soup, custards and other milk desserts, soft bread puddings, tapioca, and ice cream. Most children like mild cheese, a milk product; cottage cheese, recommended for all children, provides excellent muscle-building protein. But cheese, cottage cheese, and other milk products don't *replace* milk, because some vitamins and minerals are depleted during preparation of these products. Include both milk and milk products in the child's daily diet.

Meat Group

The meat group, consisting of meat, fish, poultry, and eggs with dried beans, peas, and nuts serving as alternates, furnishes the body with (1) protein to build muscles and body tissues, (2) iron and phosphorus to build blood, and (3) B-complex vitamins to promote growth and health. A general rule for gauging the amount of protein needed is to supply one tablespoon per day for each year of the child's age. Thus, a four-year-old would require four tablespoons of meat food per day.

Bite-size pieces of meat that they can eat with their fingers please most children past the age of two years. Those children who can manage a fork easily like to use it to eat small pieces of meat that their parents cut for them. Cook meat at low temperatures to preserve its moisture, because children prefer meat that is moist in texture and mild in flavor. Meat, liver, and fish loaves are best prepared with milk and eggs. Liver loaf will have a milder flavor if the pan in which it is baked is set in a pan of hot water while baking—the same way as is done when preparing a custard. The mild flavors of haddock, halibut, tuna, and salmon appeal to most children. Meats with stronger flavors are liable to be rejected. Bacon gives less protein than do other meats, but it has energy and flavor value. Peanut butter is a protein food especially popular with most children.

Fruits and Vegetables

This food group furnishes minerals that build bones, blood, and tissues; vitamin C, which promotes growth and health; and roughage, which aids in regular elimination. One tablespoon per day for each year of age is again recommended. This daily ration should include a dark green or yellow vegetable, possibly a potato, and a citric fruit or a tomato.

Serve vegetables and fruit in the form your child likes best. For example, he may eat vegetables raw that he would refuse cooked. Flowerettes of cauliflower or broccoli, sticks of carrots or celery,

271

and leaves of lettuce or cabbage that a child can hold in his fingers can be served to any child past two.

Eating mashed potatoes is not easy for young children; unless plenty of milk is added, the potato tends to stick to the roof of the child's mouth. Cooked vegetables are preferable in bite-sized pieces or in a form that children can recognize.

Younger children usually prefer mild-flavored fruits. After age three, however, they find that tart fruits such as plums are more acceptable. Give children over the age of two well-washed raw fruits in place of sweets. Cut cooked fruit into bite-sized pieces, and cook fruit at a low heat just enough to soften skins and fibers. Seasonings should be used sparingly for both fruits and vegetables.

Bread and Cereal Group

This group consists of whole-wheat or enriched cereals and bread that furnish fuel for the child's activity, protein to build muscles and tissues, minerals to build bones and blood, and B-complex vitamins to promote health and growth. Serve cereals with plenty of milk to be sure that the consistency will suit your preschool child. Serve cooked cereals warm, not hot. Because cereals are high in energy value, they may be served with little or no sugar.

Many children prefer toast to bread. Bread slices cut into halves or quarters can be handled more easily. Macaroni, white rice, spaghetti, and noodles are energy-producing foods, but because they have less food value than the whole-grain and enriched cereal products, they should be combined with meat, cheese, eggs, milk, fruit, or vegetables.

Snacktime

Parents often ask, "Should I let my child snack between meals?" The answer is that most preschool children seem to need some kind of food between meals. The capacity of a child's stomach is small, and his energy needs are great. Without food between meals he may become over-tired and irritable. Food between meals is best offered at the same time each day. Milk, fruit, fruit juice, and plain crackers spread with thin layers of cottage cheese or peanut butter offer the most nutritional value. Cookies, candy, and cake may spoil his mealtime appetite and are of little food value other than as sources of quick, empty energy and calories. One thing to keep in mind is that the amount of sweets should be limited.

If, in spite of regular meals and in-between-meal snacks, your child makes a nuisance of himself by going to the cupboard or refrigerator, he may need more protein foods such as milk, eggs, cheese, or meat. Consider, too, the possibility of some other cause for his desire to eat besides actual physical hunger. His need may be an emotional one. Sometimes boredom, loneliness, or a need for more affection promotes this behavior. Rather than food, his real need may be for new play equipment, playmates, or more attention from you.

How to Bring Children and Food Together Happily

Nationally recognized authorities on food give the following goals for feeding children and suggestions for achieving them.

First, assure a positive attitude towards eating. Make each mealtime pleasant. Parents either help or hinder a child's appetite by the way the mealtime stage is set. Nature is the parents' best ally: unless something unpleasant in connection with eating has already occurred, a healthy child most generally enjoys his food because eating satisfies a basic need.

Second, keep mealtime conversation happy and cheerful. Encourage interesting and pleasant conversation among children who are old enough to eat well and talk at the same time. Discourage unpleasant topics, and don't talk about personal food dislikes. Remember that even though conversation has its place, the main business at the table is eating.

Third, don't be too concerned about table manners if the child is very young. The child must experience a variety of foods, be able to handle food and eating utensils skillfully, and feel that he is part of the group before he can be expected to conform to family mealtime behavior. "Please" and "Thank you" are best learned by children as they see how these are used by their parents.

Giving positive "can-do" directions will help alleviate some of the emotional tension and aid mealtime smoothness. To the child who seems to require help feeding himself after having done so independently for some time you may say, after putting food on his spoon, "Here, you can eat it now. Put it in this hand." Say, "Hold your glass straight" to a child whose milk is about to spill, instead of, "Don't spill your milk". "Keep your food on your plate" is better to say to the child who litters the table than "Don't get your food on the table." Say, "Swallow before you talk" to the child who is talking with his mouth full instead of, "Don't talk with your mouth full." "Can-do" statements give a child direction and encouragement instead of belittling him.

Fourth, let the child serve himself; doing so allows him to develop fine motor skills. Make sure he is given foods that are easy to serve. Young hands like to feel, hold, and explore, and the child who enjoys that freedom learns to be more independent. If he does spill, take the problem in stride—spills are bound to happen at mealtime. It's all too easy to forget that children don't yet have as much control of themselves or as much experience as do adults, so exercise patience; besides, how many times have you spilled? Scolding does no good. Let the child himself clean up the spill (with your assistance when necessary), but make it as pleasant as possible. Most spills are accidents!

Fifth, don't force a child to eat. Force feeding produces an unpleasant association. Instead, motivate him to take a taste of the ignored food by saying, "Put a little bit into your mouth and tell me what it tastes like," or, "Take one taste and see if you like it. If you do, you may have some more; if you don't, leave it on your plate, and we'll try it another day," or, "Mary, do you know what 'crunchy' means? Try this celery and see if it makes a noise when you chew it." Such remarks made in a relaxed manner usually create enough interest for the child to taste the food. When all else fails, try it on another day. Don't make an issue over a particular food at the table. Enjoyment of food is more important than a clean plate.

Sixth, each child should be able to eat at his own individual pace. Competition and haste at mealtime are frustrating and hinder the enjoyment of food. It may be necessary to limit the time at the table, but eating should not proceed by the clock. Meals are served because we need food and because we enjoy eating. There is no special virtue in eating just to get through with a meal.

Seventh, keep the servings small, and let the child ask for more. It gives him a greater feeling of accomplishment and success to drink two or three small glasses of milk than one large one. Similarly, small portions are encouraging to a young child. It is better to start with a teaspoon of each food and let him ask for second helpings of those foods he prefers. As in so many other respects, we must remember individual differences: one child may eat far more than another, and to further complicate matters, each will eat different amounts on different days and may eat a great deal of one food and very little of another at one meal only to reverse preferences at the next meal. We should accept the fluctuation of appetite common in children of this age. However, it is reasonable to set some standards, such as tasting or taking one bite of each food served, or drinking a certain amount of milk. Unless he has allergies or strong dislikes, a child gains a sense of mastery from meeting responsible expectations.

Following the same principle, serve foods in a way children can easily handle them (bite-sized pieces of meat, fruit, and vegetables). Vegetables and fruits cut in thin slices or sectioned, meat and cheese cut into strips, and small sandwiches halved or quartered add to the child's interest in food, and help him learn more about it, giving him the opportunity to associate its texture and its color and flavor. A young child's need for sensory experience is great: he wants to explore the world by touching.

Several years ago a thin, rather lifeless child aged three and a half was brought into a Brigham Young University Child Development Laboratory Nursery School. When his mother expressed concern that he was still on the bottle and refused to drink from a cup or eat any solid foods, the teacher asked for full freedom to do what she felt best for the child. As soon as the distraught mother had given full permission, the teacher said that the child's bottle was to be completely taken away from him during the day—he would be allowed to have it only at night.

During the first lunchtime at school, he just sat and looked at the food. The teacher handed him the glass of milk and attempted to get him to put it to his lips. He refused. The next day she made the same attempt. This time he dumped the milk in his plate. Then, curiously, he put his fingers into his plate and swished them around in the milk, apparently enjoying the feeling of the milk on his fingers. This wasn't Emily Post's way of drinking milk, but the child was getting acquainted with the properties of milk. As time went on, the teacher put a small portion of food on his plate. The same pattern was repeated: the child sat pushing the food around, licking his fingers, and getting a sensory acquaintance with the food. Observers in the observation booth were aghast at his messiness. Little did they realize the progress he was making.

After a few weeks, the child was drinking from his glass and picking food up from his plate and eating it. No attempt was made to introduce a fork or a spoon to the child until he seemed to be enjoying his food thoroughly. But that, too, came with time and patience. And of course he was gaining weight and becoming much more pleasant. The feeding process was learned slowly—step by step, ultimately achieving adult expectation.

A third portion of the seventh goal deals with introducing new foods. Introduce them in small amounts, one at a time. Allow the child to experiment with each new food. He may want to feel it, smell it, and ask questions about it. Introducing it along with a familiar and well-liked food will help him accept it more readily. A secure child may be able to accept a variety of new foods easily, but the less secure child may feel threatened if too many new foods are pushed on him all at once. He may need longer to cling to the familiar in food, as in other things, to gain assurance.

Eighth, when you serve starchy foods, such as mashed potatoes, serve them soft and fluffy. The young child struggles to swallow anything the least bit dry because he does not have as much saliva in his mouth as an adult. Notice that as he eats he will take a bite of food, then a drink, then another bite of food, then another drink. He needs the liquid to aid his swallowing.

Ninth, serve simple, unmixed foods. Children like simple, natural-flavored foods best. Nor do fancy dishes appeal to them. Foods are more attractive to him if each one stands out separately on his plate. He may dislike casserole or meat loaf, even though he may relish each individual flavor in those dishes. Children care less for creamed foods and for sauces over foods than do adults. Make food look appealing. Bright-colored foods, such as orange carrots, bright green beans, yellow gelatin, and egg yolk beaten into white sauce will make the child's plate more appealing. Cheerful colors in cups, plates, and table mats also help make mealtime a happy occasion. How food looks and tastes and how it feels in the mouth is important in making it attractive to children.

Beware of strong odors and flavors. Children have more—and more sensitive—taste buds than adults. Our taste buds are in our tongues; theirs are in their cheeks and on the back of their throats as well as in their tongues. And because a child may hold food in his cheeks for some time to savor the flavor, a food "just right" for an adult may be too highly seasoned for a child. Similarly, foods with strong flavors and unusual textures are not popular among children.

Tenth, offer a child a choice. Often a child who has difficulty eating vegetables will, if given a choice, eat the one he chooses. Asking his choice gives him a sense of importance and tells him that you respect his right to make decisions and choices. But to assure that he will pick only nutritious foods, you would do well to place on the table only nutritious foods from which to choose.

Eleventh, adapt the eating utensils to the development level of the child. Provide dishes and flatware that are durable, attractive, and a size and shape suitable for small hands. Small, flat, heavy-bottomed glasses are easy to hold and will prevent many spills.

276

Small heavy-duty plastic dishes and stainless steel flatware are practical. A salad fork rather than a large fork and a spoon with a round bowl add to his comfort and pleasure. Likewise, he will enjoy eating more if he is comfortable. He needs a chair with an adequate footrest and a table that is the right height for him. And he will be more comfortable if he is not crowded too close to others.

Finally, let food play a part in setting a pleasant atmosphere in the home. Well-prepared meals that include favorites help make a home that children and adults love to return to. Meals should be reasonably regular, something to count on. Parents should be home at those hours and should be counted on. Celebrating birthdays with a cake singles out a person and makes him feel wanted and cherished. All members of the family should be present on these important occasions, too.

Bringing children and food together happily is an art, but tactful, wise parents can master it. Children should be fed according to individual needs and stages of development, but the easy way is generally best.

For most of us the recommendation that simple foods be served in friendly surroundings without worry about what, how much, or how the children eat is a welcome one. But because some of us learned rigid ideas about child feeding, we may sometimes find the new approach confusing or difficult. If you have worried about your child's feeding habits, you will not stop immediately. But keep trying. It has been demonstrated repeatedly that when parents do stop worrying, children start eating better. Focus attention on how to enjoy mealtime and your child, not on what or how much they should be eating.

ACTIVITY: FEEDING
YOUR CHILDREN

1. Record five specific goals or activities you would like to implement in the home during the next seven days which relate to making eating more enjoyable. The attitude of your child, his desire to eat with you at mealtime, and his enjoyment of food will help you know if you have been successful in accomplishing these goals.

1.
2.

3.
4.
5.

2. Referring to the basic food groups and their daily requirements, plan a complete day's menu for your child.

3. Plan a picnic, allowing your child to select and prepare the foods. Suggestions include making peanut butter and jelly sandwiches, frosting cookies, and peeling carrots. You will be surprised to find how much he really can do by himself. Praise his efforts and enjoy your lunch.

4. Assign your child on a long-term basis some task which is necessary for achieving a successful meal. This might include setting the table, pouring the milk, or assisting in the food preparation. When necessary, remind him of the importance of his responsibility. Encourage and praise him often.

INDEX

279